SURVIVING THE SINGLE DAD SYNDROME

KEVIN JAMES

PublishAmerica
Baltimore

First printing

ISBN: 1-4137-3342-5
PUBLISHED BY PUBLISHAMERICA, LLLP
www.publishamerica.com
Baltimore

Printed in the United States of America

For my wonderful children, and all of the little ones in my life. Thank you for so many wonderful and rewarding years. Know that you are loved.

So many people are responsible for the completion of this book. Some of them merely acquaintances at the beginning of this project I feel privileged to refer to as "friends" through their generous contributions to this writing.

I'd like to thank my friend Sue, for handing me the idea for this book on a silver platter. It was an inspired idea.

And to Trina, my "life coach," for reassuring me that this book must be written.

I'd like to thank the "ex's" that provided their stories, Naomi, Michelle, Vickie, Nicole, Chantal, and also to Ken and Mark. Their chapters were difficult to write, not so much in laying out the ideas they provided, but in the emotions their stories brought out.

I'm grateful to my parents and their unending support. I'd like to send special gratitude to my dad and Uncle John who provided the ideas and drawings for the kid's stools, without which this book would not be complete.

Also to my mother for her help in editing the book, and lending her years of wisdom as a teacher.

Thank you to my family, friends, siblings, and extended family for the many contributions in the recipe section, their help in editing, and for keeping me on track during the writing.

I'd be remiss if I didn't thank my own ex's for their contributions not only directly to the book, but also in helping to shape my life as a Single Dad, as well as the lives of my children.

And most of all, I would like to extend my gratitude and my love to my six wonderful children, Shiloh, Kiley, Danica, Camden, Sarah and Michele. I'd also like to thank their many friends, especially Kendra and Trista, that have become so dear to me in their growing years. I have been blessed to have such wonderful children as my tutors. Without their teachings, love, and energy, this book would not have been possible.

My unending gratitude to so many others that have helped when times were tough, and helped me realize they will always be there in times of need.

CONTENTS

CHAPTER 1
SUDDENLY SINGLE

I stand alone looking out to an alien place, filled with both excitement and trepidation. Tiny angels approach to take my hand leading me into this new and strange world. My loneliness disappears. I feel safe and loved.

This book is written for guys. Women may also be interested in reading this text searching for clues to the elusive male psyche. Since men and women began to form words some 20,000 years ago, there has been a gap in communication for the most part, between men and women and how they relate to each other. Simply we all have the same needs but communicating how those needs are to be met may cause some dissension.

It's interesting that we may speak the same language as our mates, English, Spanish, or whatever, but the amount of miscommunication, or non-communication is amazing. Why is it that we use the same alphabet, the same words, and phrasing do we not understand what the opposite sex is attempting to convey?

When something happens to a female, she will usually relate to the situation from an emotional standpoint first. She will want to *feel* what has happened before setting upon a logical course of action. Note I'm not saying "over-emotional," the energy of emotions is very real and vibrant and a necessary part of her process.

A male on the other hand will skip any emotion to the process and will look at it from a strictly logical standpoint. That logic is completely determined by the individual doing the thinking. A male will analyze it from a financial, security, threat vs. non-threat, long term, short term, and no term, liability, and healthy/unhealthy point of view, all in the blink of an eye! And damned if anyone offers an opposing view.

In addition to the different viewpoints both sexes experience of their own world, it's rare that either side ever clearly says what they intend to communicate!

For example, if the male half decides it's time for a new family vehicle, it would be highly unusual for him to approach his "other half" (where did that come from anyway?) and say simply "Let's go shop for a car." That would be insane! Might as well stick the old chin out and ask the wife to take a good poke! In our minds, this openness may potentially subject us to her "logical reality" of not being able to afford it or one hundred other reasons why it's the stupidest idea ever expressed.

So we modify our approach, which may take weeks. Weeks of hinting that our current vehicle is getting older, showing some signs that rust may form, it has a funny noise, the upholstery is beginning to fade. We'll discuss the idea with our best friend, "testing the waters" to see how the idea sounds. We'll do all of the research on the fair book value, and what a replacement is going to cost. We'll casually mention tidbits of information, as we happen to run across them in the newspaper, magazines, or television. We'll attempt to excite her, without ever mentioning the idea.

We'll attempt to coax *her* into making the suggestion that we might go take a look at the dealership to see what they might have. Problem solved! After all, it was her idea! She can't argue with her own idea! Well, she probably will.

Usually after weeks of dropping hints, we know full well she knows what we're leading to, but she won't bring herself to spill the words that we so desperately want to hear. We want that vehicle; we need that vehicle; why doesn't she "get it?" In reality, she probably has no idea what you are attempting to communicate. She doesn't "feel" it.

I was listening to a talk show recently with a man and wife (ages 97 and 96 respectively) that had been married for over 75 years and the marriage was still going strong. The host asked the gentleman if he and his wife had ever had arguments. He said "Sure! Everyone argues!" He was asked if they had ever had a serious argument. He replied "Only one."

"And how did it come out?" came the follow up question.

His reply, "I don't know, it's not over yet!"

It's beyond me how persons that are destined to view the world from completely different ends of the spectrum, are ever going to cohabitate together. Yet we do. The attraction between the sexes is so strong no barrier shall stand between us. Or perhaps we are all gluttons for punishment, we'd jump into this hole with blinders on, never giving thought to the doom and gloom this type of match up will bring!

In my opinion, until men can begin to listen to emotions and acknowledge them, and women begin to understand that men are going to perform a function differently, logically, there will be no peace in the home. Some acceptance and appreciation of the differences will be critical and beneficial for everyone involved. This lack of communication may be what's brought you to your Single Dad role.

A brief word on the abbreviations you will be seeing. I like to keep things simple, after all, most of us guys talk and no one listens anyway. When referring to the wife, I'll use a simple W, W1 or W2 for the 1st wife, 2nd wife etc, and SO for the significant others. (We'll lump them all together, what the heck).

At times when you have W, W1, W2 or the SO, you will be called upon to entertain or care for your "young uns" should you find your other half elsewhere. The kids may scream and whine, this may be normal, but when they begin to look a little drawn, losing some precious pounds you begin to realize they must need something!

You find yourself alone with your kids; they won't quit bugging you for something to eat, or something to drink. You *can* take them to the local fast food restaurant if you have one nearby. Kids fed, thirst quenched, they'll suck you into the playground. You don't want to go there.

If you get drawn into the playground 1) you can't get them out without a fight and 2) present will be mothers with their children, single or married, makes no difference, you are as vulnerable as a wounded zebra on the Savannah with a lion pride downwind. Every one of them is going to either *be* someone or know someone that is perfect for you, some sister, friend, relative, old maid, or bag lady that can *change* you into a decent upstanding citizen. These are the reasons the W married you in the first place. After all, a single dad is no fitting life for any decent human being, right? Bah, humbug.

I went through W1 and W2 and a number of SO's, and prior to my divorce from W2, I had come to a realization. It was time to establish some priorities. "Do I want to be married, or do I want to keep bait in the fridge?" So far, the bait has won out.

I'm nearing the big 50, and I'm wondering *is a W3 in my future?* (Shudder). Well I read recently where they had crossed a goat with some other animal (the details escape me) to breed a more productive animal. Scientists have been crossing cattle with buffalo for years to yield more and better meat.

Researchers have also done a lot of work with swine lately, for transplanting organs into humans. So *technically*, sooner or later someone is going to figure out how to make a pig fly. So I guess *technically*, one day, I may find W3.

I have a total of six children, three daughters grown and out of the house (married). None of them are or ever have been on welfare. I can't take any credit for those three; their mother did it all. Sadly, I hadn't learned my infinite wisdom, as I find myself with a young son and two younger daughters. So through the intricate process of "learned behavior principles," the younger three will receive the benefits of my learning after nearly destroying the older three. This is what I refer to as "blessings."

I've spent more than two-thirds of my adult life "technically" single and find myself with these three little ones. How do I intend to keep them from driving me to the padded room? Perhaps that's why my thinking is more than a bit jaded and cynical, though I'm not alone in my thinking.

Ah, I thought I was smart, I bought all of the video games, a television for their rooms, videos, and DVDs, to entertain them. Heck, I shouldn't have to do much, slip a bit of food under the door and I'm pretty well set.

As I said, I *thought* I was smart.

Now they come to me "I'm bored."

My response? "Go watch a movie."

"Watched them all."

"Go play a video game."

"Beat them all."

"Go watch the TV." This is the stimulating repartee you have to look forward to.

"There's nothing on! What can we dooooooo?" The whine is apparent as boredom sets in. I know you are all thinking "I've lived with these kids for years? Why are they turning evil on me?"

Here's a clue, they've *always been evil!*

When you were with W1, W2, or SO in your former castle, your other half (ha!) shielded you from them. Remember when you may have been sitting watching a ball game, and the W was talking with/at you, and you may have responded correctly, but later never remembered having the conversation? Well it's the same with the kids, you tuned out the ex, and you finely tune out the children. You can "finely" tune them out, because any lack of response on your part wouldn't cost you dearly for days, weeks or months, as it would with the ex.

It's time to open your eyes to your little ones, live in their world with them. I realize it's a new thing, but it's going to be a very rewarding experience.

This new relationship situation is a major change for all of you, the kids, the ex, and yourself. You may be a bit lost as to your direction. You may be looking to place blame. Blame isn't important. It doesn't matter anyway; nothing is going to change what has happened.

As a very wise person told me after one of my more difficult breakups, "You could not have prevented this." While I'd like to think she was referring to my particular situation, she wasn't; it was a blanket statement, and it does indeed cover most everyone.

Whatever happened in your relationship, no matter who was at fault, the breakup happened because at least one of you wasn't happy in the relationship. No blame is placed on someone for seeking happiness!

Sure people have been hurt, lives seem to have been shattered through someone's selfish desire to be happy. Life goes on. Some people are going to be miserable no matter what. At times it takes a big shake up before the lights go on. We begin to realize we have the power to choose happiness in any situation. And sometimes, it does take a major change in a person's life to find happiness.

You may be thinking that your marriage has failed. This is a common misconception. Regardless of what you may have been told, your marriage didn't fail. It ended, yes, but it wasn't a failure, and it didn't end in failure. Failure has such a negative vibration to it. The marriage was what it was. The marriage served a purpose in your life, and in your mate's life. In fulfilling that purpose, the marriage was a tremendous success. The purpose may have been nothing more than to bring these wonderful children into our lives. Other reasons may have been, it depends on your unique situation.

The marriage has outlived its usefulness, and what sense would it make to continue to hold onto it? We might do that with material things, for sentimental reasons, but how much sense would it make when your life and happiness are at stake?

The marriage has ended, simply because it has served its purpose. Of course we all like to think when we get married, that marriage will last the rest of our lives. Unfortunately, often we're wrong. Because we intended the marriage to last forever, doesn't mean our marriage failed. It means we accomplished what we intended to accomplish through our marriage, and it no longer serves us. Attempting to hold onto something that is no longer useful will merely prolong the inevitable, and you will (both) likely be miserable until it ends anyway.

Does this mean if you ever get married again, it's surely doomed after a few short years! No! That marriage will have its own purpose, whatever you have intended that to be. It has no correlation with this past marriage. You have benefitted from your past experience. When you marry again, you will surely find, it is completely different than the last, because the partner is different, the entire relationship dynamic will be different.

So wipe the *failure* connotation out of your mind; its negative, don't dwell on it. Anyone that tells you differently would likely be happy to see you miserable. Look at the positive success that your marriage was in serving its purpose and move along. No matter what your situation is, you are where you are. Living in the past doesn't move you forward. It's time to look ahead and we're going to do that. We're going to move ahead in the following pages, step by step, starting with some basic baby steps, which always work for me when I don't seem to have the energy to go on.

We're going to begin putting your life back together when it may seem futile. We're going to develop a bond with your children that will carry you through any difficult times you will be facing in the immediate and the distant future.

Backpacking in the Utah Wilderness recently, we'd stop for a break, and I'd dump that heavy backpack on the ground and rest awhile. Not looking forward to putting it back on, I always would. It was heavy. Taking a few baby steps forward, so that I could reach the goal we had set, would get me moving again. With several miles to cover that day, I would continue to think only of the next step. Knowing that with each step, I was getting closer to our evening camp.

It was a wonderful trip, in spite of the weight on my back. I experienced a peace I needed at the time. I carried on my back only the essentials.

Though the weight you carry seems too much to bear, you are packing the essentials. And through the following pages, we are going to lighten that load. Your going to redefine what those essentials are, you're going to shed some and will pick up some new ones. But as you get stronger on your journey, the load is going to be much easier to bear. You will gain a new outlook on your past relationship, future relationships, and the importance of your relationship with your children.

In the following pages we're going to examine as many aspects of the Single Dad as I could fit in one book. I've provided a wealth of information to entertain your children in health and safety. You will find insight on how you may want to treat your ex, I hope it's enlightening, no matter what your current relationship. You will also find information on dealing with your emotions, though we as men of course would rather shy away from thinking of such silliness. We're going to deal with what's "inside," to hopefully prevent ever having to go through this kind of breakup again.

Though it may not be immediately apparent, you have a tremendous amount of freedom that you may not have had in your previous marriage. Freedom is always a good thing, you may be thinking, "I didn't want to be free!" *Freedom means the opportunity to do and be anything you want to be!* You have endless opportunities and choices in front of you. All you need to do is pick one, or several, and focus on how to achieve what your life is going to be like from this day forward. After choosing, you will take the first step.

In our lives, we are faced with where we are and we've decided where we want to be. The thing that stops us from reaching our goal is, "How do I get from here to there? Such a long and complicated road! I don't know how to start!"

Well, like hiking in the Mountains of Utah, take the next step, that leads to the next. Don't be focused too much on the ultimate goal, you'll always want to keep that goal in mind naturally. Don't focus on the next mile ahead, or on the next 100 steps, nor the next 10, focus on the next step. You know what the next step is, that's simple. As you take each step, the following step will be abundantly clear, so take that one next. And so on. You're several steps closer than you were moments ago.

Your next step of course in reading this book is to finish this chapter and go to the next, if you so choose. Your life is that simple.

The ideas expressed in the following pages are the benefit of my 20 years of experience as a single dad. It may not fit the ideals expressed by many child psychologists and experts. In fact, it would surprise me if any of them agreed with what I have to say. However, I feel the things expressed are realistic, most all are from my direct experience.

I've never claimed to be the perfect parent, far from it! I've made a lifetime of mistakes, and I'm certain I'm not done making them yet. These are things that work for me. The pages will only give you options, many of them. If you disagree with any philosophies or ideas, good for you! You're thinking and are aware. Leave those on the pages and adapt your own ideas and ideals. Raise your children the way you feel is best for them. That's why you are the parent!

This book need not be read in the order I've designed, though I've attempted to have a flow to the book. If your kids are visiting shortly, and you need some ideas on what to do with them right away, jump to the chapter "Fun Projects for Kids" (Chapter 18), or if you need help right away in putting your home in order, jump to (Chapter 8) Lists to help you organize your purchases.

At the end of each chapter, you will find an assignment. These are designed to be simple and will not require much of your time, unless you choose otherwise. Following these assignments, guaranteed, will make you a better single dad, more in touch with your children and community, and will allow you to reap many rewards. Ok, so it may sound like you're back in school, doing homework again. For the few days, or weeks, (or months if you're slow) while reading this book, it will be a good opportunity to again experience homework as your children may do, every night of the week.

Start with something fun, get yourself a T-shirt that says "Parent"; get one for each child that says "Kid." You will get lots of smiles and perhaps applause from other parents when you visit the zoo, grocery store, or playground. It's also a nice reminder, when you panic, of who's who in this relationship.

Use the pages of this book to start you thinking how you want to raise your children. Use the book to help you find the next step if necessary. Be aware of the things happening around you; be creative in their activities. Please forward any of your ideas to my website, www.kevin-james.com, that other single dads and their children might benefit from your experiences. We're all on a learning curve!

CHAPTER 2
WHO IS THE SINGLE DAD?

I have been on many battlefields; I have fought the battles and won many conflicts. I find myself locked in a battle for my life and for the future of my offspring. The outcome of this engagement is unsure. My strength will lie in who I am and who I intend to become.

Men have long been in the working world. As a part of that world, we've come to let ourselves be defined by our title for whatever job we happen to be doing.

"I'm a carpenter."

"I'm a dishwasher."

"I'm the CEO of X-Y-Z Company."

"I'm an executive analyst."

"I'm an attorney." (as if we don't know that means *lawyer*) What other profession has two names?

Oh yea, "I'm a doctor/physician." Is this a more honorable profession? Try calling a doctor appropriately Mr. or Mrs. You *will* be corrected.

In most cases, I believe we're proud of those titles, after all, this is a job we went seeking, and with some extent of effort, landed. To some varied degree these positions also reflect our experience in the working world and our life experience. It is generally a stepping-stone, to get us to the next level, and thus we are defined by those titles, of who we are.

Miscommunication is rampant about single dads and exs. We run across the deadbeat dad to assume he's a deadbeat by choice. And in some cases we may be right.

I've never met a deadbeat dad that wanted to be a deadbeat! Some single women I've known have commented that Dad doesn't care for his children, he doesn't care to pay child support. I've never heard that from a dad.

Speaking for all men is not my intention. With the men I've known, as males we come with high expectancies, our peers and family expect a lot from us. No matter what our lot in life, we *want* to be successful; we want to be a good dad, husband, employee, and everything else that comes with the machismo image.

When we find ourselves single though, with little or no experience in taking care of children, no guidebooks are found, none realistic in our minds. We face a wall that we cannot climb over, nor walk around. We're at a dead end.

It's not in our nature to show weakness, nor to ask directions, especially from those that would know the most about our situations, our ex's!

Our perception for the most part is females are so bent on proving they are better than men, at anything, you name the subject, why would we open ourselves up and show another chink in our armor? And please don't try and tell me this isn't so. I have heard it many times over the years we've been put down, slammed, spit on (figuratively and literally in some cases), and the words "I can do that job as well as any man!" Seems to be the rallying cry for some mystical women's organization. Oddly enough, I have never once in my life heard a man say, "I can do that job as well as any woman!"

I've had my days when I have no more sense than a sack of hammers, but sooner or later one learns not to stick his chin out and tell his opponent, "Give me your best shot!" We remain quiet and avoid what we are not good at. It makes no sense to wade into something completely unprepared. This is not always a conscious decision. Many of us are branded a deadbeat for this very reason.

As fathers and husbands, we wear many hats. More so I think than a woman does. This of course may vary by region or by relationship. We are expected to be experts in many situations. We are the breadwinner, dad, husband, retirement planner, good citizen, protector, handy man (we should be at least a little mechanically inclined), chauffeur, barbecue chef, mechanic, banker, financier, entrepreneur as well as politician, or at least knowledgeable in politics.

I don't know of any survey as to professional titles or positions single dads' hold. I would bet for as many professional titles that exist, you would find single dads in those chosen professions. Millions of us are in the United States alone. Studies indicate that at least 60% of children born today will spend some time in a single parent household. 60%! Am I the only one that finds this sum outrageous?

We, single dads, see each other in the malls, in the fast food playgrounds, and in the parks. Particularly noticeable are dads with children on Wednesday nights or weekends in the theaters and in restaurants, that's our court appointed visitation time. We may be found everywhere, at the zoo, hiking a mountain trail, or flying with kids on a plane. It's difficult to spot us, if a W or SO is not present, we may be single dads, or we may be out with the kids to give Mom a break. But we're everywhere.

The title "Single Dad" for better or worse generates stereotypes. Many are not flattering. Dad is blamed for running around, not caring, having affairs, and being a deadbeat. Friends, family and neighbors all rally to the support of the "poor single mother." Her life has been shattered and is burdened with raising the children on her own. In some instances, this may be a valid concern, or you may be a victim of stereotyping. Shake it off, buck up, you will prove them all wrong.

The title "Single Dad" can be associated with failure, but in truth, it is a very common situation many of us find ourselves in, and it gives the opportunity unfettered to influence our children in such a way that it will carry them through their entire lives.

Single Dad is unlike a title at your employment, it generally isn't something that you were seeking. You were thrown into this position with little or no formal training, and the position isn't always a result of your efforts and life's experiences. In a deeper sense however, it is. If we were intrinsically "in tune" to the world around us, we may have seen this coming, and would have had some time to prepare.

Above all else, don't let this title define who *you* are! You *are* still the same person you were a few weeks or months ago, perhaps a bit wiser for the experience. *You* can define the title; you have previously identified *who* you are. Your values and ideals have not changed. You've stumbled for a moment on the path you were headed. You will encounter plenty of forks in the road. You have the opportunity to choose the ones that suit you best on your journey.

You also have a distinct advantage over your female counterpart, who must *always* ask directions. We know we men don't have to! It may take us a bit longer to get where we're going, but we'll know every road in the county and where it leads, should we ever find ourselves lost in this same area again. How are we ever going to find the shortcuts if we always stick to the roads on the map?

Shortcuts are available to the single dad. One of the most difficult things we have to deal with is what to do with the kids and what we *should* know. What would be most beneficial to them *and* to the ex? What can we do to assure homework is done, where should they in fact *be* in regards to their development in life? What schedule for meals, bedtime, teeth brushing, and chores in the household are going to best benefit us all? Those and the answers to many other questions will follow.

Self-identity is something we may have to deal with. We always considered ourselves a spouse and a married *partner* until the separation. The *partner* is only one, and it can be a bit intimidating.

Unique opportunities lie in redefining who we are. We think we know who we are; we think we know ourselves fairly clearly. When we look in the mirror though, do we see what other people are seeing?

It's very enlightening to notice the difference between women and men when placed in front of a mirror.

When a woman stands in front of the mirror, which she does for great lengths of time, she will scrutinize every flaw and imperfection in her appearance, and of course will think it's necessary to best downplay those imperfections with makeup. Selecting the perfect color combination in eye shadow, lipstick or lip-gloss, and blush, she will create a masterpiece that would make Michelangelo proud. She will make sure the eyes; cheeks, lips, neck, forehead, and ears look perfect. She will check to see how the dress fits, every wrinkle smoothed out. Make sure the breasts look as perky as possible, no panty lines showing on the behind. She can pick the finest, microscopic piece of lint from the sleeve if it's out of place.

A woman will carefully select from a myriad of scents and floral bouquets in perfume. She will generally try to keep the perfume selection to any one of 25 completely different scents and brands. She will not move from this spot until every hair is in place. She will be a virtual feast for the eyes and olfactory senses. And she generally is *still* not content with the result. After some time emerging from the *powder room*, She approaches us looking drop dead gorgeous. Sometimes we notice.

A man on the other hand will stop by the mirror and wonder if he let his stubble remain for the day, if he would look more like George Clooney. "Yea, I like this look.." He will check his profile to admire how the cultivation of the beer belly is progressing. Perhaps flex a muscle or two and notice he hasn't changed *that much* since his younger days. A fine example of the male physique, he may decide to shower, run a comb through his hair, brush his teeth, giving no further thought to any part of the face or body. Maybe slap a little cologne on, whether he has decided to keep the stubble or not, because the wife likes it. The brand of cologne doesn't matter, whatever he got for Christmas last year and generally no more than two to select from. Throw on his favorite pants and shirt if they are handy, a suitable replacement is at hand if not, and emerge from the *john*. He approaches her, and she will notice. Out of love, she usually withholds comment.

Though we've glanced in the mirror, do we see who we are? As in life, when in front of the mirror, we only see what we want to see. We are convinced we have a certain aura. We hope we are respected and loved, though we don't admit the latter. If our words are not carefully chosen, it's inconsequential since it's the message more than the words that are the point. They understand what we mean. "I'm one that doesn't take crap from anyone. If I have something to say, I'll say it. It's in their best interest."

We (I at least) go through life without a great deal of regard, or awareness of what others think of me. Why should we/I? We are our own men; we are on a mission. If the bills are paid, the kids are fed, and we have a toy or two, life is good.

Certainly we *must* be concerned of what others think of us. But it can be so difficult to sort out. So many opinions exist of who we should be, how we should act, and the proper manners in various situations. No matter what we do, someone isn't happy, especially *her*. We suffer from information overload and as a result, put up the shield and do what we think is best.

Every woman, including those that are married, is in search of the perfect man. They seek a man who is a good provider, and a good husband and father to their children. They want a man who is strong yet gentle; a man who is ruggedly handsome, yet boyish in his charms. This man must be knowledgeable in all things, politics, finances, mechanically inclined, even tempered, loving, and have a drive that is unmatched by any human. Essentially, take ten men from varied backgrounds and personalities combine the best of each, and you would have the perfect man! How are we as men to meet these kinds of impossible demands?

No man can claim adeptness in all fields, as no woman can meet every expectation of her male companion. As males we have learned to accept compromises. If we were able to meet the expectations put on us, this would invade on our very nature as man, our manhood, and no female would be happy with us!

We know that women have a predilection for changing their minds. Not all women I'm sure, but I have witnessed it countless times. First they want this, then they want that. That's the beauty of the female mind! If the truth is known, it amuses us. However, it's not amusing if we allow ourselves to be caught up in this push-pull in our lives. That's not what we are as men! We like, no we *need* a decision, right or wrong, so that we can begin to formulate and execute a plan.

Where did all of these expectations from women come from? It began many years ago with the women's rights movements. Of course they had been suppressed and oppressed in many areas of our lives. Females had no right to vote for our political leaders. A woman's opinion was inconsequential. They were in all ways, second-class citizens in this country. In many countries, women still are second-class citizens.

The need for change was apparent in the manner men treated women. Women have a boundless gift to give to us, to our families, to our nation, and to the world. The nature of their dissimilar perspective can help provide peace to the world. As a result, changes began through many struggles, and it wasn't an easy road for them.

Unfortunately, the final goal to this struggle is unclear. It's snowballed into the endless pursuit of perfection, and we've been on the receiving end. As with all of us, it's so much easier to see the faults in others, and to criticize than to see the improvements needed in ourselves.

In the struggle women and men of all races, to be equal we've lost sight of *who* we are. We are not much different than our ancient ancestors in that we still possess the drive to provide for those in need. Our means of doing so has changed and adapted to our modern culture. Many of us have a tremendous drive to be successful. In our society to be above average has become essential to survival. By it's very definition *half of all people are average or below in their success.* Our drive though has dramatically increased the lifestyle of the *average* person.

Can we change the opinions of women, to get them to realize this demand of perfection is unrealistic? The best we can do is to be the best person we can possibly be. Areas will always be lacking. It is not possible to be everything to everyone. However, by being true to ourselves, by being the best me I can be, I will meet that one person that fits into my life, as it was intended.

As men, we are also strong. Strength is an admirable quality. Strength can be physical as well as emotional. Much can be said for the strength a man *can* express. A man who may be focused on survival in battle with a military enemy, knows he will be victorious over this enemy to protect his country and family. This same man will kneel and put an arm around a child crying from a nightmare. He is lovingly compassionate to his life partner, and his eye sparkles when he sees her. He will stand in the boardroom with an impossible presentation and sell it to the toughest critics. He will climb the highest tree and gently cradle a chick fallen as he replaces it to its mother's nest. It's no concern that no one witnesses. He has a great respect for life in all its forms.

From our earliest days, we were the hunters. We killed things. Yet we have always had a respect for life. The earliest men celebrated the spirit of an animal whose life had been taken to feed his family. I've hunted with many men that after a successful shot would sit silently with reverence as the animal breathed his last. The remains from ancient days, a sense of veneration for a life taken, traded for our own.

As ancient hunters our offspring were very important to us. We never gave their care much thought other than for food and shelter, as long as our partner tends to the other needs.

We are much deeper than most people realize. Sometimes our life partners recognize this quality in us and they honor us for it. All too often though, we get caught up in our day-to-day struggles and lose sight of who we are.

As men, we are endowed with a gift. It's a very special gift. Unfortunately, we have for various reasons, found cause to suppress this gift for many thousands of years.

We have been imposed upon, by society, by family, our loving friends, and neighbors, to hide a very special talent that we, and we alone possess.

It has long been known that we (men) are the stronger of the sexes. I don't doubt that this is a reference to our physical prowess, if you've ever experienced a woman in labor, you will realize in the pain endurance category, they have us beat hands down. However, we have focused our attention, to be physically stronger than our female counterparts, and have lost sight of our *true* gift.

This gift whether given through our genes or inherited, or for some other reason, I'm not certain, is our *ability* to be diverse in a myriad of ways.

Because we have the *ability* however does not mean we have knowledge of the faculties of this gift.

What I mean by *diversity* is our ability to be *all* things. We have the ability to be tremendously physically powerful yet be as gentle as a child. We have the ability to be proud, yet humble, the ability to be assertive and passive. We sometimes misdirect the ability that we have, to an inappropriate situation.

A man may be tremendously strong and focused when in battle or war, trapped behind enemy lines and fighting, literally for survival. He will be resourceful, never considering anything but success. In this situation, we won't think of failure. Failure is not an option. We are focused, and we believe we will succeed. Over the course of history, many have proven success.

A man may in the obverse, also be as gentle as a lamb, when faced with the prospect of holding his newborn child, changing a diaper, or comforting the tears of a little one.

A man may be tremendously assertive in the *proper* situation with no thought of being inferior, or having to prove himself.

A man may be assertive *and* polite at the same time. I have spent many years in customer service. I know the importance of this combination.

A man may find humor in the most trying of situations, and laugh with abandon at odds that seem overwhelming.

A man has the *ability* to suppress his emotions, to deal with a particular situation without interference, and the *ability* to face those emotions when the time is right.

We have the ability to fend off an attacker with great finesse when called upon to do so, in protection of our loved ones.

We have a wealth of emotions that we have been blessed with, anger, love, confidence, fear, hate, and a drive to succeed that is ours and ours alone. Yet more, we have the *ability* to apply these emotions to fit the appropriate situation.

We are all blessed with a range of emotions that are gifts, when used appropriately. For instance, if we have purchased an item and it has not met our expectations, and more importantly the promises of the seller, it would not behoove us to crawl into their Returns department on our bellies and beg for a refund. No, the appropriate way would be to approach the counter, proud and confident, present the product to the merchant and request a refund or appropriate store credit. If you are not familiar with the term "store credit," ask your EX, she'll know.

Only when the store refuses to make good on the merchandise do we become appropriately assertive. Remember a combination of *assertive* and *politeness* is the best way to succeed in your goal. (Again, as a long time customer service representative, if you *insult* me, you will get *nothing*.) We can at the same time have our child approach us, with a tear in her eye as she fell against a post, we will kneel to console her, knowing that our request from our friendly neighborhood merchant will be met. We are not showing weakness, this has nothing to do with the merchant issue.

We get so caught up in labels sometimes; we lose a sense of who we really are. I have been living by myself, more on than off for 20 years, so I do it *all* in my house. I cook and do dishes (many dinner parties), vacuum, dust, and take out the trash (my son and daughter are great at helping with this). Essentially in my home, if I don't wear many hats, I'd live like a pig!

After Thanksgiving dinner recently, I was doing dishes to help my ex clean the house before I left. Her daughter commented, "A man doing dishes? Go figure!" I thought how odd, she knows I live by myself and have for many years. If I didn't do the dishes at my house, who would? I can't afford a maid, nor do I desire one.

Labels are very prevalent in our society, probably most apparent between the "Men Things" and the "Women Things." We teach our children these labels from the earliest of ages. The truth is, we have all been blessed with both *tendencies* in our personalities. That, which we choose to nurture however, grows and becomes stronger.

We all have experienced lawyers, used car salesmen, door to door salesmen, mothers, grandmothers, and we all have our expectations of how those particular people must act to fit the label we have put on them.

The most obvious example currently in the forefront in my world is Shania Twain. She has recently returned from an absence after having a child, to recharge and write more music. A great debate continues in some circles whether her newest music is country, or pop, or something else? I am a tremendous Shania Fan and am also a *country* music fan. I am not passionate about country music, but anything Shania sings stirs my passions. I'm not referring to the obvious.

The label wouldn't slow me down for a minute. If you want to call Shania's music pop rock, it wouldn't matter. I like Shania's music, Shania, if *you* are singing, I am there! It's what she does and who she is, it's not the label. It's how I feel when I am listening to her sing, or watching on a DVD, it's the spirit she projects when she is doing something she loves. If she gave a damn what label was being put on it, I think she would be very limited in the type of music she produced. If Shania chooses to leave music altogether and do something else she wants to do, I say GO!

When Shania is doing anything, from mothering, to cooking, to skiing or writing and singing, she is laser focused on the moment. A quality I would like to have! Watching her interviews she exudes childlike innocence. She's playful and shy, which belies the confidence displayed on stage. Does it matter that she is not the Shania diva at all times? She is being the person she was born to be.

As so many feel they must put their own label on Shania's music, so it fits their little way of thinking, we are all subjected to the labels from those around us. Oddly enough, Shania grew up singing many forms of music, to make a living in her younger years, rock, country, and many others. She *is* all of them. *We* labeled her country.

One of the greatest compliments anyone can possibly give you is "You are so YOU!" This is unique. You are one of a kind. You are not like anyone else, and you are not fitting a label.

It's our duty to shed the labels. *Be* who you are. You cannot make use of your gifts, all of the wonderful emotions, strengths and weaknesses that you alone possess, and still fit a label.

Now and then we must be aware of how others see us. Things may have been said in the relationship, perhaps in an angry moment, if we had listened, might have given us time to pause and reflect. Take time to look back, remember some of those issues that your partner had with you. She likely knows *you* better than most anyone.

If the problems were financial, work toward balancing your talent in that area as you have in others. If problems were with intimacy or being unemotional, perhaps you will want to search out books, a support group or professional assistance in balancing issues that may need attention.

It can be beneficial to sit with a close friend, and ask them honestly yet lovingly to give you some advice on how they see you and what things you may want to work on. (Add this to your Assignment below if you are ready.) I wouldn't rely too much on the ex for help on this one unless you have a very close relationship. She may be a bit partial, or vindictive, in presenting those ideas. This is a great opportunity to round out your personality to best benefit you in the future, if for no other reason than to keep from repeating this pattern, or at the very least, creating a pattern.

One of my ex's recently made a comment on my language (foul) which I can let slip at times. My gut thought was, "Would you like me to list all of your faults?" I was immediately defensive. I held my tongue though, not wanting to start a fight. But I must admit whether or not she was right, I was insulted. I have made a mental note to learn to watch my tongue. It's been said that a person using foul language hasn't the intelligence to use the proper words. It is another reminder that I'm not perfect, and is another goal in my striving for perfection. At least my own version of it!

We find ourselves in this single dad role, and we, as well as others, seem to think this automatically strips away the centuries of knowledge and instinct that have been bred into us. *It doesn't change a thing, other than our circumstances.* We still have the same instincts for survival, for the protection of our offspring. We still have hopes and dreams of being in a loving relationship and being above average in our success.

Being a single dad is yet another opportunity to shine. Forget the stereotypes that have been born in ignorance. You *are* who you *are* and you will be as good at this, or better, than you are at everything else in your life. You will have and will work toward fulfilling your dreams. The success built from being a great single dad will carry you well on in your life and toward fulfilling your goals. Children are wonderful at helping you fulfill your dreams and goals. How many times have I had one of my children tell me "You can do it, Dad. I believe in you!" I need little further inspiration.

Single dads are everywhere. We are everything. The *commonality* is doing what's right for the kids while making ourselves happy. We have a great contribution for our children, and *through* them, to the world. It's all perspective.

To do this effectively, we need to deal with the past relationship and perhaps, grieve its loss.

ASSIGNMENT

Identify what title you wear (doctor, lawyer, etc) and remove that barrier. What does that mean anyway?

Make a list of traits you would like to have, and who you would like to be. (i.e.: Loving, warm, gentle, patient, healthy, etc.) Keep this list handy; review it first daily, or weekly to see how well you are progressing at becoming the person you want to be.

Identify those areas that are lacking (i.e.: financial organization, patience, housekeeping etc) and work toward improving those areas. Identify the best and fastest way to improve those areas of your life. Find a financial advisor, or a class on personal finances, find a support group for single dads or parents in your area to learn more on being a parent. Most classes only last a few weeks.

If housekeeping is your shortfall, identify which nights of the week and which duties you will perform on that night. An hour a day (laundry aside) in keeping my house clean, works for me. More on Sunday when the kids leave, keeping a regular schedule allows me to complete these chores. I'm more content with the condition of my home.

CHAPTER 3
HOW TO GET THROUGH
THE GRIEVING

An ache fills my chest piercing deep in my heart. It speaks to me. Dwell on it and I ache from every pore of my being. I grieve not only the loss of a loved one, but of the memories and dreams yet to come. Dreams faded into night. I have lost a piece of myself.

If you are going through the grieving process or have yet to grieve over your separation with EX, *read this chapter*. If you *think* you have taken care of the emotions involved with the break up, *read this chapter*. If you *have* taken care of all of the emotions, done the grieving and are ready to move on, Congratulations! *Read this chapter*.

Not long ago, I was given the opportunity to make a walking stick for a dear friend that loves to hike in the mountains. Knowing at the time, this could not be just any walking stick, this one had to be special, to match the unique qualities of my special friend.

On my search in the mountains, I had a picture in my mind's eye, of the exact piece of wood that would be needed, and I also knew precisely where it would be found. During the hike to the place I knew, I passed by many saplings, that would make a staff suitable for most, growing straight and true, but I knew these were not ones to be selected.

Arriving at the appointed place, and looking around for the oak I knew would be there, in short order it presented itself. Growing from the ground it had been damaged by some thoughtless campers, determined to tear it from the earth.

Apparently, the sapling had proven too strong for their undetermined efforts, yet had been damaged at the base and would die in the months to come.

In the spirit of the Native American culture, I informed the sapling of what I intended, and requested permission to cut it from the ground to take it home with me to be worked. It was with a certain sadness that the oak consented.

After arriving home, I began peeling the bark from the wood. As the outer covering was removed, the twists, and knots and knurls at one end of the stick were revealed. Between two sets of these knots a straight section that would make a perfect handle to fit into the delicate hand of my friend.

I spent some time working this piece of wood, not "making it," but merely brought forth the beauty of the wood. The Creator, in all its perfection made the tree. The twists and knots were scars of tough winters, and lack of rainfall, snow slides, high wind, and other assaults sustained. Yet in this rugged environment the sapling endured, a unique character was sculpted.

So it is with us. We see our imperfections that make us different. We curse these imperfections! Rather these imperfections make each unique, they allow us to be who we are. Typically when we suffer significant loss, we are reminded of imperfections.

Yet when we seek a mate, a partner, or friend, it is the imperfections that draw us, due to the uniqueness of their nature. And rather than appreciate the differences, we try to make them more like us, to match our own perceived imperfections.

The beauty of this particular walking stick was unmatched. The knots and twists in its shaft, giving it a distinct character. It is unique and was made as it was designed.

I could not change an atom of its makeup. I was only allowed to show the beauty that was natural.

To my joy, my friend was very pleased with the walking stick and has treasured it as the precious gift it was intended to be.

Please take the opportunity in your life to appreciate the uniqueness of each individual, though they may not fit the mold of what we consider perfect. My friend and her walking stick were the first to teach me this elusive but valuable lesson. For this I will be forever grateful.

What boring world would we live in, if every sapling, every tree grew tall and straight and true? What if every rock was perfectly smooth and every day sunny and bright? This would be a world I could not envision, nor want to live in.

As I write, I notice similar imperfections in each crystal that I am currently collecting, and in the dents my children put in my beautiful coffee table, making it more beautiful with each little nick and bump. I am surrounded by imperfection! Perfection in Imperfections!

To my special friend Kelly, and to each of my friends and loved ones, a special "Thank You" for being exactly "imperfect" enough to be who you are. Without you, I would not be unique and "imperfect" enough to be me.

We all know nobody's perfect. We all tolerate the faults and flaws in our loved ones. We can however be extremely intolerant of our own imperfections, especially when we are not happy with the direction our life may be taking. This is a time for a change in our lives, to move on to something bigger, better, and much more wonderful. Our former life has outlived its usefulness to us, and it's time to move on.

Studies have been completed evaluating the most emotional times we may experience in our lives. Much like when someone dear to us dies, and passes on, a large hole is left when a relationship ends. The impact can be one of varying degrees, depending on the length of the relationship, if children are involved and how close we were to our *life* partner. Losing someone that has been very special to you a family member or in a relationship can be quite a blow emotionally. The added impact of *losing* the children, one's home, a portion of income, and our worldly possessions can cause a sense of loss, what we would consider devastation.

Let's look at the word *devastation*. Certainly we are torn, perhaps a bit lost, but devastated? Can we liken this to the bomb being dropped on Hiroshima with thousands of lives lost, The World Trade Center *devastation*, or a natural catastrophe, which changes the very world, as we know it? Devastation is a bit harsh, so work on redefining how you are *really* feeling. Changing the word will help change your outlook on the situation. "I'm a bit troubled" perhaps?

During one of my worst breakups, I'd been asked to leave my home and my two daughters. I didn't have time to pack my things, only a few clothes in a suitcase. The soon to be ex had assured me she would pack up everything I owned, and I would be able to pick them up after a few days.

This whole breakup was a real shock to me. I should have seen it coming, as all the signs were visible for years. I loved her very much, or at least thought I did. I was completely taken with this woman. I thought I had done everything right, whatever that might mean. I had been a good cook, good at helping with the kids, helped around the house whenever I could. I thought I had done my best to provide, in the best way I knew how. Sure I was a bit down on my luck, but things would change. Thing always change.

So with a few dollars in my pocket and a pickup truck, I left. With no place to go, I tried to contact one of my best friends. I had lost touch with he and his wife through the relationship. I was able to reach his daughter, and she said they were out of state for a couple of weeks. She gave me a number where I could reach them.

I called him. My friend said he was sad to hear of my plight. I was more than welcome to stay in their trailer home until they returned, which would be a couple of weeks. I retrieved the key from his daughter and went to his trailer.

I didn't feel much for the first few days, numbness I suppose. I've always considered myself a "thinker," and I thought a lot of things. *What had I done wrong? What could I have possibly done differently that would have made any difference at all?*

It was unusual for me not to at least hope that we might get back together. This time I knew it was over. This didn't make things any easier.

The first few days, while tough, were not the worst. I contacted as many old friends as I could. Wanting sympathy where I could get it. I contacted old girlfriends. All of them were very sympathetic, but all were involved with their lives and didn't have time for anything more than a phone chat. Looking back, I can't say I blame any of them. I would not have wanted to be around me at that time in my life. I reeked of negative energy.

I had called my boss, let her know I was going through a very tough time, and I wouldn't be into work for an indefinite period of time. I couldn't be in a position to "perform" at this time. She assured me the job would wait and was very gracious. She asked that I at least keep her informed of my plans.

In retrospect, not going to work was a huge mistake. I needed some sense of normalcy in my life. Whether I thought I could handle it or not. A few days back in the flow of life and I'd at least have some break from the depression I was going through.

So I subjected myself, day after day, to my own thoughts.

If anyone were to stop by, it was only for moments and our words brief. I drank heavily and smoked frequently. I couldn't sleep, which of course made the whole situation worse. My phone contacts were rapidly drying up, I assume my negativity was too overwhelming for those I contacted.

I couldn't remember the last time I'd cried. Perhaps it had been as a child or during one of my past breakups. I wasn't a crier. I wasn't in touch with my emotions, and I certainly could think of nothing worse. I cried. When everything started, it didn't stop. I had cried before but nothing like this. I'm not so certain I *needed* to cry as much as my physical body was incapable of containing all of the emotion any longer.

Not long after purging those emotions, being the man that I was, I had lots of room to suppress any other emotions. I had cleaned out the warehouse, so I thought, so I could compose myself and move on. But I wasn't done yet.

After several more days of being alone with nothing but my brain to entertain me, I had been drinking and smoking particularly heavily one day and evening. I hated when the darkness came. To me this is when everyone else would be soundly sleeping. The chances of someone taking pity on my poor soul and stopping by, which I so desperately hoped, was gone until the morning light would bring new hope. I'd been through enough of these nights, enough of this futile hope. The dialogue in my mind began, wrestling with decisions I did and did not want to make. I sat on the bed, not quite ready to crawl under the covers yet.

I'm tired and drunk, maybe I'll go ahead and sleep like everyone else. As I sat on the bed, knowing that sleep would not come for a long time.

Surely things will look better in the morning.

What is possibly going to be different tomorrow than it was today? Nothing. Absolutely nothing

Contrary to what I should have been doing, building my self up, I began to run myself down. *You've sure done it this time. Six years wasted with that bitch, and you have nothing to show for it. It is no wonder she wanted you out, you have nothing to offer.*

What the hell are you going to do? You have nothing. You have no plan. You have no money, no food. You are going nowhere. You have no friends left, you ran them all off. You didn't have time for them when they needed you. Now you need them, and they are returning the favor. You're a leach, a bum, you're 43 years old, and you have nothing. You're incapable of loving anyone, and anyone loving you. You are a worthless asshole to everyone you've ever come in contact with.

Oddly enough, I wasn't feeling much. The alcohol was clouding my judgment. Sure I was worthless, but if I had been sober, I'd at least have known this line of thinking was leading to nothing good. My eyes raised and immediately settled on the glass door of my friend's gun cabinet. It contained several hunting rifles. I stared at the beautifully crafted wood, the blue steel of the barrels and the cold steel triggers. *End it all, be done with it, no one is going to give a shit. Those rifles aren't so long you can't just put the barrel in your mouth, pull the trigger and have...peace. The pain will all go away.*

I didn't catch myself or stop my thoughts. I thought long and hard. *I wonder where he keeps the bullets. Perhaps in the desk drawer or maybe in his dresser? I could find them, only need one.* I still wasn't moving from the bed.

I thought of my friend and his wife, coming home after how many days? *Who would clean my brains off the wall?* This was not something I wanted to do to my friend, or his wife. *Take the rifle and the bullet and go somewhere else to do this.*

Then it came, thoughts of my children. I could see their faces. I could see their smiles and feel their loving hugs. *The girls love me. My son loves me. How are they going to get by without me? They think I'm worth something.* A peace came over me. I began to know, beyond anything I had ever known, doing this thing was not an option. Thank God I still had enough of my senses to realize this.

I also realized that I could rebuild the few worldly possessions I once had. I knew I would find someone meant only for me. This process I was going through was merely a step to getting me closer to that relationship. The amount of the *loss* of my children would to a great degree, be determined by me. Realization of this was the first sign that I would get through the grieving process.

I had been on a roller coast of emotions, perhaps some or all of which may be familiar to you. It could change from moment to moment. I shed many tears, didn't care if I ate or not, I certainly had no appetite. The simple sound of a friendly voice on the phone would bring hope, and was faced with the end of hope as I hung up the phone. I didn't want to do anything to take care of myself, wash clothes, go to work, do any banking or bill paying. What was the use? What difference would it make in anyone's life, if I were to disappear from the earth?

Men are tough; men don't cry; men bury their emotions. Don't we? You've all heard it from the females most of your life. We were taught this at the earliest of ages of course, "big boys don't cry" etc. We are guilty of teaching it to our children, and the women taught this to us, our mothers! The ones we hold so dearly and precious in our lives. *But* when we become men, they want to magically undo these years of programming. It's ok for their little guys to be tough and to be men, not crying, being able to take it like a man, but not their husbands! Keep this in mind when raising your children.

It is what it is guys, "you ain't gonna change 'em." I've heard that a man marries a woman hoping they *won't* change, a woman marries a man because he has potential *to* change. Often we disappoint them. But guess what, that's ok! We are who we are. Popeye was a man. One of his favorite sayings was "I am what I am and that's all that I am." Popeye was way ahead of his time. But along came Olive Oil…well you probably all know the story. Popeye was *very* cool.

On the surface, the breakup appears to be a very tragic situation for everyone involved, especially the children. What you do from this moment forward will make a difference to the child, and there is no one more important.

Understanding at first that this is a great thing can be difficult but not impossible. When your guts are all wound up, your chest hurts, your head pounds, and your brain spins uncontrollably, it's hard to look at this as a good thing. You may decide to visit a doctor, thinking surely you must have contracted malaria or some other exotic disease. He'll shrug his shoulders and say, "I dunno."

If you are fortunate as I was, beyond this pain comes numbness. No emotions. This condition can last for days, but it will pass. It will pass more quickly as you begin to realize that life is continuing, whether you choose to be a part of it or not.

We certainly don't want to play the blame game. We discussed earlier the heat men take when a relationship breaks up. I've known many instances when mom didn't want to be married any longer and did the running around to cause the eventual downfall of the marriage. It is difficult for anyone outside the relationship to see the truth. Short of a professional counselor, it's no one else's business. It's also difficult for anyone inside the relationship to see truth. We each judge from our own emotional needs and are blinded by our perspective.

Men take a lot of heat because we're supposed to be strong. It's no wonder we bury our emotions to prepare for battle against those that would see us to our doom. Despite which partner made the first move, the burden of responsibility for the breakup lies on the shoulders of both. We attempt to justify that we did everything we could by being a loving father, husband and breadwinner. Accept your part of the burden *by knowing that this is what it is*.

A relationship rarely ends as the result of a single action. One of us doesn't decide one day we're going to be unfaithful, go have an affair or walk away from the relationship for no reason. Numerous emotions and issues are involved. These can include money troubles, communication problems, that we are unappreciated and don't fit in this home and family. It's the result of many months or years of broken down communication between the partners.

It takes at least two to communicate, whether it's humans, animals, or radio signals. When one stops broadcasting, or stops receiving signals, the other may continue to broadcast for a period of time. After awhile it's a huge waste of energy to continue. Soon we both shut down and don't communicate effectively. Yelling at one another is not a valid form of communication; it is however a form of expressing and releasing pent up emotions. This can be accomplished in other ways, by exercising, doing something creative, or taking a walk. When the intensity of the emotion is reduced, it's time to fix the problem by talking with your partner. In most cases a breakdown of communication is the first step on a long and winding staircase leading down.

I heard a story recently of a marriage that surely seemed doomed due to the little snipping between the husband and wife. They were unhappy and felt unappreciated for the things they did daily. This made the children unhappy feel unloved and afraid for what the future may hold.

One day, the husband said to his wife, "Do you know I have magical dresser drawers? I want to thank you for making them magical in that whenever I open them, there are always clean socks, neatly folded inside! I appreciate that you do that for me."

His wife, skeptical as always of sarcasm, didn't say a word, but it gave her cause to wonder. At least until his next comment, "You look wonderful today! I appreciate that you always take the time to look so nice."

Again, she had no comment, but was taken aback, as she had been the first time.

Well, these compliments continued over several weeks. After several days, his wife had to assume he was being sincere and complimented him on how regular and thorough he was with the yard work: "I appreciate that you always keep our yard looking so nice!" He replied, "Thank you, honey."

Soon the father was complimenting the children, for doing things so well and being such a valuable part of the family. It was driving the teenaged daughter nuts!

Needless to say, these little extra comments began to make a big difference in their lives. They could honestly sit and talk together again of things that bothered them. Knowing they *were* appreciated gave them the strength and confidence to discuss other issues.

To this day, no one has been able to get father to tell what caused his sudden change of behavior. His wife has pressed him time after time. He smiles slyly, gives her a peck on the cheek and says, "I love you."

You are still the same person you were when you attracted that wife. You may have "advanced" a little bit and sooner or later you will attract another, when you're ready. Your dreams don't need to change, you may need to change the person you are going to fulfill them with, but the dream need not change.

Having dreams and goals is a wonderful thing. They give us purpose in life. You may want to rethink some of your dreams, but overall, hang on to them. It is time to start making your dreams a reality. *You will be more of who you are as you fulfill some of those dreams*

If you have the means, a vacation you've always wanted to may be in order. Surely you have a friend or close acquaintance or family member that would love to accompany you. If not, consider going by yourself as an adventure. Get out and explore. Be someone you have always wanted to be, go do it.

Unfortunately, some men (and women) in our society become so obsessed with the ex they feel it will make things better if they can watch every move the other makes and know everything they are doing. They want to have some dirt to throw, or to justify they were right in the breakup. It may be victim justification. Sometimes it may resort to stalking. I don't want to make light of the stalking problem in this country, it's a very disturbing trend that causes fear for many of the victims and will certainly prolong the healing process for the perpetrator. This is a crime in America, and it is a serious invasion of privacy. This may involve someone being subjected to physical harm as well as a great deal of mental anguish.

That being said however, let me tell you, stalking is not all it's cracked up to be. I have a good friend that I had a tremendous crush on a few years ago. She is a wonderful great spirited lady, happily married with two children. In order to satisfy my obsession with her, and being the polite person I am, I notified her that I would like to stalk her. I advised her though my schedule was extremely busy, and I wouldn't have the time to try and find her all the time. I asked if she would be so kind as to write out her schedule each week, it would make my "job" much easier. Happily, she consented, with a laugh of course. Fortunately, her husband was also a very understanding man.

I'll tell you that she is one busy woman! She is constantly on the move with work, running her children to all types of school activities and sporting events. After a couple of weeks, I was exhausted! I found I was also running low on funds for vehicle expenses. With her help, we came to an arrangement. Since it was the summer months, she would set a lawn chair out on her deck, with a stocked cooler of beer. I could wile away my afternoons, soaking up the sun, enjoying a cold brew, and she would call in regularly on my cell phone to notify me of her movements. This was a much better arrangement! Ok, so I failed miserably at being a stalker.

Avoid such contact with your ex. Seeing *anything she is doing or the places she is going will only lead to more suspicion.* How far must she go with her actions that will make you feel like you are justified in what you are feeling? We don't think with a logical mind when in this emotional state. We tend to only think the worst. "She is doing everything she can to hurt me," preoccupies our thoughts. Indulgence in such behavior can quickly escalate into a tragic situation. *Whatever we nurture, will grow and become stronger.*

Seeking to understand will go a long way in your dealing with your emotions. Understand the pain the ex is going through. Because you don't see it doesn't mean it's not there. She is not prepared to show you any weakness.

She is *also* going through a loss of her dreams, a loss of a loved one. Someone she has spent a great deal of her life with, someone she began her family with. She is probably in turmoil trying to figure out how she is going to provide for her dear offspring. Perhaps she is at a point of being overwhelmed, has shut down, and can't cope with life. She is going through many of the emotions you are.

Since the relationship ended, at least one of you decided you did not want to live *this way* any longer. One of you decided they had done everything they could to resolve this situation albeit unsuccessfully. It is what it is; it's time to move away from that relationship. The sooner you realize this, the sooner you will have your life on track.

If you want to know how your ex is feeling, I'll give you a general "rule of thumb" on how to do that. This is a completely unscientific formula, and comes from some deep dark area of my mind where I rarely venture.

Take all of the pain that you perceive and multiply it by one (for her). Take that and multiply it by the number of children she has (x2, x3 etc) because as a mother, she also hurts for her children. Take that number, let's say you have three children, so we have taken your pain and multiplied it by three to give us a total of three. Since she's a female and works greatly on emotion, multiply this number by another three for a total of nine. Because she is in touch with her emotions, it's a good chance she is hurting nine times as much as you are. Factor in the state of her financial affairs and how she is going to provide for the fruit of her loins, and multiply it by another unknown figure.

Know that she is not doing all of the things to *hurt* you. She is, as you are, in *survival* mode. She *has* to be strong, she *has* to move on, and she *has* to do this quickly for the children. She does not have the luxury of taking days or weeks without caring for her needs. She must maintain the daily routines and necessities of life, because she is not the only one dependent on them. She may also be blaming herself for taking her children's father away, for what may seem to her at least, her own selfish desires. She fears every day that the children will also blame her. She alone can answer their questions and comfort their fears that *she* will not go away also. That *she* will be home for them. That *she* will not abandon them.

She fears that if she were to have some life threatening medical problem, or God forbid, be killed in a car accident, *She* will have lied to her children. Her children will be without mother or father.

She is experiencing the pain you are and perhaps more.

We seek to diminish the pain with a fix, *something* to take away the pain if only for a short time. You may witness yourself or the ex in another's company, seeming to be moving on with their life, as if the other had never existed. *Things are rarely as they appear to be.*

This fix of being around someone else is very similar to a narcotic, and provides the same stimulus in the brain of a false euphoria. The term associated with this is a *rebound relationship*. We fool ourselves into thinking this other person is the dream person we have always waited for, because only they can provide what we *need*. And sadly, many people in the world, for reasons of low self-esteem or other issues will jump at the chance to pick up on someone in such need.

As a drug dealer will feed his product to his customer to keep them hooked, this *rebound* partner is in a position to exert a great deal of control over someone in such a broken mental state. But as with a narcotic, the effect is going to wear off, and *eventually* the single person, is going to be forced by circumstances to face the reality of the loss.

When handled in a healthy and productive manner, a *rebound relationship* can be an extremely helpful relationship. For the person formerly in an abusive relationship fearing they don't have the strength to stay away, a nurturing loving and emotionally secure rebound partner may help them work through these emotions. Allowing them to regain the strength needed to get back on their feet.

I was fortunate after my first divorce to be in a wonderful loving, rebound relationship with another woman. She understood what I needed. She held me close when I needed it, and gave me room when I could handle it. She kept me at arms length, so I wouldn't become attached for the wrong reasons, and when it was time to move on, she gave me a big hug, a kiss, and a tear rolled down her cheek as she wished me well. She always knew it would one day come to this, as we one day must release our children onto the world. God Bless you, Vicky.

Conversely, when the rebound partner is a sexual predator, has control issues or other personality defects, it can be a very dangerous situation. Unfortunately in this type of situation, *you* (the former partner) may be the *last* person that can help the ex. Anything you say about your ex's social life will generally be interpreted as *sour grapes,* jealousy or the like. Your best recourse is to casually alert a mutual friend or family member that may be able to influence the situation and *leave it alone.*

Trying to break up the rebound relationship, or influence it in any way on your part will generally make that relationship stronger. Both partners in that relationship identify only one enemy to their relationship, *you.*

Should you feel you are in a rebound relationship, take a look at it objectively. See it for what it is, for what it *should* be to serve you *both* effectively in your growth process. If you or your partner sees yourselves becoming dependent on the other for happiness, you are in this relationship for the wrong reason.

Rebound relationships are rare when they last. They serve a very useful purpose, and once that purpose has been met, we are able to view it in a different light. The result of this enlightened view is generally both partners moving on separately.

In an unhealthy rebound relationship, when taken far enough, it can lead to the emotional breakdown of one or both partners, and may escalate to physical harm, or to the death of one of the partners involved. Very intense emotions are involved, and keeping things in perspective is crucial.

If you do not find yourself desiring an intimate relationship at this time, other options can be considered.

Use this time in front of you to clear out baggage. You will not want to cart this icky stuff around and certainly not into your next relationship. Use this time to begin rebuilding your self-esteem. Take an objective look at yourself. Clean up your appearance if you like, work on your physical health and get in shape. It's not unusual for any of us to be involved in a marriage or serious relationship, and get comfortable with our appearance.

This is a good time to start a new hobby, or to restart one that you had in the past but had given up. You won't do this to avoid grieving, but we all need a break from that grieving once in awhile to give our minds and emotions a rest. Spending some time doing something you enjoy in a hobby, will recharge you, clear your mind, and give you the strength and desire to continue on your path. Possibly some activity you always wanted to get involved in, but held back because of your ex. Well, it is time to go do those things!

Find yourself some social outlets. I spent a great deal of time in the bars and nightclubs. I soon learned though, this is *not* the place to meet anyone of significance, at least not the type of person (male OR female) that I'm going to want in my life. A bar type establishment should be provided for entertainment and socializing. I think this is the purpose designed by most club owners. However, the patrons may take that to another level. They seek companionship, a sexual partner, and a life mate. I'm not certain this is a wise idea.

Don't get me wrong; when you need to get 'out' sometime and be entertained, meet new people, have some laughs, this can be a great place to go. Over the years (and I do mean *years*) frequenting the bars and nightclubs, I've no doubt met a couple of thousand women. Only a handful were people I prefer to pursue a relationship with. This isn't a great set of odds! Go out; enjoy the environment for what it is, keep it in perspective. The bar owners and patrons will appreciate your fresh outlook. And we all know, when you aren't looking, that's when the right person turns up! You are more relaxed, you are yourself, and this is the type of person that will attract that special someone.

When I divorced from W1, we were living in a small town for a short time. I had no family and few friends. The soon to be ex, packed the kids up and moved back to her home town, close to family and friends. I want to say, straight up, I had put her in a position due to infidelity that she had no choice but to make the split. Yes, I cheated, more than once for no fault of hers. We had tried to work it out, and *she* was the only one trying to work it out. If blame were to be placed, it would have to go squarely on my shoulders.

My therapy at that time consisted of hanging with the guys, frequenting the bars, chasing and sometimes catching any little bunny that would come along. Drinking was the order of the day; I took up smoking as a hobby to keep me occupied. By god, I would show *her*.

Assuming we are all in agreement some wiser choices were in front of me (hey I was young and stupid), let's move on.

Consider joining a social group of some kind, depending on your interests. Communities offer a wide variety of groups you may want to get involved with, bowling leagues (mixed and singles), Gold panning organizations, Four Wheel drive clubs, fly fishing groups, skin diving clubs, car clubs, photography clubs, science and astronomy groups. Anything you are interested in, chances are a large number of other folks are interested and have formed a social gathering for people like yourself. They will appreciate your support, and it will be a great outlet for your needs. This doesn't have to be a lifelong commitment. Step out of your comfort zone and go try it.

If needed, professional counselors and clergy are trained to provide any support you might need to get through this process of grief. These folks will have knowledge of area social groups and activities. You may not want to be around people, but it is very important just for a break if nothing more.

Not long ago I made a major investment in a complete home theater system for my home. Having laid out a large chunk of cash to purchase the system, I decided I would do the installation myself. I soon found the project was going to involve some major electrical work, running some new wiring and installing a new circuit breaker to handle the amperage.

Electrical work has never been my strength. In fact an electrician that I worked with several years ago had given the sum of my knowledge to me. He taught me that electrical wires contain smoke. As long as you keep the smoke *in*, you've done it right. With his sound advice, I was intelligent enough to know if I didn't do things correctly, retribution from the electricity would be swift and sure.

Being faced with this type of situation in the past, the choices were simple. I could go through the yellow pages and hire a qualified electrician, or I could seek out the advice of those qualified professionals and perhaps reassess my skill level as it related to the job.

I first visited the local Home Improvement center and approached an obviously experienced gentleman working in the electrical department. He was kind and extremely helpful. He showed me which parts I would need and carefully explained in detail how to shut off the main power, how to make certain it was shut off in the areas I would be working and assured me the job wasn't as difficult as I was imagining. I felt a tremendous sense of relief after speaking with him. I purchased the parts and tools I would need and left the store.

I remembered another friend who was a licensed electrician. I immediately called and ask that he meet me at my home to give me some pointers. He was more than accommodating, and it wasn't long with his assistance, I had my theater system up and running.

Seeking out advice from professionals in their chosen fields is nothing new for any of us. We all do it with great regularity. However, when it comes to seeking out professional assistance when it relates to our feelings or emotions, it's not open for discussion. "Nope, not a chance, I don't need a shrink, don't need anyone telling me how I feel."

This is certainly a ridiculous way of thinking isn't it? I have to admit though; I've done it. It's a guy thing and we're very, very good at it. There is no shame in it, any more than seeking the help of the electrically qualified. I was proud *I* had done the work, and with their helpful advice, had not found myself frozen to the end of a live wire, going through various break dancing contortions on the floor.

As I felt relief when I spoke to the gentleman in the store, a therapist can help you realize that what you are feeling is perfectly normal. After all, your life, your hopes, your dreams have all been turned upside down. That's the way it *looks* anyway. Whatever you are going through, it's likely normal. Trained professionals are ready to serve you! Be selective in who you choose for assistance. Trust their judgment but rely on your gut to do what is right for you. A qualified therapist can help you find a step-by-step approach to getting back to normal in as short a time as possible.

You may want to set a specific amount of time to go through the grieving process. A time limit gives you a defined time to hash out all of the junk, get over the guilt, the crying and punching the walls. Learning how to repair the drywall may be a great hobby!

Healing has no set time, days, a few weeks, maybe a bit longer. The rewards healing provides are tremendous. You will find yourself at the end of a process, a much better person than were before you began. Certainly you will be wiser.

The amount of time for you to get through this will depend on a number of factors and will be specific to your particular time involved and the closeness of your former relationship. It will also be determined by how badly you may have been blind-sided and how well you may deal with stress. If you are a champion at dealing in stressful situations, you may find you will bury this along with all of the other crap deep down inside. Sooner or later you *will* deal with it. Keep this chapter handy. You may find you always thought you were great at dealing with tough situations but this one has stripped you of everything you thought you were. Rest assured, all of this is normal.

Should you find yourself still wandering around after a month or more, glassy eyed, unable to concentrate, unable to perform the every day responsibilities of your life, you are *way* past the point you would have wanted to seek help. Typical signs of this may be alcohol or drugs, or as simple as referring to your-self in the third person "Bob is going to the store now!" Get help now. Keep the humor though; it's a good thing.

Consult with a friend or family member, someone very close. Make certain this is someone that would have your best interest in mind. Let them know you are a bit lost and need some help finding some direction (we *do* hate to ask for directions!) Ask them to help you find someone that would be appropriate for your needs. Many friends will offer advice, and take that with a grain of salt. Seek someone professionally if you've come to this point in your life.

When a family member dies, it is a time to lay them to rest and move on with your life. Realizing that a relationship is over, and it's time to move on is very beneficial in our healing. It's time to let this rest also, and get on with the rest of your life.

A situation to best avoid is the *suddenly single* friend imposing on a married friend's relationship. This is a natural tendency. We've lost someone close to us. A hole is left in our hearts; we seek to replace it with *something*. The urge to *bond* with someone, anyone, is very strong. This of course isn't going to work, but we seek temporary relief from that ache in our chest, the nausea in our stomach. Something, someone to stop the mind from reeling into what may feel like an unending abyss of pain. We feel subconsciously that if we can perform this bonding, it validates us as human beings, as being someone important. It's not unlike the fix described in the rebound relationship.

Few things can end a marriage faster than a single friend, who needs to party and socialize, dragging his or her best friend away from their spouse and family to party until the wee hours. We may in a perverted sense, subconsciously want to take some one with us into our misery. If you value your friend and his family, ask to spend some quality time with he/she and the spouse. Don't overdo the amount of time. They may enjoy it, be willing to support you, and you may benefit from double the experience from a male and female friend. If you do not have single friends, respect the relationship of those friends that are still in a stable partnership. The need for *validation* is an illusion. No one is going to be able to give you what you already have. You are important; your existence is vital to many friends and family members, to your *children*. The pain may blind you. *It is temporary*.

You may find yourself with some thoughts of ending your life; this may also be normal, regardless of what crap a shrink might tell you. But because it's normal doesn't mean it's a *good* thing, it merely *is what it is*. If these thoughts are surfacing, immediately think of those loving children and the pain they are going through, but would be all the more subjected to for the rest of their lives. Think of how much they love you, those little arms wrapped around your neck as you receive raspberry kisses on the cheek. Your children need you around for as many days as you have left. As soon as you are composed, call that family member or friend and ask for some help. In these types of situations no time of day or night is inappropriate to call. Do it now.

Your friends and family will understand. If you find yourself calling them night after night and you are *not* seeking counseling, they may not be so understanding after they have lost many nights of sleep. This is *your* problem, not *theirs*, ask them to find you someone immediately.

Many people don't require professional help in my opinion. The love and support provided by friends and family will help you on your road to recovery. Rely on your own gut instinct when friends offer advice. Take it with a grain of salt. *Take the love and support unconditionally.* Regardless of your particular emotional state, seek the level of help *you* need. In some cases I did not, and the road to recovery was very long because I felt I could go it alone.

Your friends may choose to support you in some very strange ways. They may talk of your ex and to run her down in a number of ways. They will report to you every time they run into her on the street, or is with some other guy. Why they do this is beyond me. It certainly doesn't say much for my integrity when I hear their opinion that she is a slut or worse. It doesn't help me any to hear how unstable she was. It doesn't say much for *me* that I spent years with this person. She hasn't changed *who* she is; she may be expressing it differently, spreading her wings. Hearing words like this can hurt deeply. It doesn't help in your grieving process. Ask these *friends* to refrain from speaking ill of her at all, and avoid keeping you well *informed*. If they continue, it may be time to find some better friends.

At times you may feel unappreciated. Seek to see the smallest blessings in life. My youngest Michele frequently provides the opportunity. Days ago I had the children when I had taken a break from my cleaning to fix them lunch, for her favorite, some of her quick cook noodle soup. She had been pestering me for some time that she was hungry, but not wanting to stop my cleaning, I put it off as long as possible.

One of my downfalls in fixing her meals in particular, she's still a bit young to get her own drink with her meal, and I always forget until she reminds me. It bothers me that she always wants something, and I was a bit irritated at being interrupted from my cleaning.

As she sat eating her lunch quietly, I asked her (still a bit irritated) if it was good. "Are you happy now?"

She nodded her head in affirmation, and added "But I'm angry because I don't have a drink."

I had forgotten yet again! Off I went to get her drink, mumbling to myself, but still chuckling. "Angry."

Later in the day, she made an attempt in her little way to make up for it. I had gone back to my cleaning. I had just finished polishing the coffee table, and was wrapping the cord on the vacuum after cleaning the carpet. I heard her come in the door from outside. I wasn't paying as much attention as I should have. I heard something plop down on the coffee table as she landed on the couch. "I brought you some flowers, Dad!"

I looked up and saw a fresh picked bundle of grass on my coffee table, roots and dirt still in tact, except for that which had come loose and landed on my shiny coffee table!

I would like to say I immediately saw the little silver lining from this bundle of joy. I'm not perfect, I chased her out of the house with her flowers. I'm sure that sent a nice loving message. We talked later and I had to once again apologize, for not appreciating her lovely gift.

Some days of this grieving process will be easier than others. Hopefully the children, as mine do, will inject enough humor to keep you balanced. An overall trend should be that it gets easier with time and you can begin to put things into perspective. If it's not, consider another approach. It may be difficult to understand exactly when you are past the grieving process, but when you find you are smiling and laughing again occasionally, it's time to begin putting your life back together.

ASSIGNMENT

Determine if you are grieving, or merely ignoring the situation again. Make the decision that it's time to grieve.

Assign your own definite time period not only for the grieving, but also to the whole process. Assign yourself some time daily, or weekly, to grieve. Assign an appropriate time period for this grieving process to take (i.e.: weeks or a month). Mark the final day on the calendar. Be ready when it comes.

Find a method to help you get through the grieving process as quickly and thoroughly as possible. Don't avoid *anything*! Seek out wise friends or a counselor to best help you work your way through this.

Write your ex a letter, telling her all of the things you want to tell her. Be as angry and vindictive as you like. When you're finished, tear it up and throw it away. You're done holding on to those things.

Make a list of everything you hated in your ex. Read it over carefully. Forgive. Tear it up and throw it away.

Make a list of all of the wonderful things you enjoyed from your ex. Read it and cherish it, thank her (silently) for all of these wonderful things. Put it away and forget it. You'll run across it in the future, and it may seem much more precious.

You may prefer, as I did, to make more of a ceremony out of letting go of the lists, which contain all things you want to let go in your life. I found an isolated spot out in the desert, I made a medicine wheel of stones burned some candles and incense, read through them all, and said everything I had to say to everyone I could think of. And I said PLENTY!

When it was finished, I burned the lists and spread the ashes (ecologically minded of course) to the earth. You can make this ceremony as simple or as detailed as you wish. Take some time to plan it. Go with your gut. You may find it is a deeply rewarding experience to let things go in this manner. Later, we'll discuss another ceremony to bring good things into your life. As any recovering addict knows, if you remove something bad from your life, you must replace it with something healthy.

I would suggest reading through the next few chapters before beginning your ceremony. Some great ideas are presented. Compile your lists, set them aside until you've completed the next chapters.

CHAPTER 4
SOUL MATES

A divine harmonic dance begins when two perfect souls meet. The elusive mystery is to permit the dance to brand itself onto our very souls. Brand deeply, that the everyday music of the world cannot drown our melody. Allow this symphony to play, and experience life, human nature in its purest form.

The following are my ideas on the attraction between you and anyone to whom you may be connected in your life. I don't wish to convert anyone to my way of thinking I only offer this as an idea to get some semblance of the destiny in such meetings. Perhaps to offer hope during what may be a frustrating time when we're alone.

I was in a cowboy bar in Grand Junction, Colorado a number of years ago. This was my regular hang out during many of my single years. I was as usual with my friends, mostly my guy friends. We were having a terrific time on a Saturday night, unwinding from the weekly stresses.

We had all noticed the little cowgirl standing not far from our table. She had platinum blonde hair that cascaded below her shoulders. She wore tight jeans, and a western style cowboy shirt that complimented her sky blue eyes. I swear the folks at Wrangler had her in mind when they made jeans!

She appeared to be alone. Since we were all regulars, we determined she was new meat. Someone new to the area that none of us had ever seen before. She was ripe for the picking.

Though she was alone, she seemed to be enjoying herself, dancing with several of the local goat ropers, and sipping a beer in between. She seemed to be aware of our table of testosterone so intent on her every move. We had scared off many new prospects over the years with our obvious male prowess.

I was never one for much confidence in meeting women in such situations, something that has held me in the past.

As another hour or so passed, she was more aware of our table. With a lot of posturing among us, as to which one of us she was checking out, perhaps more than one. One of my buddies got her attention and made an obvious come on, we all laughed. I was a bit embarrassed at my friend's advances, and was sure we had seen the last of her, at least for that night.

I had underestimated this little spitfire, she laughed and approached our table, and we were silent, waiting for her opinion of us all. Her pearly whites continued to glow contrasting her red lipstick as she smiled wide inquiring as to whether we were having a good time. We all nodded that we were. She asked why none of us were dancing. We all lowered our eyes in schoolboy shame.

As she looked squarely at me, I was captivated by those eyes, "How about you, cowboy? Wanna polish your belt buckle?" (A term for close, slow dancing).

My face immediately flushed as I stammered something. I bounced off my chair, and snatching the beer from her hand, placed it on the table, and took her by the hand to the dance floor. I was intentionally moving quickly, to escape the snickers from the pack at the table. Better to be me on the dance floor, than sitting at that table watching I figured.

As we danced, I learned her name was Wendy, and she was indeed new to the area, coming from a little town down south that I don't recall the name of. No ring on her finger, I still asked if she was married, she wasn't. We were always suspicious around new people in "our bar," making sure we weren't setting ourselves up. I didn't want to be "explaining" things in drunken lingo to a jealous 6' 7" husband later in the evening.

After the dance, we made our way through the crowd back to the table. Wendy asked if she could join us. I said "sure!" as I glanced around for a chair to pull up for her. She put her hand on my chest, sat me in my chair, and plopped herself down on my lap.

Not a sound from the eye-popping guys, they were stunned but happy to have some female company.

Wendy was a pure delight. A cool spring breeze wafting through a dark smoke filled barroom. Her laughter lit up the immediate area around us. She was loaded with personality, outgoing, immediately adopting all of us as new friends. She made her rounds dancing with each of the guys, and would find her place back on my lap after each.

My attraction to her, though a bit reserved at first I'll admit, was soon falling into the comfortable zone. She wasn't one to spend all of her time talking about herself, rather she asked after each of us, wanting to know who we were, what we did for a living, the usual small talk. Though I got the impression she was interested, not making simple idle chatter.

When it was time for the bar to close, she turned and gave me a soft kiss on the lips, and asked if I'd mind giving her a ride home. This lady was of such a class I had no doubt she wasn't inviting me for anything other than transportation. Quite unlike the usual women I'd meet in the bar. How could I decline?

We had a pleasant ride home. The drive was all too short for my tastes. We sat in her driveway and talked for a couple of hours before I headed home, alone.

Wendy and I spent many nights together, dancing and talking at the bar. We spent a few nights together outside of the bar. We had a thing going. I never took it any farther for some reason. Something I've regretted, though I shouldn't I suppose.

She was always beautiful, always herself, always upbeat and positive. She was very appreciative of any small gesture of kindness. She never pressed me for more.

Though we never took our relationship to another level, Wendy gave me something I needed at that time in my life. I needed female companionship. I needed her smile, the glint in her eyes, I needed to hold her in my arms as we danced. She made my heart flutter; she made me tingle all over to watch her approach. She gave me peace in an unsettling way.

As with Wendy, when we meet someone special in our lives, we fill some void in our lives, some small space. It's not important how large or small that void, the person brings something out in us, that we need to exercise.

When we meet that "soul mate" or as I call it our "twin flame," our connection to that person makes us more of which we are. More of who we were meant to be, and it feels wonderful!

The distinction, for me at least, between a soul mate and a twin flame is quite profound. When we are in the heavenly realm, before coming to this life, we have close friends, even family as we do on earth. These are what I refer to as soul mates, and we have many. They are very close to us; we know each other well. When we meet one of these spirits in human form on earth, the connection is often quite intense. It can be a bit unnerving. That spirit has a purpose, to help fulfill something in us. It can feel like being home again. It's like we've always known them (and we have!), we can't remember the connection. It feels so right. It's not unusual for these soul mates to meet, and be so overwhelmed by the strong connection, to marry in this life. Or to have children, after all, everything is perfect.

As I mentioned, the soul mate is to bring out something in us. To help us exercise a *part* of ourselves. They help us to feel that strong connection, which allows us to be more open to the idea of *love*. No doubt a very strong love is passed between soul mates.

Some of us will remain with this soul mate through our entire lives, being perfectly content that we have found our soul mate, and we have! This can be a great-married relationship, we grow old, and we die together. It's not always without problems of course, everyone argues and fights, but a connection exists more powerful than any petty worldly problem, so we get through it.

Sometimes we divorce our soul mate, or separate, sometimes for life. When the need we both had has been fulfilled, the relationship may naturally "sour" and both of us will move on. From the human perspective, we can be bitter, angry, and hurt. This can make it easier, dealing with our human emotions, or ego, to make the split, from someone that was, and still is, so important to us. From a spiritual perspective though, we've exchanged a wonderful expression of love. Even the *love* expressed in the need to separate, that we might *both* pursue that magnificent twin flame connection.

It's not unusual to have some meeting, or relationship with several soul mates, allowing us to bring out more *parts* of ourselves.

As wonderful as this soul mate connection is, the twin flame experience is something much more powerful.

When we are in the spirit world (or heaven) we exist as a complete being, we have tendencies for both male and female traits. We are perfect in our existence. A twin flame is born when we, as spirit, split into two halves. The split usually results in one male and one female. A slightly different thing happens when you have two gay persons. For the sake of brevity, we won't delve into this. But rest assured the split still happens, and it makes the same wonderful connection when we meet our other half.

We laid out a plan for this earthly life, prior to the split of the twins. The split occurs to help facilitate the plan of our life. After all, can you imagine coming to earth, as a complete being? Both female and male tendencies strongly enhanced, perfect, with all memories of past life in tact? Has such a being ever come to this planet? I don't know for certain, but I would tend to think probably.

With the plan of our lives etched in our subconscious we come to this earth to begin our journey. We have mapped out many experiences, and determined the time we will meet our other half, our twin flame to make us a perfect *one* again, to live out the remainder of our lives.

At times, one half will remain in spirit to be a spirit guide for us. Angels are different. Realizing our other half, our twin flame may not be on this earth can be terrifying! It doesn't need to be. If this is the case, a soul mate exists for you on this earth and will assist in fulfilling all the needs of your life plan when you meet. One half of the twin remaining in spirit is an exception rather than the rule. By being on Earth, both halves can fulfill double the experiences that only one could accomplish alone.

Rest assured, that if your other half remained in spirit as your guide, you have some great things to accomplish in this life, and it will take *both* of you together to achieve these goals.

We go through our lives, stumbling along, trying to fulfill our life's purpose, without a hint as to what the purpose may be. We seek to know our twin flame as quickly as possible, to make ourselves complete once again. This is a natural tendency for our human emotions. After all, who wouldn't want that connection?

We see signs when heading in the right direction of our life plan. You may have moments of déjà vu; we've all had those. This is when you hear something, smell, or see something, which connects. We swear we've been here before. If we pay attention, we may know how someone is going to finish a sentence, or what he or she is going to do next. It's spooky!

This is plainly a road sign for the map you made in your life. It's spirits little way of saying, "You're on the right road, and you're heading in the right direction."

Let's say we were taking a cross-country trip, driving from Los Angeles to New York City. When we take such a trip, we'll find ourselves on the right highways, to get to our destination. We may also take little detours. Have you ever been on a road trip, taken a wrong turn and nothing looks familiar? The road signs don't look familiar, the countryside is foreign, followed by the sinking thought, "Gee, I screwed up somewhere." The situation is simple to fix, at least usually. We pull off the road, pull out the map and retrace our steps, or find where we are and map a course to get back onto the highway leading to our destination.

It's the exact same thing when dealing with our lives. We might take a bit of a detour. This isn't wrong. We have purpose in the experience alone. Simple enough retrace your steps until that last road sign, and figure the direction you were heading on and get back on the road.

No life goes smoothly, this wouldn't be the Life experience! We will run into what we perceive as obstacles when we are on the *right* road! It may be a snowplow that slows us down, it may be a sign reading Bridge Out, forcing a detour, or a traffic accident that lays us up temporarily. It's all part of the experience.

On the cross-country trip we focus on the goal ahead. We take whatever detours we must to continue the journey. After all, can you imagine giving up on your road trip at the halfway point? You would pull over in some sleepy little town, unload your stuff, and make your life, falling well short of your planned destination "What the heck, we tried, we'll meet the goal half-way, New York can come to us!"

This wouldn't serve us very well would it?

It's not unusual for twin flames to meet, before it's time. It may be bumping into one another in an airport, a casual meeting at a cocktail party, or a brush against another in a shopping mall. It's something, but you don't recognize the connection. That's because it's not time yet!

This may be another road sign telling you, "New York City—500 Miles," you're on the right road, and you're not there yet.

To my knowledge, I've not met my twin flame yet, but I know she is close. For me, it's dreams of her. I have seen her face in these dreams (something that started recently); I can feel her presence, sometimes when I'm awake. I have heard her voice in my dreams; once heard her call my name when I was awake. This voice from thin air, with no one around, but the voice was very clear. And my soul as well as my ears heard it. On our road trip to New York City, as we get closer to the destination, the signs become more frequent and more apparent.

When twin flames meet at the right time, it can evoke a variety of reactions, though all of them are equally wonderful. You may feel this person is too good to be true, you may feel overwhelmed. You may experience nausea, feel sick, your head and energy spinning like a whirling dervish. The connection *will be*; you will *just know* it. It will be so much different than anything you've felt before; it's unmistakable.

Your spirit self will go through a molecular transformation as you join your two halves together again, and this can be a bit disorienting at first. You will know you have met the one that you will spend the rest of this life with.

Do twin flames ever meet and separate again, after recognizing the connection? I can't say that it *hasn't* happened, but I don't see the purpose. When your pre-determined time comes for you both to meet, the goals for each separately have been accomplished. It's time for you both to take on the world together to live in your world as one and experience life with another.

Wendy and I experienced a strong attraction. I only hope she received the same blessings from our relationship that I did. I don't remember the relationship ever ending. Neither of us made a determination to end it. It seemed we simply drifted apart, and I heard later that she had moved away.

The whole relationship came in such a sudden, unexpected, and wonderful way. It also ended so subtly, and in such a manner that I have to believe Wendy was a soul mate. We were very close, very comfortable with each other. We provided something very needed for both of us, with no expectations. The natural sensation is very difficult to put into words. It was as normal as going out to my car, putting in the keys and driving.

The end was also eerily normal, natural, so natural it didn't seem I had ever lost anything. To this day I feel very blessed to have experienced her wonderful spirit. I would love to see her again one day, to see the flash of those pearly whites again and the sparkle in her eye. I wonder if those jeans still fit as well as I remember? I'd like to thank her for being such a wonderful influence in my life.

Understand that your ex played a very important part in your life. The connection still exists. Hopefully it will remain long after your children are grown. It may not be the ultimate love connection of a twin flame, nonetheless; it's a very important part of your growth process, and hers! Putting it in the right perspective is also an important part of your growth, and your preparing to move on with your life.

ASSIGNMENT

Please take stock of all those in your life closest to you. Recognize the "soul mates" that may be with you your entire life. Evaluate the shared connection and lessons you both experience. Do your best to make their experience as wonderful as it is intended to be.

CHAPTER 5
THE POWER OF THOUGHT

Most of us go through life a product of recycled thinking. Our thoughts are given to us from our friends, parents, family and acquaintances. My goal is to one day have an original thought, one that no one has thought before. This will be my doorway into a new and exciting world.

Perhaps you have a strong sense of who you are and how the world and universe works. Perhaps you have some strong religious convictions and beliefs. If so, I encourage you to cherish those. The ideas presented in the next two chapters are some of my ideas and beliefs. They can be used to enhance any form of belief, religion, and personal conviction. My intent is not to change your way of thinking or believing rather to enhance your conviction of control over life and circumstances.

Use what works for you in the following pages. If it is something that doesn't fit with what you believe, this is certainly all right. Leave those things that don't work and take what does.

If something isn't working in your life, a lot of energy is wasted in repeating the same over and over. So it's time to change, but how?

Let's start with basic fundamentals. The entire universe is composed of only one thing, energy. We have come to know this energy in its scientific terms as atoms, protons, electrons, and neutrons. Scientists are continuing to discover smaller and smaller components of this energy and it looks to continue in an infinite direction. Most of us have heard at least of atoms, protons, and neutrons. Smaller particles exist (subatomic particles) called quarks, and smaller still, gluons. All of these make up our universe, and us as humans.

Everything in the known Universe is made of the same components, the protons, electrons, etc, vibrate at different frequencies (or speeds if you will) to make each thing unique and different. Your body is composed of the same basic elements as your desk; you simply vibrate at a different frequency, so you appear differently (hopefully!) than your desk.

Some theologians believe that God is energy. Before the beginning of time as we can conceive it, all that existed, was energy. My belief also is that

God is energy; God also vibrates at a different frequency than we do. This does not make Him any less of a deity.

God, or the All that Is, the Supreme Being, the Force that Connects us all, The Great Spirit, The Great Mystery, call it your conscience if you like, whatever your belief, whatever name you choose to call it, organized all of this energy into the Universe we know today. The Universe is not only composed of energy, but is *driven* by energy.

You have your own energy vehicle, designed to guide your life and actions in any manner you wish to direct. This vehicle is your thought process.

Despite what you may have been taught, or have learned over your lifetime, you can and do control your thoughts. You do it every day and every night, every moment of every day. Is this working for you?

Unfortunately, we are taught to *react* to situations, rather than listen to that inner voice guidance. It is a matter of choice.

To direct our thoughts, it's first necessary to decide what's not working, and what we want to accomplish. Write down everything in your life that doesn't work for you. Sorry, *everything* is a little broad; certainly some things do. Make a list of the ones that don't.

Next, understand certain aspects of your life you cannot control. Specific Universal Laws are true whether you believe them or not, it makes no difference. Your perception of those things that you cannot control is what makes all the difference in *your* world. If someone around you is having a bad day, week, month, year or life, listen to them, let them vent, but don't own the emotion. It is so easy to be sucked into having a bad day if the person working with you, or sitting next to you is in a bad mood, griping, complaining, and crying; it is *their* emotion, not yours. Distance yourself from it. *You* decide what type of day you are having. Eventually you will not attract these types of people any longer. And perhaps they will learn from your example.

You can however control your own thoughts, ideas and actions. Your thoughts are energy, and as a result, they have a great deal of power. Everything that has ever been created first began as a thought. Those thoughts of yours, like it or not, go directly into the universal pool of energy, and begin to set a series of events in motion. Your life will be a direct result of your thoughts. Scary isn't it? It can be! Direct your thoughts positively, lovingly and wonderfully, and that is exactly the type of life you will experience, because that's what you chose!

Is this hard to do? No! It is impossible! If that's what you choose. It is very easy, if you choose.

A suggested book on positive thinking (and I'm sure many more) is *The Power of the Subconscious Mind* by Dr. Joseph Murphy, D.R.S., PhD, DID, L.L.D. (don't ask me what all those titles are!). This book is simple, has some wonderful thought process exercises, and will save us from having to go into a lot of the detail here.

Through directing your thought in a positive manner, your life begins to reshape itself, in ways that are absolutely incredible. People see you differently; things come your way, because you are ready for them. You will begin to gather things because you know how; you will treasure things because you know how valuable they are. This does not make you materialistic! Purely appreciate *all* of the things in life you are entitled to.

The key, never give up, never revert back to old patterns. Surround yourself with things that make you feel good. Surround yourself with people that uplift you, that make you more of who you are. Eliminate the negatives, the people that make you feel bad, that bring you down.

How do you eliminate these things and people? Please, don't kill anyone! Simply bless them, (silently) do it with love and understanding. Bless them that they are on their own path. Be grateful that they were a part of your life because you have learned many things from them. Bless them that it is time for them to move on. Wish them well; wish them all of the blessings the universe has to offer. In a very short time, you will notice they happen to be a very small part of your life. You may lose contact altogether if this is what you choose.

You will have much more time for those things that help you grow, and certainly much more energy!

Unquestionably what we've covered so far on the power of thought is not a new concept. But this is only the beginning. Thoughts can be used in much more powerful ways.

Let's begin by letting go of those things you have decided don't work any longer in your life. Add to the list any traits, habits etc you wish to be rid of. It's necessary to get rid of the old stuff to make room for all of the wonderful things to come into our lives.

When you have the list compiled, it's time to release those things, back into the Universe. Many rituals or exercises have been written by some wonderful people to release this energy. I prefer the Life and Death Arrow Ceremony written by Lynn Andrews in *Teachings from the Sacred Wheel*. Essentially you make a Death Arrow, symbolizing all of the things you want to release, and a Life Arrow to symbolize all things you want to come into your life. (Please refer to her book for the details). Go to a place you choose, preferably outdoors, and perform two ceremonies in a Sacred Circle, one for the Death Arrow in a lower setting geographically, such as the bottom of a hill. The other ceremony for the Life Arrow is to be performed in a higher place such as the top of the hill. You will release all those things you wish to let go of in the Death Arrow ceremony and the Life Arrow ceremony opens your energy, and invites all those good things to come into your life. It is an enlightening experience!

Anytime you are letting go of something, it's essential to replace it with something else, the reason many smokers have so much difficulty quitting. Compile a list, of things to bring into your life. Better traits and habits (be very specific), other people or loved ones, new friends, again, be as specific as possible.

For the sake of simplicity, I will outline this very simple ceremony that works for many people, though you can certainly design your own, or use another that you may have seen or read.

Once you have your lists compiled, set a date and time to spend some time alone to perform your ceremony. Give it a few days if possible. Spend the interim time contemplating the things on your lists. Blessing all of those things you are letting go, visualizing all of the new wonderful things you will soon have in your life. This sets your thought energy in motion, and makes it very powerful.

When the appointed date and time arrives, go outdoors to a place very special to you. If you don't know of one, find one. The particular place is not as important as the energy you will bring, and awaken in this place. Bring some personal items with you that make you feel good; make you feel strong and loving. You may also bring some items to let go of if you wish.

When arriving at your desired place, spend a little time, again contemplating first all things you are going to let go. Get yourself centered, feel at peace; let your Higher Self be with you and take over your thoughts. Feel what is taking place. If you wish to pray, pray. If you wish to burn incense, this is a wonderful thing; anything that helps set the positive or spiritual mood.

When you are ready, take your list of things to let go, read it over one last time, contemplate each and every item on the list. Say goodbye and bless each and every one. Set it on fire, let it burn, watch the fire consume and convert all of these things back into pure energy, releasing them back to the Universe. When it has finished, scatter the ashes, leaving them to decompose and again become part of the Earth.

When you are performing this ritual, and when finished please be mindful of the environment. Leave it at least as nice as when you came, leave no trace of your visit. Any other items you have brought to leave can be buried (I wouldn't suggest burning any others).

It's time to get on with your Life Ceremony. Pick another place close by. A place up a hill works very well, but this is for your own choosing. Take your list of things you wish to come into your life, choose your place, and repeat the ceremony similar as you did the first. Read over the items on your list, welcome them into your life, and bless each and every one that it comes to you for your highest good. Pray if you like, burning incense if you like. Get yourself again centered on what you are doing at this very moment. Set the list on fire, release its energy into the Universe so that these good things may come to you. Again when it is finished, scatter the ashes, knowing that it is done, things are set in motion to come to you.

Again, please scan the area before you leave, be mindful of the environment, and leave no trace of your visit. Keep this as a special place to you. Leave it better than you found it.

These ceremonies can be repeated anytime, as you need them. Once a year is a nice remembrance, more frequently if you need it.

The ceremony itself is merely a process to put yourself in the frame of mind needed to bring out your Higher Self. How you do that is entirely up to you, the details of the ceremony are insignificant.

The power of thought is a wonderful thing. All thoughts you experience influence your life in some way. Everything that has ever been created first began as a thought. Some Greater Power created YOU because of a thought that took place. Bridges have been built, civilizations have formed, and entire empires have been built and destroyed with the simple beginning thought. Your thoughts are no less powerful. The only difference may be in consistency and focus.

Be aware also that Spirit works in a strange way. It works in an absolute literal sense. For instance, if you say to yourself "I need money," your Spirit (the Universe or God, whatever) says "Ok. You need money." "But that's not what I meant!." It doesn't matter what you meant, that's what you said (or thought) so that's what you get, need for money, and lack of money.

Retrain your thought process, instead of "I need money"; think, "I have money." Or "I have all the money I need for whatever I decide to do." Spirit will see that it is so. Once you have entered that thought with Spirit, let it go, know that it has been done. It's not necessary to keep reminding spirit, He

(She, they, It, and whatever) has a very good memory. If you've ever known a great artist, you will grasp the concept; they don't know when a painting is finished! An artist will complete a beautiful painting, and they will not be happy, they'll keep picking, keep adding to it, a little here, a little there, until it looks horrid! Take the painting away from them before they ruin it! So it works with Spirit. You've directed Spirit in the direction you are heading, leave it at that, and let it happen. Unlike the artist though, Spirit will know when you've met your goal.

I don't usually dwell on negativity and we won't, we'll mention it in passing, that's all it's worth. Eliminate all negative thinking. Eliminate people with negative thoughts. Eliminate things that don't make you feel in step with your Higher Purpose. Don't waste your energy. Negative thoughts are just as powerful as positive IF you give them the power. Don't.

What is your Higher Purpose? It's different for everyone, yet the same. All of us have done something, maybe one thing in our lives that helped someone. We did it unselfishly, and many people may have benefitted from one unselfish act of kindness.

A domino effect begins when an act of kindness is performed. For instance if I'm heading to work one day, as I do five days or nights a week and some pretty woman I've never seen smiles and says "Hello!" it feels good. I might say the same to the next person I meet, it gives them a warm sensation, and they do the same. It continues on to several people throughout the day. As a result of that one kind person telling me "Hello!" the effect has rippled to an unknown number of people, and who knows how many individuals had their day a little brighter, because of one simple kind word. This is a simplified example surely, but how much influence would a thought of paying the toll for the person behind you, or merely holding the door for another, male or female, and a friendly "good morning" greeting go?

When you performed this act, you were working from your Higher Self, toward your Higher Purpose. Remember that feeling? Keep that in mind; it will be a great guide.

Understand that everyone is on his or her own path. Imagine you're walking in the hills, alongside the ocean on a beautiful sunny day with someone very dear to you. You are hiking to a favorite place for an afternoon picnic. You come to a fork in the path; one goes left, downward, the other to the right and up the hill. You have walked this path before, you know on the left is a darker, swampy forest, filled with insects, snakes, and on your last visit, a black bear chased you up the path.

The path to the right goes into beautiful serene flowered meadows. It's so peaceful and refreshing. Your partner wishes to enjoy the day choosing the path to the right. You on the other hand being a bit more adventurous want to experience the excitement of the forest once again. So you agree to go your separate ways, and meet as the paths join up again. Off you both go, your partner to the right, you to the left.

When the paths meet up again, your partner is joyful, thrilled with the beautiful things he or she has experienced in the beautiful meadows. You on the other hand, have a rapid pulse, adrenalin flowing through your body as the bear has chased you once again up the path. But what an exhilarating experience as you both share what each has seen throughout the walk.

So it is with our journey. We choose different paths, however they always arrive at the same destination. It's impossible NOT to get to the place you are going. The only difference is what we choose to experience on our journey.

Your thoughts and perceptions control these conscious and unconscious choices.

Acknowledging that our lives have changed is a big step in our growth process. More so, understanding to the deepest parts of our soul, when we look back at our lives, at the big picture we will easily see the reason for these changes.

Many of us have been in the position when we've lost our place of employment, or we choose to move on to something else. It's funny how the Universe works. If we get that it's time to move on, we take the steps necessary to fulfill that which our current occupation is not satisfying within us. On the other hand at times we are ready to leave and we don't get it. This requires our employer to help us make that step out the door. It's a subconscious thing on our part. We took the steps necessary to cause our employer to make that career choice for us. We look at it as a very stressful time. We can be devastated, feeling unwanted and unappreciated.

In reality, we should stand up in our termination meeting, and shake our employer's hand. We should thank him or her for all the wonderful experiences we've had with them. And know in our hearts, they helped us move on to something much more wonderful in our lives.

After all, we couldn't possibly keep *this* job and still have another full time career! The whole thing may not unfold as we would have liked in our conscious minds, but it is all something we had planned for ourselves many years before.

Finding yourself in this single role, you should be equally as delighted that you find yourself on this new path. You wouldn't go out and find that perfect mate to bring into your life, while you are still married, would you? Ok, some us of would, and have, but it sure makes for a sticky situation!

I sat with a gentleman in a downtown Chicago bar. We were having a pleasant conversation. He's a big tall, dark haired and muscular gentleman. Rugged cut features in his face, a bit of curl in his well-groomed hair. As we chatted, he was approached by one of the most beautiful blonde women I had ever seen. They would surely make a handsome couple.

The blonde offered to buy my newfound friend a drink. She was obviously drooling all over herself. He respectfully declined.

She announced to him she would very much like to take him back to her place and make passionate love to him.

My friend, polite as could be respectfully declined again, saying he would very much like that too, but was trying to save himself for the woman he loved.

The blonde impressed with his moral character replied, "That must be very difficult for a big handsome man like you."

My friend replied, "Yes, well, it's not too bad. But it sure has my wife upset!"

Until you have made room in your life, for another person to come in, you will not find her. When married persons have difficult times in the relationship, one partner or the other may believe they have found their soul mate. Someone else they've met.

The breakup of the marriage soon follows, tearing the children out of the home they've come to know, and is devastating (there's that word again!) to the remaining faithful partner.

It breaks my heart when this happens. I'm not saying it can't happen, or hasn't happened, but this isn't the way the Universe works. It's more likely the person they met, Mr. or Ms. Right Now is displaying some quality they feel is lacking in their mate. It may take some time until they realize this. They fall into this wonderful relationship and appear to put their lives back together, and they are so happy.

It's not unusual for a relationship that begins this way to outlive its natural life. Once the person realizes this is not the one for me, they absolutely feel they must make this relationship work. Otherwise, they broke up their previous marriage on a whim!

Some of you may find yourselves on either side of this fence.

If you are the person that left for your soul mate and have come to realize that you had your head up your ass, get out of it! Take the time to at least treat your current partner with more respect than you did the last. Sit down and have a heart to heart talk. Chances are, they feel it too. express your heartfelt gratitude for their love and devotion, and beat a hasty retreat.

It may be time to go to your ex, and apologize. I know, you're afraid to hear "I told you so!" But apologize for the hurt you've caused, and again, beat a hasty retreat! Don't try to go back, you've obviously gotten out of that relationship for a reason. It's an opportunity to settle into single life for a time, and get your feet firmly back on terra firma.

If you are the one however that was dumped so your ex can experience her soul mate, and you have found out it wasn't working for her, go into a closet, close the door and yell out "I told you so!" It's your right! Saying it directly to her can only do more harm than good. Let her know you understand, and praise her for at least acknowledging it wasn't working. Let her know she is a wonderful person. Treat your ex the opposite from what she expects! She will love you (in a way) for it. It will help give her the confidence she needs to pick her life up and start getting back on track.

When you begin to start doing the things above, essentially not thinking, or acting the way everyone else would act in that situation, you are seeing your Higher Self. It won't take long before you will be thinking and hearing yourself say loving, gentle things, when they seem to have no place in the conversation. This is a big step in becoming the person you want to be.

ASSIGNMENT

Be aware of your thought patterns, both the positive and the negative ones. Turn the negative thoughts into positive, in every situation. A positive *always* exists. Look for it you may find it. Use what works for you, write them down if you have to, and keep track of your progress if it works for you. But be aware that what you are thinking has been learned *somewhere*. Determine how you might change that thinking to best move you toward your goal in life.

People are turned off and tuned out by negative speaking. The same people are *drawn* to positive, uplifting and complimentary people. You control what you think. Use the most powerful tool you have, to guide your life in a positive direction.

CHAPTER 6
RESPONSIBILITY

The five-letter word spelled BLAME has determined the course of countless lives on our planet. This simple word has provided endless numbers of excuses for tragedy and failure that befall us. Two individuals alone have a direct influence on what my life will entail, My Creator and myself.

"Men are from Earth, women are from Earth, get over it." I chuckled as I read this on the Internet recently. I don't know if the author of this sarcasm was seeing it in the same light as I, but it gave me reason to pause.

I've spent years in Customer Service in one form or another. If what I've experienced is a reflection of the state of the nation, and the world, and I believe it is, this planet is in desperate need of a wake up call. I have experienced my customers blowing a gasket over the silliest things, and most of the time, it was their own fault, due to lack of knowledge on their part. They want to raise hell and blame someone else for their own ignorance or procrastination.

I have a female friend, who lately has been on this kick of exerting her feminine power. Always regaling anyone with her latest tale of how she ripped her car mechanic or another individual (usually a male is the offending villain) up one side and down the other for some seeming attack on her lack of intelligence for being female, or for any other reason. Is this worth it?

I've been witness to countless conversations of the poor unfortunate female victimized in some manner. Or some race of people had been oppressed. I have yet to hear a male say to a potential employer "I can do that job as well as any woman!" They bring this oppression on themselves. "What? I brought this on myself? No, no, someone else has done this to me!" That's our first reaction of course, why have more blame heaped upon us.

Someone please answer for me, what great mysterious power or authority this person or persons have, that they could heap such blackness on your entire life?

Maybe I've merely gotten old and cranky, but it appears an awful lot of folks are bent on blaming bad things in life on someone else. The constant, subtle male bashing that continues into the 21st century makes me cringe. Few people, men or women have chosen to take responsibility for their own actions.

We've all probably heard the story of the person that bought a cup of HOT coffee at a drive through fast food restaurant one day to spill it on his/her lap while driving. The victim in the story sued the company responsible for this heinous crime and won a large settlement in court! You have got to be kidding me!

The coffee is HOT, dummy! Coffee is supposed to be hot when you drink it! Don't dump it on your lap! Don't drink it while driving! At least wait until it cools down before you dump it near any private parts! Did your mother not teach you to think?

I don't profess to know all details in this hot coffee incident, but I find it hard to believe that some malicious employee, knowing that this helpless and obviously uneducated person would decide they would rather wear the coffee than drink it, so in the spirit of education, throw an extra ten degrees on the coffee machine to let this person know not to do that again.

We see countless incidents in the news, and if you listen, of people all around every day, someone is taking the poor me attitude, and blaming all of their troubles on someone else.

The "New Age" movement today concerns me. Some teach past life regression, and take one back in their past lives to find out why they are the way they are. Well bingo! That's why I wanted to murder all of the people around me, because they killed me in a past life!!! Well holy Toledo Batman, what a revelation.

If you believe in such things, generational healing, past life regression, etc is a wonderful thing. But you *still* created it in your own life, no matter which life it was! That was your *past* life, you've moved beyond that! You have a responsibility to take control of *this* life, and all of your coming lives. Blaming it on someone else in a past life is still avoiding responsibility.

Unfortunately also, once we've identified the perpetrator of our oppression, love goes right out the window. This person is abusing me, so I hate them, I don't want to be around them. Take a look at your own issues, and why this other person's actions affect you so. Deal with your own stuff. I think you'll see the other person in a whole new light.

Understanding that you create your own life literally is not so hard to understand. Consider if I am in need of a loaf of bread and I want to go to the store to get more. What is the plan? For me, it would be check my wallet, make certain I have something beyond the pictures of my kids and grandkids, grab my keys and head out the door to my car, start the car, drive down the road to the store, pick up the loaf of bread, take it to the cashier, pay for it, go out of the doors to the store, get into my vehicle, and drive home. Good, I've created 20 minutes of my life.

Creating an entire life is on a slightly larger scale. What of those little tragedies and unforeseen things in our lives that seem to upset the apple cart? Well Sherlock, unforeseen means someone didn't see it coming. Who would that be? *You*! You still created it though, if not on this level of your understanding, certainly on another level.

"But I don't remember asking for this!" Of course you don't remember, that would ruin the whole purpose of the lesson!

One of the most predominant beliefs in our Christian religion is that as we come to this earth, we are somehow predestined by God to live a certain way, or that He has mapped out certain things we are to experience in our lives. For those of us with a human mentality, this fits our "blame it on someone else" mind-set. Many of us seek the divine benevolence of our Lord to get us out of this pickle we are in.

I don't buy into this one. And I have tried! It doesn't work for me. I believe rather, that before coming to this planet, you (you in a Spirit sense), sat down (maybe not, maybe you stood up or lay down) and mapped out the basic design of your entire life, which *you* wished to experience on earth. Certainly in Spirit we were much more knowledgeable than we are in this life. I prefer the term *lessons*, but it's not something to learn in a knowledge sense. When we were in Spirit, and connected to All that Is more closely, we knew everything. Yes, Everything, this includes all secrets of the universe.

The only thing we didn't *know* was the *experience* of it all. What is it like *not* to know? What is it like to be surprised, with a great surprise, or a tragic accident? What is it like to feel that ache in your chest when you've lost a loved one? What is it like to finish first in a track meet on the high school track team, all eyes are upon you as the crowd stands, cheering, stomping their feet, yelling your name? What does that feel like? We didn't have any idea. Now (hopefully) we know what it is to *feel*.

Getting back to your mapping out *your* life, you have the basic outline done. You begin to fill in the details, right down to the seemingly minute eccentricities of your life, leaving nothing to chance. You have many Spirit friends and Soul mates, family and acquaintances that also have their own lives they are mapping out. With all of you together, you find how each being fits their lives together, so *you*, and *they* can each experience all of the wonderful things on earth that each experiences every day. Your ex was a part of this plan for the time she *was* or *is* in your life.

The thing that intrigues me, we each have this plan, yet we are unaware of it. We still try to change it! Why? Simply for the control and the sake of change. Some of us wouldn't be happy no matter how it turned out! Others are not so concerned with the outcome, as long as we got to engineer it.

The difference in the people that come into my life has long fascinated me. The varying lengths of time that I have other people around cannot be coincidental.

Being one that never stayed much in one place for long, particularly when I was younger, I had a lot of people come and go from my life. This can be quite perplexing. I moved across country from my family when I left high school, like a salmon following some homing instinct, I headed west.

I never realized at the time that moving so far away and building a new family would have consequences I will likely feel the rest of my life.

Throughout the years though, a few old friends have remained in contact. Others are a distant memory.

As with all of us, I experienced people that would come into my life for a very short period of time (perhaps days or weeks) others that would come in for months to a few years and others who have remained in my life for many years and some for decades.

However, each person contributes greatly to my life. Whatever lesson I have to learn (and I like to think they learn also) is played out like a beautiful cosmic dance. For some it may be a fleeting moment, for others it's the experience of being together, doing exciting things together. It all prepares us for our life ahead and allows us to experience this wonderful thing called life.

Be mindful of the roles those in your life might play. Perhaps some persons you would like to contact again. If you do, and you find the "connection" isn't there any longer, that they've moved on, accept it as such. Enjoy what you had in the past for the wonderful thing that it was. Realize that the lesson they had for you was learned and likely the connection won't be again.

Acknowledge that those that have been in your life for many years, will likely remain, your ex is possibly one of them. The two of you are connected through your children.

I was a bit melancholy when I realized after leaving my first couple of ex's, that when the kids were grown and had left school, our roles as parents would be over, and I'd likely lose contact with them. I couldn't have been more wrong!

After the kids are grown and leave the home, birthdays, weddings, anniversaries, and holidays may all be celebrated together. Often the ex's are present. The grandkids are born and of course we both would like to be involved at the hospital. Fortunately, I've maintained a loving relationship with those two ex's, and these events don't cause any of us concern.

Unless you are unusual, it's likely your ex will be a part of your life for as long as you are alive. It is time to begin to build a new relationship with her that will make those years ahead as comfortable for you, her, and the children as possible.

As for others in your life that may have been for a short time, appreciate them, know that you are both benefitting from the relationship and bless them for the wonderful spirits that they are.

Others have been in your life for a very long time. Know that these are beings you've likely been with long before coming to Earth. You have probably experienced many lifetimes together and may have many more. These are the types of friends that you can count on always when needed. Make certain *you* can be counted on when needed. A wonderful exchange takes place between such friends, and the score is always even. No one ever owes anything. It is the way it is because the two of you are beyond petty material things. You are both allied to help and experience the other in life, to both reach your final goal, to lead an exciting and interesting life! Never think you are alone. If you are lonely, you have these particular friends to reach out to, always.

Take some time in your life to observe what's going on around you. Don't jump in and try to control every situation in your life, simply watch. Watch what parts the others play in your life and try to guess the outcome of any given situation. A very valuable lesson to learn is, do not have a preferred outcome to a situation. This can of course be very difficult, but it can be done. Trust that a power greater than *You* is at work. We all know it is, but how many of us *know* this to the very core of our being? When you master this, you will be the Master of your own destiny. You will experience the pure magic of your entire existence on this earth, not before.

Sometime later, look back on the very situation that you were concerned with, and see how it turned out for the best, without any help from you! You will see this same pattern repeated time and time again.

Certainly though, we wish to take an active role in creating our lives, otherwise this whole life experience is wasted time. Don't sit around and watch it all go by. Yet don't place the same importance on the outcome, to either a seemingly trivial situation, or on the more grand ones. Accept the outcome, whether it's what you think you want or not. It will unfold as *You* wanted it to. Most times you will understand why in a short amount of time. Sometimes it may be more difficult to understand, perhaps until the time you choose to leave this earth life. One day it will all make sense, and it *all* fits into your grand map of what you had intended for your life.

Does this mean as I go through my life and I have someone physically abusing me, that I should stand by and let it happen? If this is a horrible thought to you, most likely, this is not what you intended your life to be, so change it! The change itself is part of your master plan.

If you absolutely *cannot* change a situation (and most always we can) for some reason that *you* designed, this is the plan. It will all become clear at some time.

We've all heard stories of great athletes and leaders that came from humble beginnings, possibly abusive homes or homes that were poverty stricken. It is because of those very things that we rise above the challenges of daily life and become the great athletes, healers, musicians, and leaders that we do. Without that experience we would not have obtained the desired skills or drive it takes to become such a person.

I've witnessed countless individuals anger because of some bad hand that life has dealt them. Yet I've seen others, very successful, unless you know them well, you wouldn't know of the tragedies they've experienced in their lives. All because of choices made, as well as the understanding of what life is, and how it works.

I'm proud to say that in two weeks, my parents will have been married for 53 years. Not a small feat in today's world of the easy and convenient divorce.

My parents have been wonderful examples of *good people* all of their lives. Some of my earliest memories as a child were going with my father to his parents' house, or my mother's parents' house, to do repairs. My dad is a jack-of-all-trades and a master of several. The most impressive thing is his talent and how he put it to use. He was always mindful of the little things that would make their lives better. He would always go to any length to do the job right. Yet, he would never accept any money for parts or the supplies he needed to complete the job. He did so because he cared for his parents. He had enough respect for his wife to do the same for her parents. It was not unusual for him to do the same for friends either. He did it because he could, and because it made their life experience much more wonderful.

Once you have your relationship stabilized with your ex, when you see little projects around the house that need to be done, offer to do it, or assist, if it's something you feel you can handle. It must be a tough situation for a single mother, strapped for cash and fighting to make it one more day, to deal with simple plumbing or electrical problems. Anything you can do to help not only benefits her life, but the lives of your little ones. It teaches them a great deal about *who* you are. If she declines your offer, honor that.

Don't use this as an opportunity to get back together, do it because you *are* a good person. Don't accept any payment; don't deduct it from the child support. This is a part of your responsibility as a protector and provider for your children. Leave it at that. Your reward will be doing something nice for someone when you didn't have to.

Bottom line, *you* chose to buy the hot coffee and drive. You chose to dump it in your lap. Did you not know the risks of such actions? You were the one that decided to bungee jump without knowing a damn thing about it, putting your life in another person's hands. Perhaps he/she didn't make sure the cord was short enough, or tight enough. If you don't know the risks, don't do it! Don't come back and sue someone for your own laziness. Do the proper homework! Don't place blame on someone else, take the responsibility and change your life yourself, everyone else will if you let them!

You also choose to be an example to your children. Like it or not, they watch every move you make and hear every word you speak. They have memories longer than your ex wife, and it may come back to haunt you or bless you, it's entirely your choice.

You have an astonishing amount of power in your thoughts and your choices in life will influence precisely who you are and where you are going. Learning to use these gifts is a lot of fun and will relieve a great amount of stress. Doing little things for your ex out of kindness will benefit you, your ex, and your children in ways that cannot be measured. Know your life is a direct result of your choices. Your life forward is determined by your power of thinking and the choices you make.

ASSIGNMENT

Recognize the cycles in your life. We all go through ups and downs. If you were to map your ups and downs, it looks like a sine wave, or a roller coaster ride. The secret to having a peaceful happy life is to bring those peaks and valleys closer together. The ups aren't as high, the downs aren't as low.

The method I use to bring those peaks and valleys into more uniformity is to attempt to find the good in every little down or valley in my life. I find the lesson and realize the incident or "tragedy" provides me with a lesson or a learning opportunity. Everything happens for a very *good* reason. If nothing else, how would you recognize the highs, if it weren't for the lows? When I feel I've been dealt an injustice, I determine why it happened, what can I do to prevent this from happening again? Where is my lesson in this?

I've also learned to appreciate and celebrate the wonderful blessings in my life; they are all peaks or *highs*. But I also keep it in perspective, this is not the final chapter in my life, I know the cycle will again turn, so I relish my success for as long as I can.

The more tragic or *low* the valley, the more learning opportunity is presented. If it's a small low, it may call for a change in behavior, such as reassessing finances, or driving more carefully. If it's a big valley, it may call for a change in life style, just as a heart attack signals the need to quit smoking or drinking.

Be aware of these cycles and recognize them for what they are. Changing your perspective on any situation may change your reality of the part you play in that situation.

CHAPTER 7
PUTTING YOUR LIFE
BACK TOGETHER

I came to a fork in the path. As I could see only a short way down each, my decision was difficult. I realized the only right decision, was to choose the path with complete commitment, no matter which direction I chose, it would be the right one, because I had made a choice.

Hopefully we all realize we have choices in our lives. We choose to get up every day, go to work, and pay the bills. We choose vacation destinations, how many children we will have, and the names of the children. At least most of us do.

I'm ashamed to say, during my many relationships, I was not the best father to my three older daughters; in fact I was a father in absentia. I spent little time with them; their mother struggled to raise them on her own for many years and struggled harder to get child support from me. I wasn't terribly responsible in my business "careers" either; I was too busy seeking companionship.

Fortunately, their mother raised them well. They have learned forgiveness for my sins, and have spent some time instructing me on being a better father. I have been blessed to have a second chance with the little ones that I still have in my life, my *second three* as I call them.

I'd like to think I was given this second chance, as it was what I had planned for my life, before coming to this life, to get parenthood right during this lifetime. I don't have it right yet, but I'm learning. I've been so blessed with six wonderful children, who are every bit as adaptable, born with a resolve to survive under any circumstance, as I was in my younger years. I was blessed to be married to two wonderfully patient women, and have a relationship with a third that allowed me to complete my family.

The results of my life's experiences are a result of choices I've made in one sense or another. We all choose our circumstances, whether we'd like to believe that or not. If you think you find yourself in a situation that you didn't appear to have any control over, you did. As a result of those choices, the experience is going to be what you need to lead a more beneficial life from this day forward. The sooner you come to this realization, the sooner you will begin to not only rebuild your life, but to *make it better than it has ever been in the past.*

With change, such as the one you've been through comes a tremendous amount of freedom. It's all a matter of how you choose to see it. You may pick any path you like in proceeding with the rest of your life, with very little influence from anyone else.

I had the benefit of a life coach that came into my life at one of the lowest points in my life. She was my savior, my angel, and assured me to *see this* was the best thing for my direction. It *always* is. That was six years ago. Looking back on it, I can see that I have had some absolutely *wonderful* experiences and relationships that I would not have been able to experience, had my ex and I not separated. I am a much better man for having been separated and to have experienced the things I have. I wouldn't have missed it for the world!

No, I've not been able to afford the Caribbean cruises, trips to Mexico and Hawaii that I would have liked. Happiness is *inside.* Yea, blah, blah, but it is. I know a lot of people that go to bars, cruises, trips etc, to escape. But no matter where *you* go, there *you* are. You cannot escape yourself, even when you sleep. *You* are still in most of the dreams.

To some, facing our inner demons can be terrifying! I recall going through my first visit with this life coach, and cleaning out all of the crap that was inside. She never explained what it was, some pretty terrible junk came out. I could literally feel these pockets of past crud finding their way out of the deep hidden areas of my body, and surfacing to be dealt with and discarded. It was an experience I won't soon forget. We all have a certain amount of this rotten energy buried deep inside, and until it gets out, it's left to fester. It's this exact energy that surfaces at times we are stressed, or we over react to a situation and think "Where the hell did that come from?" I may go into those processes and how I was able to accomplish this purging in a later book.

Going through this process need not be a scary experience. You will likely deal with some things you don't want to, but you will sooner or later. Through it all you will regain yourself, your own best friend.

I'm working on the cruise and the trips. I've dealt with the inside stuff, I look forward to going on a trip and taking *me* along. *Me, myself* and *I* will have one hell of a good time without having to face stuff when I get back.

If you were married for any length of time, it may seem as though you are stepping into a completely foreign world. You remember little of what it was like being a single guy. Hanging out with the single friends, dating, playing the game. It takes some time to re-learn the language, and the customs of the single people you'll meet.

Remember back to a time when you did something for the first time. It may have been trying out for a sports team, learning to scuba dive, or joining your first group of people in a new activity. You may have experienced some fear, hesitation, or resistance. Since it was something you desperately wanted, you acknowledged that resistance and participated anyway.

Being single again can bring on those same types of fears and resistance. The important thing to remember is, we usually resist the lessons we need most. We are afraid to take that step into the unknown, for fear it will change our lives forever. Isn't that what we'd like to accomplish though, to change our lives forever? And change our lives in a good way, in a great way?

To help you get past this, acknowledge that fear. Admit to yourself, you are afraid. Make a list of the things you fear most if you like. And tell yourself it's ok to be afraid.

Acknowledge everything has a process. You don't plant vegetables in your garden, and expect them to yield enough to stock your dinner table after the first week. Seeds have a growth process. They need time to sprout, need to be nurtured and coaxed along. They will grow into what they were meant to be, and they will yield the wonderful fresh vegetables you want to harvest.

So in our lives, we go through the same things. Few individuals step on the ball field for the first time as star players. Learning and growing has a process. We learn by practicing, and listening to the advice of coaches, and other players that have played longer than we have. No matter where they may be on the learning curve, they generally have something to teach us. At one time, they experienced the same resistance you were when first stepping onto the field.

Acknowledge again you have these fears, take the bat and swing away! You'll hit that ball. As you practice more and more, you will get better. Soon you will be in your comfort zone and be playing right along with the other players.

Learning the single father role has no set time. In fact, it can be a never-ending process. After the years I've been doing it, I am still learning things every day that can help me be a better person, and a better father to my children. I hope they grow up soon! My brain is overloaded!

If finances are not one of your strong points, you'll want to make up a budget. You can find information on how to do this online, in bookstores, or in your local library. It's critical to have a clear picture of what your income is versus your output, and what you can afford for a new home. Make certain you figure in your child support. You may want to choose a specific date each month to have it paid. Your ex will appreciate this tremendously. Once you have your finances in place, it's time to start making your space.

You are faced with the situation of paying another rent or house payment. You need the means to build your space from the ground up, new bed, new furniture, and new cooking utensils, new everything. Many of us are not in a position to consider new. Adequate is the best we can hope for.

If you find yourself in this position, don't hesitate to let friends know your needs. You'll be surprised at the number of folks that have extra furniture, pots, pans, dishes etc they've had in storage for years and are more than happy to donate to your cause. This is *not* the time to be so full of pride you would be ashamed to accept charity. Don't be ashamed to accept a gift from someone that will benefit you, and more importantly your children. The time will come you will be back on your feet, and you'll be in a position to donate some of your extra items to those in need, whether it's those that have found themselves in your same position, or to local charities or homeless shelters. Put that huge ego on the back burner for a while and tackle this with the same intensity you would at your employment. *This* is your job now.

For some of us, it's not terribly tragic to wander around homeless for a short time. Getting your home set up as quickly as possible will not only offer you some stability, but will provide your children with a sense of comfort. Our children worry tremendously if we are not being taken care of, or are in danger in any way. Do this for your children and make them as much a part of the process as you can.

Should you find yourself being seriously financially strapped, speak with friends search the newspapers or the Internet for rooms to rent. Many people in our state are renting rooms to supplement their income in these troubled times. You will have the benefit of much lower rent than you would generally have in an apartment. You should have access to the kitchen, bathrooms, a yard, and parking space, all thrown in a package. Usually your room rent will also factor in the cost of utilities, so you won't have to come up with deposits for the utility companies. You may find a place furnished or partially furnished. In any case less furniture will be needed, which saves you some huge initial expense. If you do rent a room make certain to decorate it with a few of your personal items. Give it your sense of home. You'll feel like less of a visitor and more at home. Make certain with the landlord or owner before renting that your children will be welcome in your new home.

Pictures of the kids are essential. Looking into those angelic faces will help through some difficult times, and serve as a reminder of why you are doing all of this. Pictures of W1, W2 or SO are up to you, but I wouldn't recommend it. It negates the good energy of the children. (No offense ladies but this is my book, I can say what I want).

If you need communications service, and in most cases you will, consider purchasing a cell phone on a low priced package. You won't always need, or be able to afford a Home Phone or landline. Cell phone call plans can be obtained for $40 per month, and some lower. You generally need to purchase the phone, but again, ask your friends if they might have one that can be reactivated. I have a perfectly good cell phone lying around the house that's been deactivated. I use it as a battery charger to charge spare batteries for my existing service. You may find a friend more than happy to donate one.

One of the most obvious places to search for essentials will be your local Thrift Store. Most items can be purchased for pennies on the dollar to what you might pay at a store for new. Once you have essentials in place, consider re-visiting the thrift store and look for a few things to make your house more of a home. Purchase or acquire pictures, a cheap centerpiece for the tables and lamps, candles, curtains and any decorations for the walls. Be creative.

Check the classifieds in the newspaper, you'll find great deals, and the seller is generally in a position to haggle. This can be a lot of fun, make a game of it. You'll find you might get some items much cheaper than you dreamed! Use a tactic I use when I go to Mexico. I'll see something I like, but don't care one way or the other if I take it home. Begin to barter at a low price; the vendor will name his or her price. Get them down to rock bottom. When they are ready to walk away, they can't afford to sell it any cheaper, grab their last quoted price and run with it. Chances are it's a fair price. But have some idea going in, what the item is worth, and the worth to you.

Flea Markets, garage and yard sales in season are a treasure trove of items, and you will generally find items much more reasonable than in thrift stores. This is a fun outing for the kids as long as you don't overdo and try to hit too many sales in one day. Get the items you *need* first. The essentials for day to day living, dishes, silverware, plates, pots and pans, a bed to sleep on, some furniture in the front room. Food always comes in handy. You can expand outward after that; get some things to fix the place up a bit, as long as it fits in your budget.

Make your new home comfortable for you. *You* get to decide if grape colored curtains go with a flaming yellow/orange couch. And if they don't and you're happy with it, let everyone else go pound sand.

For years you may have been subjected to matching curtains with floor tiles, doilies on the tables and dust being declared extinct in your realm. This is your opportunity to assert your personality. Make certain it's something you aren't going to grow tired of in the months to come.

When we first become single, we all want the Ultimate Bachelor Pad. In my case, reality soon set in. It's time to look realistically at what I can afford, and what my children can be comfortable with. Remember that child support is coming due, and it may tap your financial plans more than you know. If you can afford to purchase the furnishings you've always wanted, go for it! Make your house yours. Let it speak to who you are. You'll find it tremendously inspirational. I'll come hang out; we'll have a great time!

When you have the home situation handled, it's time to learn *how* to be single dad. You will be spending a great deal of time with the children. Still a social life is going to be very important. Let your friends know, if they were associated with your ex, they aren't doing you any favors by badmouthing her, or keeping you informed of her activities every time they see her. We've covered this before. Some of us are a bit dense so it bears repeating.

Our friends mean well, but if they're constantly slamming your ex, that doesn't say much for your intelligence in ever getting involved with her in the first place! Let them know no *blame* is placed in your mind, and it's time for you both to move on. How you both choose to handle that is entirely up to you. Hearing constant talk of your ex drains your energy and doesn't allow the wound to heal. If you feel the need to talk to get past it, seek a qualified therapist that will be impartial. Your friends of course won't be objective; they'll *always* take your side! That's why they are friends!

If your friends don't seem to *get it* and continuously harp on your ex, find new friends. At least establish some distance from those that drain your energy. You don't have time for this. You have more productive things to do with your life.

Men's support groups are a great means of talking and venting, and finding the emotional support you may need. Again, our pride may get in our way, but we're talking *survival*. If you were to find yourself stranded on a desert island, or in a wilderness situation, most of us would take any means necessary to provide food, shelter, and water for our basic needs. We would also take any extra time to make ourselves as comfortable in the environment to allow us to make the most of the situation even to *thrive* in this world. When you find yourself in the situation of being stranded in an alien world or as a single dad, the difference between survival (and not surviving) and thriving, is going to be knowledge. You'll find a great deal of knowledge imparted by the members of a support group that will help you thrive in your environment. Sadly, not many books are written on the subject, seek out any you can, if reading is your *thing*. I'm going to assume it is your thing, or you wouldn't have made it this far in the book. Good for you reach around and pat yourself on the back. You are on your way to becoming *The New Man*!

A *New Man* is forming in our society. It's been so for several years. I was completely blind to it. I think many of us men, as a whole, have realized that what we've been doing all of these years isn't working any more. Many men are seeking the *New Man*, and are making their own definitions of who that man is going to be. For too long we've let the female gender define the types of husbands and role models we should be. Enough of that! We weren't happy, they obviously are *never* happy, so let's take the bull by the horns and make our own definitions. Their only other option is to move to another planet. Bravo to those who pave the way!

I'm going to catch a lot of heat for those statements. Am I serious? Ask me sometime, I *might* tell.

Change is inevitable. Without change, we don't grow, we don't advance, and we're destined to repeat the same mistakes that have put us in this situation. "If we do not learn from history, we are destined to repeat it," this may be a paraphrase, but it applies to our lives as well. You may still be in the mental state that "I didn't do anything wrong!" And you would be correct. If this isn't the situation idealized in your mind, or societies, that doesn't mean you've done anything wrong, nor has she.

In your mind over the coming months or years, be specific. What do you want to be different, or the same in your next partner? It may be too early to start thinking of another partner, but it will come. The need for a companion of the opposite sex (or the same sex in an alternative life style) is as old as human history. We've all been drawn to finding that perfect mate. Not only for the perpetuation of the species, but rather to work as a team in the domestic chores and raising the family. We also began living in tribes and in communities many thousands of years ago, to protect us from the dangerous forces of nature, creatures and natural disasters. These are some very ancient instincts we're dealing with.

I've had some wonderful experiences in my life. I've seen some of the most beautiful sunsets, have been so close to herds of wild Elk that I could reach out and touch them. They never knew I was present. I've walked through the most beautiful dew covered forest as the morning sun began to peak through branches, and strolled on a glorious white sand beach as the sun set into the sea. Through many experiences, I had no one to share it with. Not having someone special in your space, when extraordinary things happen robs the experience of its grandeur. And at the same time, can make it that much more special.

Few of us are meant to be alone. Regardless of how it feels at times. Some of us spend years alone, some decades. Others don't know what it's like to be our only companion. After spending years alone, happily, I can't recall what that was like.

Both you and your ex are where you need to be, to best follow the course of your life that you had set out in the blueprint of your life before coming into this world. A wealth of opportunities await that you could *not* have experienced had you remained in the situation you were in, or in the direction you were both heading. This will all be clear some day, and how long someday is will be entirely up to you. To how much you accomplish today, this week or this month.

Feel a sense of peace knowing that you are where you are for reasons that may not be understandable yet. And give *her* the same respect. If things ever come up with the children along these lines, do your best to explain it to them in terms they will understand. It's critical *not* to badmouth the ex. Make it clear to your children that agree with the decision that's been made. Let them know you are content with the situation, and that though it may not seem to make sense to them, it's best for all of you. Let them know, unconditionally you are still their dad and Mom is still Mom and the both of you love them as much, or more than you ever have. My children know I still love their mothers. It is a different love than the love expressed by a couple. Children are very intuitive in understanding love. They are closer to love and know love better than we have since we were children.

Talking bad about the ex, especially to the children can only instill resentment for her, for you, and may instill fear in them to even be around her (or you). No one benefits!

When you mention the ex to the children, it is imperative to raise your vibration. I know this is a new age term and may not be familiar. It's very simple. To raise your vibration, calm your voice and your thoughts. Anger and hate if you feel them are for another time and place. When your voice is calm and peaceful, it will reassure them. Speak only with love and compassion. Practice in front of the mirror first if you must. You'll know you're on the right track when your heart is warm. When you have a tear roll down your cheek, big macho guy that you are, you'll know you are *there*.

If the ex is going to be vindictive and vengeful, you cannot control that. Nor should you want to. Hope that she will begin to understand the negative affects of this thinking. And it's not for *you* to tell her.

Put yourself in a higher form of thinking. The children are going to need your assurances that nothing has changed in your feelings, or mother's feelings for them. Without removing the fear, it's tough for them to enjoy your time and their mothers. They don't have a means to begin to put *their* lives back together. Enough damage has been done. It's time for healing. Let the wound begin to heal.

When you come face to face with the ex, do the same. Keep yourself in another vibration. Only deal with issues that must be dealt with (kids, expenses etc). Don't get into the whys and wherefores of what happened, what she's doing, or what you would like to see her do. *It's none of your business!* She is an adult and is entitled to run her life as she sees fit. If you feel the children are endangered, or not in a situation best for their safety and well being, take it up with an attorney. However when you are dealing with her directly, show her respect and speak kindly. She is not having an easy time of this either, regardless of who made the decision. This may have been a decision she didn't *want* to make, but had to, due to circumstances. Respect and appreciate her strength for doing it. It's doubtful she went into this with a blind eye; she knew what difficult circumstances this would bring to *all* of you.

Reconciliation of course may be an option. That is up to you and to her. I certainly wouldn't be wise to provide any advice. However, doing it for the sake of the kids is crap. The kids aren't going to be happy if you and your mate are miserable. Best to leave well enough alone unless you find other reasons you two would like to be together. If you feel that way, you're certainly entitled to speak with her. Do it without the children being present. If you are going to approach the subject, be prepared. Have definitive plans on how to correct whatever went wrong in the marriage or relationship. If counseling is involved, have the names and phone numbers of the counselors or therapists ready. Speak with one of them first before approaching your ex.

After you've said your piece, if she decides it may not be in her and the best interest of the kids', respect that decision. You may not be aware of the details of her present life, or of the issues that led you to this place. If she decides it's not best for her, accept it. Paying attention? One "No" is *final*. Don't keep revisiting the subject. That is your *final* clue to move on. If she should change her mind, it's up to her to let you know. If you should need something better, someone once said, "Living well after a divorce or separation is the best revenge." Go with that.

Living well doesn't necessarily mean financially or worldly, it also means *emotionally* well. Get yourself some help if you need it. Don't bury it, deal with it and begin to live your new life. Live well and be happy. That's what life is. Prepare yourself and your home for the new people and experiences that are coming your way. Prepare yourself with constant smiles, laughter, and snuggle hugs from the joys of your life. It's very rewarding.

ASSIGNMENT

Make a list of only 5 things that will make a big difference in your life. Under each write down why you do not have this in your life. No fair blaming it on anyone else! Lay out each step as to how you are going to accomplish each. This may be as simple as buying a few things for your home or may be as complicated as finding a significant other. All will require only your time and effort to accomplish this goal.

When you cross one off the list as accomplished, replace it with another goal. Continue this until you have no more goals, which should be the day after "Never."

Take conscious steps to surround yourself with only positive and inspirational energy. This may come in the form of music, movies, videos, people, or books as well as other sources. Be aware of what brings your energy up and helps you feel at peace in your world. Don't attempt to bring negative people or items into your world; they seem to find their own way of showing up!

Make one place in your home a priority. If you like to read, set up a reading area with a comfortable chair and lamp. Maybe watching television is special to you, set up a recliner and the nicest television you can acquire. Make at least one little place in your home something very special only for you. Use this place to energize yourself, and perhaps for a temporary escape. Not as a hiding place.

Never underestimate your potential, or what you can do with your life. Never.

CHAPTER 8
LISTS

I believe strongly that each person we meet, offers a little something we can gain from our time with them. This is especially so with relationships. A quality, habit, or trait, be it good or bad that holds a lesson for us in each of our partners. If I could go back in time, and have the opportunity once again to spend time with one of my ex's it would be with Edette to learn her talent for keeping lists!

I'll be honest, when we were together her compulsion of making lists drove me to the edge of insanity! But as I've grown older and have come to the stark realization that I'm not the most organized person in the world (quite the contrary) I wish I had a penchant for making lists as she did.

Don't get me wrong, I don't want to become obsessed with them, she would make lists of her lists! But I would very much like some of the organization she had in making her lists. Her goals and whole life are neatly written on paper, to see at a glance, where she was, and where she was heading, what it would take to accomplish, and specifically what she would have and how it would improve her life once the dreaded list was completed. And these lists have served her well in meeting goal after goal.

In keeping that spirit alive, and in my attempt to become more organized, I've compiled a few lists the recently single dad may find useful in organizing his life.

Feel free to use these if you'd like. I've tried to write them so you can either write them out, or slap them on a copy machine to make your own checklist of things you have, and things you'd like to acquire to make your home more safe and comfortable.

The composition of these lists come from years of attempting to keep a workable household for myself and my young ones and hopefully it will give you a head start on getting things comfortable for you and your little ones.

This is organized with a pretty basic functionality. As your house becomes larger, or your income increases, you may want to add as you go along.

I've provided a few blank lines after every category, to add any items you may need that I've not accounted for.

Furniture:

I'll leave most of these items up to you and your budget. Keep the children in mind with your purchases though. Try not to limit yourself to a recliner and television. Kids don't feel at home if they have to sit on the floor all of the time, and you may find you are sitting in your recliner less than they are!

Coat Rack—kids coats will land on furniture or floor unless you have a designated place for them.
Stools—for little kids to watch you cook, or for them to reach cups and glasses. You'll find some simple building plans in Fun Projects for Kids Chapter 18. Have your child help build it!

____
____

____

Kitchen:

You may want to add or subtract to this list, to fit your number of children and the amount of guests you may have on an average. It's best to purchase or otherwise acquire items that you can match later, in case you decide to add more pots and pans, silverware, dishes etc.

Pots and Pans:

I wholeheartedly recommend cast iron if appropriate. The maintenance is simple it will last you many more years than some of the more expensive cookware when properly cared for, and the costs have come down in the last few years to make them reasonably priced. Aside from that it has a health factor, as it doesn't pass aluminum to your cooking. The taste of a meal cooked in a well-seasoned cast iron pan is unsurpassed. You'll find them at most outdoors sporting good stores, or your local superstore.

1 small saucepan w/lid
1 medium saucepan w/lid (though I wish I had one more of these)
1 large cooking pot w/lid
1 6-inch skillet w/lid
1 10-inch skillet w/lid
1 14-inch (or larger) skillet w/lid
1 9 x 13 roasting pan (I prefer the glass tempered but some dishes, like brownies, cook better in metal.)
1 broiling pan (These are tough to find unless they came with your oven. I use a heavy aluminum cookie sheet.)
1 Wok (for you yuppies)
2 large cookie sheets (I've found some heavy aluminum that won't warp under high heat, one of my favorite cooking pans! Also used for hot wings, bread sticks, biscuits, cookies, etc.)
1 small cookie sheet (great for broiling a single serving of fish or chicken)

____

____

____

Cutlery:

Buy the best you can afford, you won't regret it. I've never been one for serrated knives but that's a personal preference.

1 small paring knife
1 vegetable peeler
1 larger butcher knife aka: 1 big ass butcher knife
4 steak knives
1 filet knife—It's a guy thing and can be extremely useful for things like carving the raw breast from a chicken, useful after fishing trips.
Cutting board—buy a mid-price range or better you'll get a lot of use out of this.

____

____

____

Cookware:

Ingenious dishes that you cook in, and goes from the oven/microwave to the table.

1 small casserole dish w/lid
1 medium casserole dish w/lid

____

____

____

Dinnerware:

Stoneware is an excellent choice, you can beat them up pretty well without damaging them, and they look nice!

8 dinner plates
8 small plates—Younger kids like smaller plates.
4 coffee cups— If you don't drink coffee, as I don't, they are handy to have around.
8 cereal bowls—Trust me, you'll use them for a variety of things.
1 large serving platter
1 gravy boat (optional)

____

____

____

Silverware:

Serving for 8
8 butter knives
8 dinner forks
8 salad forks—The little ones will use these for dinner.
8 dinner teaspoons

8 dinner tablespoons
1 large solid serving spoon
1 large slotted serving spoon
1 large serving fork—Used in combination with the serving spoon for serving salad, or pulling hot chickens from a roasting pan.
1 silverware tray—for organizing silverware in the cabinet drawer

____

____

____

Cooking Utensils:

1 large spatula
1 medium spatula
2 wooden spoons or spatulas (These work well with cast iron cookware.)
1 rubber spatula (buy a good one that won't melt when you forget and leave it in a sauce)
1 hand potato masher (This has many uses!)
1 grater (For cheese and vegetables, I prefer the tall 4-sided, since it has a variety of grating sizes on one grater)
1 colander (The bowl with the holes in it for straining pasta, vegetables, etc.)
1 wire whisk—Optional, but I would have a hard time living without mine

____

____

____

Cups and Glasses:

8 medium water glasses
8 small glasses (like a rum and coke glass only a bit bigger)
Plastic cups (have two for each child, they'll have friends over!)
1 big ass beer mug (for when the little ones go home)
4 wine glasses (for when the kids are gone, entertaining guests, or for special occasions for kids to drink their punch from. Experts will argue that it promotes alcohol abuse, let them argue. You decide what works for you.

Oh! And teach the kids how to make the crystal glasses sing by wetting your finger and rubbing the rim!)

____

____

____

Bowls:

1 large bowl (salad or popcorn)
1 small mixing bowl (small, but large enough to beat two eggs)
1 medium sized mixing bowl
1 larger mixing bowl
Storage containers (for leftovers to be placed in the refrigerator)

____

____

____

Miscellaneous:

4 good hot pads
1 bottle dish soap—for the sink, don't use this in the dishwasher until you have a pail and mop.
1 pail
1 sponge mop
1 drainer for dishes
1 bottle dishwasher soap
1 bottle floor cleaner
1 bottle floor wax
Dish scrubber—buy 3 or 4.
1 brush for washing bottles. If your children are out of the baby bottle stage, still handy for washing cups and glasses with our big hands.
2 dishcloth—one will get dirty and sit in the laundry!
2 sponges—large and small—Please don't use the same sponges from the bathroom as you do in the kitchen. Keep them separate. If you need an explanation on this, think harder!
2 kitchen towels

Oven cleaner and rubber gloves
Paper towels
Plastic wrap
Tin foil wrap
1 can disinfectant—use once a week or so on counters and sinks
Cookbooks
1 canister set (flour, coffee, sugar etc)
Broom and dustpan
Note pad and pen—for using as a grocery list. I like the little ones with magnets to put on the refrigerator, but the kids seem to think it's their personal sketch pad, so you may elect to keep this out of their reach.

____
____
____

Small Appliances:

1 electric hand mixer
1 blender- optional
1 food processor
1 steamer (Optional, though if you like steamed vegetables, it's irreplaceable.)
1 coffee or cappuccino maker—I've never had a cup of coffee in my life, but I find a small 2-cup coffee maker essential for guests.
1 toaster—You won't find one in my house. The only time I'll use one is for making garlic toast; I do it in the oven, but what a waste of energy!

____
____
____

Medicine Cabinet:

Children's aspirin
Children's cold medicine
Children's cough medicine or cough drops
Band-aids—Depending on their age of course, get the ones with the little

cartoon characters, and make sure you have a lot of them!

Aloe plant— in your house an aloe plant should be growing. When the children have minor scrapes or burns, bug bites, etc, break off one of the stems, cut it open and put some of the liquid on the affected area. It's very soothing, and is a natural remedy; it helps tremendously in the healing process. Children like it because it's natural, and it has no burning or stinging.

Diaper ointment—Again depending on the children's age. This is critical for a baby in diapers.

Baby powder-—good for babies, some of the out of diaper kids will still like to use it after a bath.

Rubbing Alcohol—keep it around for cleaning scraped knees, cut fingers, etc, before adding a band-aid.

Baby oil—good for all ages

Vitamins—children and adult

Aspirin—adult (you'll need them!)

Medical tape

Gauze

First aid kit—optional, has a few of all items you'll need

____

____

____

Bathroom:

Waste basket—When girls begin their period, this is essential.

Tampons or Feminine napkins—age appropriate of course. You may want to ask your ex what size and type, etc. It may embarrass your daughter. (It's a female thing.) I know this is *not our favorite thing to shop for!* I will generally go to a store or market that I don't frequent, so no one knows me when I have to pick up female items.

Diapers—age appropriate, ask the ex what size, brand etc, it's important.

Baby shampoo

Bubble bath

Soap—Something mild, many of us like to use something stronger for men, it may not be best for a child's skin.

Towels—You may want several bath and hand towels and wash cloths.

Scrubbing brush or natural sponge—Normal kids get muddy and greasy when playing, this helps a great deal at bath time. I like having a long handled back scrubber for this.

Shower curtain

Toilet paper—*Always* keep at least two extra rolls on hand. Children seem to use a *lot* of this!

Toilet lid and tank lid covers

Bathroom rug—If possible, match it with your lid and tank covers, as well as the shower curtain.

Soap dish—makes cleaning the bathroom counter much simpler.

Liquid hand soap—optional.

____

____

____

Bathroom Cleaning Items:

Scrubbing powder—for cleaning the tub or sinks

Pumice stone—these can be tough to find but most professional cleaning supply houses will carry them. It's essentially a rectangular stone that works miracles for scrubbing hard water deposits from porcelain. This little item will save an enormous amount of time when cleaning.

Bathroom cleaner

Glass cleaner—for cleaning mirrors

1 large sponge

1 medium scrubbing brush for the tub

1 toilet brush

1 plunger—if you don't have a wastebasket, feminine napkins *will* go down the toilet, well, part way at least.

____

____

____

Kids' Bed room(s):

Bed

Linens—sheets, and pillowcases.

Pillows
Blankets or quilts
Clock Radio or radio (optional)
Television (optional)
Wall Pictures—Some age appropriate inexpensive pictures make their room so much more comfortable.
Lamp (optional if needed)
Nightlight—This is good especially for the younger ones. Remember, they are not in their bed at home yet.
Chairs—Kids' chairs can be inexpensive, and will be extremely personal to them.
Dresser or chest—to keep their clothing
Clothes hangers— for the closet
Nightstand—depending on the size and configuration of the room
Wastebasket—It will help keep their room much cleaner! Kids don't always like to take their pop cans all the way out to the kitchen wastebasket when involved in a movie or project.
Toys
Books

———————————————————
———————————————————
———————————————————

Dad's Bedroom:

Bed
Linens—sheets, pillowcases, etc.
Pillows
Blankets or quilts
Night Stand(s)
Lamp(s)
Clock Radio or alarm clock
Dresser or chest of drawers
Candles
Clothes Hangers
Earplugs (optional—I work nights.)
Safe or some other concealed area to keep valuables.

Pictures or wall hangings

____

____

____

Laundry:

Whether you'll be using your own washer and dryer, going to the Laundromat or going to your Mothers house to do laundry, you'll want to have some of the basics.

Laundry Soap
Bleach
Dryer sheets (for fabric softening)
Borax (not too many people know of this one, in my circles anyway. Add a bit to the laundry and it helps get clothes extremely clean, and removes odors. It's also useful for cleaning the bathroom, tub, toilet etc).

____

____

____

Miscellaneous Household Items:

Vacuum—If you can't afford it right away, consider getting one of the non-electric push type sweepers.
Dust buster—Small hand held vacuum that is a blessing to have with kids around
Feather duster—On the whole, men see no reason to dust. This little item makes it extremely simple to dust a lot of items in minutes.
Furniture polish
Lemon oil —for furniture
Chamois—The same ones we use to dry our cars can be used for dust rags. If you have plenty of these, and something gets spilled, wet them down good, wipe up the spill, rinse them out, spread several layers on top of the spill and let it sit for several hours. They are wonderful for drawing spilled liquids out of the carpet.

Carpet cleaner—for cleaning all of those spills
Blankets—Kids love them if the house is too cold, watching TV, having picnics on the lawn, etc.
Night Light—Use in the hall between bathroom and kids' bedrooms. One in the bathroom is a nice idea also.

____

____

____

Other things you may want to figure into your budget:

Television
Entertainment center
VCR or DVD player
Stereo
Telephone
Candles
Wall paintings or pictures
Magazine rack
Reading lamp
Kitchen table and chairs
Lamps
Microwave and stand
Barbecue grill

____

____

____

You may use your own judgment on the above of course. Some items you may need more or less of. Others you may not feel you need at all. The lists are only to be used as a guide to help you equip your household with a minimum of organizational effort.

CHAPTER 9
UNDERSTANDING THE EX

Chances are, the goals of your ex and yourself are not terribly different. We all know our basic physical needs are water, food, and shelter. Emotionally, all of us seek happiness, security and love. The means we choose to pursue meeting the goal is where we conflict.

It's been so long ago it seems as in another life, I had a friend named Dean. Dean was more than a friend; he was my hunting partner for several years when I lived in Colorado.

If you have had the experience of having a regular hunting partner, particularly one that you hunt big game with (deer and elk) and spend many nights together, alone at a campfire, you will understand the bond we two might have had. Few things men in this position won't speak of. Add to this setting a half-gallon of whiskey, and taboos vanish.

I've never been one to mix alcohol, men and high-powered rifles, but with Dean it was an exception. Dean was smart when it came to hunting. We both knew the alcohol didn't come out until the rifles were up for the day, dinner had been served, perhaps a large T-bone with all of the fixings, and the fire was the only light, save for the stars and moonlight on those special fall nights.

Dean had things to say, and these hunting trips were the rare occasion when he would dare to delve into that realm. It was only when he was many miles from his wife and children, a full stomach, with few ears around, that he would bless me with his memories of Viet Nam.

With Dean it had an atmosphere of authenticity since he didn't brag. Not like those "firefighters" as he called them, the guys that had or had not been on the front lines (but said they were) and seemed to thrive on the action, the bloodshed. He thought they were a half bubble off.

A mountain of a man he, was, six feet four inches and Three hundred plus pounds. He possessed a laugh as jovial as his enormous body would allow. Dean loved his wife and children dearly. They were the twinkle in his eye, and they deserved such an honored place. He had a heart that was bigger than his own massive frame.

The nights we were in camp, usually alone, Dean would reminisce. Under the frosty fall moon, with the Milky Way as our protector, perhaps sensing his insignificance, a change would come over him. He would begin to speak of life in another time and terrifying place.

Dean had been captured, fairly early in the U.S. involvement in "Nam." It was ok for vets back then to call it "Nam" or "the Nam," which is not so any more. He was taken into North Vietnam to a prisoner of war camp. He existed for more than seven years, not always at the same camp, but after awhile they all seemed the same.

He told of the cold damp nights, the creative torture, the beatings, the forced marches late into the night through the jungle, sometimes barefoot, sometimes completely void of clothing.

For seven years he endured physical, mental, and emotional torture. No nourishment to speak of. If they ate on any particular day, it was a good day. He couldn't count the times his captors told him the war was over; they were going to go home, only to be disappointed, again and again. Trust was difficult for the prisoners with whom they would whisper through the walls of stone. Anyone that remotely kept them in their prison was the enemy.

Of course they plotted to escape those first few years and some tried only to be brought back with all of their limbs broken, or worse. Some were captured but never brought back. Their fate remained unknown for many years.

After a few years, came resignation. Resignation was a fate worse than death. This mountain of a man was told, along with his fellow soldiers, what to do, when to eat, when to sleep, when to wake up, which was frequent. Resist and they were beaten or worse.

One torture device he experienced on more than one occasion they called the cage. The cage was built of bamboo and partially submerged, at the edge of a river, or a rice patty. A prisoner was put into the cage with his ankles bound and his wrists bound behind his back. If he were to survive, he could press his face upward between the bamboo stalks on the top of the cage to breathe. The cage had just enough room to get most of a face out of the water. He would remain like this for an hour, ½ a day, or longer. His captors would decide when he had been properly disciplined.

Personally, I cannot imagine a worse hell on earth.

For some reason, during several of the interviews I've had with single mothers, this image of the prisoner of war kept flashing in my mind.

The similarities are not a far stretch for some women sharing their stories. Some not wanting to become pregnant at an early age, in their young naivety. Others chose adoption, only to be overridden by parents or the father of the child. They had given up their dreams of an exotic exciting life, in a few short weeks. Dreams were stolen through what some considered no fault of their own. After a time, they resigned themselves to the "dream" of motherhood. "Maybe one day I will be rescued," the same thoughts echoing in their minds as those of the soldiers. They could only hope it would not be seven years as my friend had experienced. Many of these mothers have children aged well into their teens, and still they wait.

I spoke with mothers whose teenaged sons beat them, probably as badly as the captors in the prison camp. One mother's ex had committed suicide years earlier, so he wasn't around for support of any kind. She had no male role model to step in and teach these boys how men should treat women. The boys blamed their mother because they had no father. The anger was so dark they couldn't see a way out.

Sadly, I talked with mothers that had not resigned themselves to this maternal life. They resented their children, blamed *them* for the loss of any dream life. Convinced without these "blessings" in their lives, they would be living an exciting, very wealthy, *good life.* If your ex is not one of these, consider yourself blessed.

Women have secret thoughts they would never dare speak. As they sit and chat with their closest girlfriends, discussing dreams that would terrify them if secret thoughts formed words. The role as mother sacred, to speak any hidden thought that might indicate otherwise, would be a sin against mothers of the world. The fear of being judged for a secret wish of another life is too great.

Because a woman had children doesn't *automatically* make her a mother. As men, we certainly understand that those fatherly instincts don't always *kick in,* as we believe they should. The same with mothers in many cases, they learn to adapt. They learn to nurse, they learn to change diapers, and they learn to program their body clock to wake at the slightest fuss from the little angel, no matter how many hours of sleep in the last week. No matter if the child is up at 2, 3, and 4 am, they learn to awaken for them. Some mothers do not *want* this. They don't *want* to do this.

Our first judgment of course is their selfishness. Let's take another look at that.

Too many husbands and fathers seem to think with a bit of organization, the mother of their child or children would be much better off, a much better mother, and have time for themselves to unwind. These fathers evidently are completely blind to what is going on in their own homes!

Shortly after my second child was born, my wife was recovering from the birth. I was faced with not only caring for our two year old, but also moving my family to a new apartment. This was a simple undertaking, I thought! During long 20-hour days most of the moving was done while my two-year-old, infant, and wife were sleeping. The rest of the time was spent bathing, feeding, cleaning, cooking, and various household chores for the family. I had no time to organize, barely enough time to reason with any sense of rationale! I could not imagine the single mother with a job and more than one child, having a moment to gather her thoughts!

If you are one of the father's that subscribe to this more organization belief, you will likely learn one of two lessons. Either you will have yourselves and your children in what can only be described as a military regimen, with no one happy, or you will find you've seriously underestimated the amount of organization a child will adhere to. Children have all they can do to remember to clean their rooms or brush their teeth, they have much more important things on their mind. So if your organization plan doesn't work, don't give up all hope. Take time to reorganize your organization plans to include only the most important items, and use the fly by the seat of the pants method on everything else. If you can get them to the age of 21 alive, you've done well!

Many of the mothers that I spoke with had resigned themselves to living on welfare. Others, quite wealthy by many peoples standards were still forced to live in substandard conditions, certainly not the life they had always dreamed of. All were pressed for time, never getting enough sleep, or if they did, it was a fitful sleep. Many could not remember the last time that they had a good undisturbed night's sleep. If their children had gone off with the fathers, they would wake worrying, not able to sleep because the house was too quiet. They may interpret their paranoia for mother's intuition thinking something must be wrong with their babies.

Many of them ate less than they should, and not as nutritious, because they couldn't afford to feed their children *and* themselves. As one mother mentioned, her children were convinced that her favorite part of a chicken was the wings. She would eat only the wings, to allow her children the rest of the chicken.

Phones were shut off, gas and lights had been on and off for years as they struggled to make one paycheck ahead of the bills. Heaven forbid if one of the children needed an unexpected doctor or hospital visit. This could seriously set them back for months. These women were forced as the prisoner of war, to live and survive at all costs. With a very slight glimmer of hope, their only motivation to take one more step forward. Tomorrow might be different. In all of these however, they took their motherhood seriously.

Let's take a closer look at the woman that has children but doesn't want to be a mother. Unfortunately, I've experienced these also. I'm not particularly proud to say I have had many relationships in my 30 years as an adult and have seen many different approaches to motherhood.

The mother that does not want to be a mother keeps the children for a variety of reasons. She may feel she has failed as a human being if she gives her children to the ex, or up for adoption. Her parents, peers and her ex expect it of her. After all, someone has to do it. But this is a smoke screen.

If the children tell their story, they rarely see their mother, not as other children do. They are left in the care of anyone that will take them, sometimes for days, or weeks at a time. Often these caretakers are not fit parents themselves, but will take the children anyway, for a variety of reasons.

Mother is living the life she intended to live; she's taking cruises, going to exotic locations, or partying at the club late. She *knows* that the one man, or that one event that is going to change her life is close; she simply must find *him* or trigger that life-changing event. For some the belief in the fairy tail we were raised with dies hard. Surely Prince Charming or that winning lottery ticket is just beyond her finger tips. She may be attempting, for a few short hours, to escape the stress of this life that was forced upon her, that *nightmare,* which has become her life.

As mothers and fathers we choose our own level of involvement with our children, whether we are married, or single. We choose on a daily basis whether we wish to see the children, or call them on the phone. Whether to buy them a birthday gift or if a card will suffice. We choose the activities we share with them when they are living with us, visiting (or we visiting them). We choose how involved we want to be in their lives physically and emotionally. We sometimes don't talk to them, because we don't know what to say!

One of the most terrifying things for a newly single father is when the teenage daughter needs to visit the store because she began her first menstrual period. You go instead. You don't take her with you! Let her relax, get the ex on the phone and ask her what you do, what do you buy at the store? When you get these things taken care of, come home; lock yourself in your room for a few minutes (after you know the children are taken care of) and P A N I C!

Our first instinct as men may be to load up the deer rifle, head for the forest and kill something, reaffirming our manhood is still in tact. But this is hardly the time or the place. Hopefully your relationship is in a place that you can at least ask what you can do for her. Tell her that you don't know about this, but that you love her. This is a big step for her and anything you can do, if only dialing Mom on the phone helps, do it. At your first opportunity, learn all you can of women's menstrual cycles. One tip from experience, make sure to put a trash can in the restroom so that they can dispose of things easily (Seriously, this is important to them).

In most cases, since you're a "male" and the very reason that every woman has had to experience this since Adam and Eve were banished from the Garden of Eden, don't push it. Remember back to when you first said something to your first love, and you made her cry. That helpless feeling comes rushing back in a wave of inadequacy that can only be met with your drowning. No matter how much you clamber for air, you'll not find it.

The level of involvement you choose in your relationship with your children and your ex is very important, it can also change at any time. So be vigilant. The child did not choose you as their father, and they did not choose their mother. As far as they know, they were thrown on earth with you and she as their parents. They didn't buy into this whole mess. And if they were to verbalize it, you may hear that you really suck as a parent!

Your children are very intuitive when it comes to your feelings. Unfortunately until they are teenaged or beyond, they don't have the ability to say "I didn't do anything wrong! Don't be mad at me! Just love me!" Even when they're teenagers, some can't seem to form these words.

Children have no way out, unless they run away. And how hopeless must that seem? They cannot change their situation. Their parents can't even live with each other. And they *will* blame themselves. They cannot find the words to comfort their mother's tears when she can't keep the car running, or loses her job. Still they feel what she feels.

Be mindful of how *you* are reacting around them. If you are upset with the ex, or some situation at work, or in your life, they will pick up on that. Especially at early ages, they seem to know you are upset. And don't let them fill in the blanks on the things that go unsaid. A child will *always fill in the blanks so somehow; the way you are feeling is their fault!* If you are having a bad day, no matter what their age, snap out of it and take the time to explain it is *not* their fault, explain the situation as best you can so that it's age appropriate. And make certain you *don't* make their mother the villain.

We are living our lives separately. It's important to understand the ex is going to be an integral part of your children's lives and your life for many years. This continues after the children are grown and married. Chances are you will have contact through discussions concerning the children, arranging visitations, attending parent/teacher conferences and as they get older attending children's weddings, being present for the birth of your grandchildren and other events.

It's not absolutely critical to have a civil relationship with the mother of your children, but it *will* make both of your lives easier and will have a profound influence on the children.

Whether she or you were the one to make the decision on the separation and the divorce, understand that you and she find yourselves in identical circumstances. She also has suffered a great loss, she also has had her dreams shattered, and she also is living the pain you are going through. It's all too easy to lose sight of this as we both stumble through our lives, wearing masks that guard us from the pain.

Both have spent a great deal of time together while beginning this family and building the home. It's a great gift you have given each other in the birth of your children. This gift was presented with love and divine purpose. It's not something that can be rescinded.

It's become all too customary after a separation or divorce for the parties to become adversaries. Despising the other can be very easy; at least it appears so. In reality, it's very difficult anytime you dislike anyone. You lose energy over the many years to follow by thinking ill of another, and feeling resentment. Because the majority does it, doesn't make it right.

The alternative is to appreciate the other half, for the time you spent together, the many gifts of love you've shared. You and she can define your relationship, as it is and will be for the next number of years. You alone may decide on how you are going to treat your ex and to a great extent, how you treat her will affect how she will treat you.

This is one of the greatest gifts you can bestow upon your children. The example of a greater form of love, they will learn much by your example, and they will be watching with intense scrutiny.

This may sound difficult, but it's not. Begin with baby steps. Speak softly and kindly when you have occasion to speak with your former spouse or SO. It's not your place to guide her life, or to give her any form of direction, including issues involving the children. If it is safety or health concerns with the children, you two will certainly want to discuss those issues. When it comes to advising her on her life though, this is not your place any more than it is her place to direct yours.

If both parties cannot suitably address the safety or health concerns, legal recourse may need to be considered. For the sake of the children and your own peace of mind, this should not be undertaken lightly.

When you begin slowly, treating each other with respect, you will build an amicable relationship and eventually you will begin to discuss most any issue without offending the other.

Your children will delight in watching the relationship develop between you and your ex though the relationship is much different than in the past. They may feel comfortable speaking with either or both of you concerning their lives, knowing they will not add to the source of contention between you.

It's ok to feel a certain sense of love for someone that you had spent such great deal of time with, someone that has given you the gift of children. Obviously, a romantic love between you is gone and it's best to keep this in the context it is *today*. Life will come easier with time. You will find that you wish the best for your ex partner and hope that they find happiness.

All persons, regardless of gender, race, creed, or color wish to be treated with respect. Treating your ex with respect at *all* times is admirable, especially in the course of disagreement. This may have been one issue in the relationship bringing both of you to where you are, but it's never too late to reverse that trend. Great opportunities to grow exist in *any* situation.

Being a Mother is a very difficult calling in life. As Fathers many of us don't appreciate the bond between a mother and child, regardless of the *capabilities* of some women to perform their motherly duties. A strong bond is present with Mothers and their children. exceptions are few. Mothers fear for the safety and well being of their children, when everything in the home isn't perfect.

In my specific situation W1 and I always found it a bit uncomfortable to be amicable, but we did it anyway. It began as soon as we separated and grew over time. It was easy when she met the man she would marry to treat him with respect also. This was someone I had known many years before, and it wasn't a difficult adjustment. I sincerely wanted her to find happiness.

W2 and I had it a bit more difficult since our divorce was a bit messy, but we kept things in perspective, and today we are extremely close. Through the ongoing relationships all three of us still had with our former partner, W1 and W2 have become good friends over the years. It's not uncommon for W1 to call W2 and arrange to pick up the child from W2 to spend time with she and her husband. When they do get together, they will talk at length on the subject of children. They discuss anything they feel is important.

My last SO has not been as easy to keep a relationship with. We separated 6 years ago and have had some issues concerning the children and some legal matters. Yet we continue to respect each other's space and ideas. Sadly many weeks pass between our communications leading to misunderstanding, which continues to cause some suspicion in how effective we both are at parenting. This relationship will likely prove more comfortable as time passes. We have both learned a great deal from one another.

An interesting push/pull goes on between ex's and can take a number of forms. I've been through it, and also witnessed it in other divorced couples.

One former couple that I'm well acquainted is going through this, which brings it to mind.

They've been divorced a few years, and live in towns an hour or more apart driving time. Unfortunately, the father to this point must be classified as a deadbeat dad. I can't say I know him well, but I have met him a few times, I've witnessed him around his children, and mine, and in some interactions with his ex.

He's not a bad guy. He's very pleasant to be around quite friendly with a great sense of humor. It's very obvious that he loves his two girls, and they him, so his non-involvement wouldn't appear to be for lack of caring.

The ex wife is very attractive, well cared for and has become at least a very confident, independent, and outspoken woman. She is raising her children on her own, and she won't hesitate to make that known to anyone interested.

Not long ago, the Dad moved up so he could be closer and more involved in their lives. Whether he had thoughts of getting back together with the ex wife, I can't say, though his intentions seemed honorable.

Rumors circulate about involvement with drugs, which may be a contributing factor, but I wasn't convinced that was the whole story. He's never been strung out to my knowledge when I've been around him.

When he and his ex are together, she dogs him, not being involved enough in the girls lives, not having a steady job, he looks unkempt, and "for God's sakes, you've never paid child support!" I was only with them for a couple of hours!

(Ding, ding, I think I have a clue, Bob.)

Before long he had his tail tucked between his legs and was heading south!

You may be experiencing some of this push/pull with your ex, or another type, which we'll discuss next. I'm sure she has good intentions, it may be out of frustration, and it may help her ego to put him, or any man in his place. But her intentions are not meeting her apparent goal of getting him more involved in the children's lives, rather it's driving him away.

Intentions are only a first step. The IRS doesn't care if you intended to pay your taxes. Intending to fix dinner doesn't fill your belly. Take your intentions and develop a plan of action that will meet the goal you intend.

If she would let him get his foot in the door, start seeing them, at least that's better than nothing. Child support and emotional support for the children are very important yes. Let him get to know his daughters again, and soon all of that support will likely be as important to him as it is to the rest of them. Mom could do a bit better at supporting the dad's relationship with his girls and leave her particular issues between them.

Let's not put all of the blame on Mom though. Dad does indeed need to perhaps revise his approach. Perhaps paying child support will at least show that his intentions are more real, in her eyes at least. I think they are both reading the same map; they are speaking in different tongues. Keep this in mind when you and your ex have a disagreement. Are you both perhaps trying to reach the same place, but maybe beginning at opposite ends of the map? Does it matter *how* we get there as long as we get there?

The other type of push/pull many of us go through is with our love relationship with our ex. We may find ourselves visiting her more than the children. Sometimes it may be at her invitation. We may be involved in some flirting, taking us back to our courting days, before marriage.

Relax, this is normal, be aware if it's happening, and why it may be happening. In our marriages, we became comfortable with each other, and dependant on each other emotionally and sexually. We choose to express, or release those emotions through sex. And it's *not* only the guys' ladies; many of *you* do it too! The difference being, the guys are less subtle, and are branded as pigs.

It's all too easy for both parties to find they long for that companionship again, to break the loneliness, or to hop in bed together and relieve a bit of sexual tension. Both should be aware of intentions. Do you want to get back together? Have the problems that ended the relationship been reasonably discussed and resolved? If so, it may be time you take a look at the relationship again. If not, zip up your pants and go home, for now anyway, at least until we've discussed the future.

Some adults can go into this fling with eyes wide open, and be perfectly fine. If that's what you *both* choose, not a problem and may not cause future problems. Yet make certain you are *both* on an even ground and reading the same map. If not, you or she may be leading the other along a path that is only going to result in another break up with one of you being hurt again.

This past weekend, I had the opportunity (or misfortune?) to have an ex girlfriend and my ex wife over for dinner (with all of the children). This was the result of some miscommunication on my part. Was I a bit nervous? More than a bit! I spent most of my time cooking avoiding what I was sure was going to come.

The two women were alone together in the living room, chatting. *Not* a good situation for an ex husband/boyfriend. These two had met before in social situations and seemed, at the very least, to tolerate each other. I had long known they had a lot in common (besides me) and if given the chance could be at least casual friends (again, *not* the best situation for me!).

As the evening wore on they continued talking of their children, as well as the situations that had led to each being single. Heavy girl talk going on. I eavesdropped from the kitchen, I could tell they were reaching some common ground.

After a time, they were acting like their own little support group as several hugs were exchanged when the evening came to an end. They were also both kind enough to tell me how special I had been in their lives. Of course I hadn't always done things right. It was a very surreal situation in a way, but at the same time, it was quite natural. Caution to the unwise, as they say on TV, *don't try this at home, these are trained professionals!*

I know I learned some lessons of how we are all together in this life, like it or not. These two had taken the opportunity to take that experience one step further and chose to support each other, rather than to let the claws come out. Since the children from both families are such close friends, I know they all enjoyed it.

Children are not capable of getting into all of the intricacies of jealousy that *could* be apparent in this situation, but they are very accepting of the love exchanged between two mothers.

We all want to be loved and respected. Though we may not completely understand our ex, nor her direction or motivation, we can at least afford her the same respect as any other individual we meet. Since she is the mother of our children and we have shared so many wonderful things together, it's not inappropriate to still possess a certain love for her, and the sincere desire to see her reach her goals.

Through love comes understanding. Through understanding comes peace.

ASSIGNMENT

Write down what you think your ex's goals might be in her life. Understand the similarities between her goals and your own. Allow her to meet hers through any support you might appropriately provide. She will return in kind.

CHAPTER 10
IF ONLY...

*"I never could find any tracks on a woman's heart... But I swear a
woman's breast is the hardest rock the almighty ever made on this earth,
and I can find no sign on it."*
Bear Claw played by Will Geer
Jeremiah Johnson *(the movie)*

My first wife, Edette has been an exceptional mother over the years,
though I'm not certain my daughters fully appreciate that yet. They are young
mothers themselves, and I'm sure they will be learning a lot of the wonderful
mother they were blessed with. I asked Edette if she had any words of wisdom
for single dads.

W1.Edette writes:
What did I want the father of my children to know?

*That it was extremely helpful to get child support the first of the month, so
bills could be paid and not have that added stress, because raising children
as a single parent is not easy and it is horrific when you have to worry about
finances.*

*That I was glad we kept a friendly relationship. We didn't fight, and we didn't
badmouth each other*

*I was glad he would take the children every other weekend. It was a good
break for me*

*I was glad we both went on with our lives, and we didn't keep hooked into one
another.*

*I also wanted him to know that paying child support was not the equal half to
raising the kids. I would be frustrated that he could pay child support but that*

didn't cover all the emotional things that go on with raising children. It didn't pay for the nights getting up with a sick child, or going to the emergency room, or doing homework, or going to school functions or making money stretch for food, clothes, birthdays, Christmas, doctor visits, tears, arguments, cleaning the house, doing laundry etc.

I hate that women use children as a leverage to get child support. Some women won't let the father see his child if he has not paid child support. In reality, the child doesn't care about the money; the child wants to know they are important enough to spend time with their dad. Thus, it puts the innocent child in the middle of an adult battle and poor behavior.

Men don't talk as much as women do. They hold a lot inside, but maybe it would be beneficial to talk more or join a support group (not a badgering group) to help with all the emotions that go on with being a single dad.

Being divorced can be very emotional. A friend of mine told me to never bad mouth my ex-husband in front of my children. It ruins their self-esteem and it puts children in the middle of a battle that shouldn't be their battle. They love both of their parents and they want security by knowing both of their parents love them

Edette was also kind enough to include some Free Activities to do with the kids. I've included those in the chapter on Fun Projects for Kids (chapter 18).

Well after reading her words, I realized I might not be the all knowing ex that I thought I was. I had several other women around that were also ex's (though not all mine, don't give me *that* much credit!) so I asked a few of them to share some ideas that might be helpful. Following are only a few of their stories but the range of experiences spans the spectrum. Chances are, you may hear some of your ex's words. All of them are important in the stories they tell, what *is*, what *could be*, and at least one that tears my heart out for the things the entire family has experienced, especially the young children.

Naomi is a 28-year-old single mother of two young boys. She and her husband mutually decided on a divorce after five years of marriage. Naomi and her boys have been a single family for over three years. Naomi was kind enough to share some insights into her noteworthy relationship with her boys and her ex husband.

My ex husband lives in a town nearby and has been gainfully employed since we were first married in a job he loves very much. He has been very responsible while paying child support on time. He knows how important it is to the family, and what a difference he makes in his sons' lives. He is very involved in the boys' lives, and it means the world to them.

He often coaches and manages their sports teams, takes them to games and practices, provides and pays for their equipment. This keeps him busy since they are active in basketball, football, and baseball!

Other events he also takes them to are professional basketball games, he takes them camping and fishing, and they go on road trips in the summer. They'll also go to movies or swimming.

We've both made a commitment to each other to be the best parents we can be to the boys. We've gone to extra efforts to make certain one can always contact the other in case of an emergency or any other problems that may arise. We've also stayed in touch with each other's families, so that we can easily discuss any issues that may come up with the boys.

Of course this type of relationship isn't always easy at first, and it takes having some mutual respect from both of us toward the other. We realize that our differences are ours and need not affect the kids. At first of course it took a lot of time, and patience. Treating each other with respect was the best for the boys, and each day that we did this it became easier. After a time it just seems natural. We still have disagreements, but we have both learned to compromise, and always come to an agreement that is acceptable for all of us.

My ex's great quality is he puts himself as a Father first. I have seen a lot of Dads that only see their kids every other weekend, if that, and most are content with it. My ex is not an every other weekend Dad, he will want to have the kids any time I want or need him to. He will ask to keep them longer periods of time than what is "expected." We do not believe in having a strict schedule for the kids when it comes to whose weekend is it? Or "who had them last," or whose turn it is to do what. Whatever goes with the kids and their happiness goes with us!

I'm certain all of our lives would be very different if the boys had a dead beat Dad, thank heaven they don't.

I had to ask her at this point if anyone is that perfect. She laughed and continued:

Well, if there were anything I wish he would do differently, it would be for him to not leave messages for me, with the children. He doesn't do this often though. Simply a phone call, leave a message for me, so the boys don't have to worry, then *he'd be the perfect ex!*

The boys would tell you they have the best dad in the world! Because he is such an active influence in their lives, it takes a lot of the pressure off of me, and allows the boys and I to have the relationship a mother should have with her sons. When I'm not so worried with housework, schoolwork and have his help with child support, which allows me to pay the bills, the boys and I can relax and enjoy our time together. We go to the movies, I go to their sports games, shoot hoops with them, we go to arcades and play games at home.

They'll bake with me, and we'll do craft projects. We like to jump on the tramp. I get them to help me around the house, and we'll make a game or a contest of it. They love to help with the chores, raking leaves, hosing the sidewalk, sweep the garage, watering the flowers etc.

I'm taking advantage of this before they become teenagers! (Laughing).

My older son is into getting an allowance, and is learning the value of a dollar. I don't know if he understands it all yet, considering he still thinks I have a money tree growing in some secret hiding place.

Finding yourself as a single mom is certainly a learning experience. I think sometimes we tend to over compensate, or give in to them, so to speak on a lot of things. We want to make up in some sense for an incomplete family.

Sometimes it's hard playing both roles, and not having that extra hand of help when you need it. At the present time though, I have a significant other, and he is a tremendous help and is great to the boys. He enjoys them as they do him.

Don't get me wrong, being a single mom is no bed of roses. During the separation and divorce, we had plenty of disagreements and occurrences that were not good for our kids to be put through. Like everything else, we learned from our mistakes.

My ex and I have a relationship that works very well for us and for the boys. I would like him to know, though I don't ever show it, that I really do appreciate him being involved with the boys. I also am very glad he is their father and has taken on that role, no matter what relationship he and I have. I'm thankful for the communication and relationship we've been able to maintain, even though we are not a couple we are still a couple when it comes to parenting. This is much better than two half parents.

I believe if both parents keep the children's best interests in mind, and stay with this attitude of respect, it works out better for everyone involved.

What a wonderful relationship Naomi and her ex have developed over a few short years. You have to ask yourself, what are these boys learning concerning relationships through all of this? It can only help them in their coming lives, in dealing with all sorts of situations that may not appear simple at first.

Naomi brought up a couple of points in particular that I believe are especially worth noting. She emphasized the importance of child support, that receiving it regularly not only allowed her to pay the bills, giving her a stable home for the children, but also relieved stress on her. This allows her to spend more stress free time with her boys, and allows her to be the mother her boys need.

Dad's roll in his boys' lives is more significant than being a father and provider to them. He is actively involved in their lives, and they know their accomplishments and failures are important to him. He listens and coaches them along in life. This dad should have a long loving relationship with his sons for the rest of their lives.

Michelle is a 31-year-old mother of two children, a son and daughter. Seven years ago, she made the decision to divorce her husband of six years and take on this single mother role.

It's been a tough road for the kids and I in our relationship with my ex. He lives an hour and a half away and unfortunately hasn't taken a real active part in their lives.

At first little communication, but over the years we have been able to talk more about the kids. This will sometimes end up in arguments as I get frustrated with him and want him more involved in the children's lives.

When he does pick them up, he'll take them shooting, or fishing, or camping

It's so important for him to be involved more in their lives. They would like him involved in their activities, schooling, or to be there to talk to. I think they wouldn't mind if he were involved in their discipline! Kids understand that parents administer discipline because they care.

It would make such a difference in their lives if they had him there to talk to, or if it's a frequent and regular phone call. Something to show them that he cares, and he is trying to be a part of their lives, and to be there to support them.

He pays his child support regularly through the state, so I won't accuse him of being a dead beat dad. He's always been good with the child support.

I hear from the kids that they love him, they care for him, but would like to see him more, to spend more time with him. They've also learned he doesn't always do what he says he will, and it causes some trust issues.

Time is a big thing for the kids and I. I don't always feel I can give them the quality time I'd like to spend with them. I'm too busy cleaning, doing laundry, cooking meals, doing dishes, as well as working and generally maintaining the home.

When we do get fun time, we like to go to the movies, go to dinner, go bowling, or have dinner together at home (while watching movies!) and hang out together.

Being a single mother is tough. You have to play both mother and father when the dad isn't involved. Mom has to be the nice person and the disciplinarian, so you can easily teeter on both sides. I would prefer to be the healer and the friend, rather than always having to be the one to put my foot down. It's important to have a strong male influence in their lives; they seem to have a sterner hand.

I do want to express though, I don't think my ex is a bad father. I know that he loves his kids very much, and would do anything for them. I would like to see him more involved, more interested in what they are doing, if for nothing other than to gain their trust and respect. Respect works both ways, him to them, as well as them to him. Because he is their Dad, that doesn't make him a father. As I have had to work and to learn to gain their love, trust and respect, so should he.

I desperately wish he could see how much they need *him in their lives on a regular basis, not an every other weekend father.*

And most importantly, I want him to know his children love him unconditionally, *and will always be there for him.*

Though it could be worse for Michelle and her kids, I have doubts of the healthy ideals the children are learning through this strained relationship. As my daughter mentions in an upcoming chapter, Kids Words (Chapter 14), having a dad not actively involved in a child's life, plays havoc on their self-esteem. Michelle's children are young yet, and they have unlimited potential. That potential can most easily be met with Dad in their life to show his support, to cheer them on, to express the love they so much want and need.

My conversation with Michelle brought to mind something I've seen in some women, though she vaguely brushed over it. Sometimes when speaking with your ex, particularly when discussing difficult issues, you may hear her always take a stance of, "The kids and I feel…" or "We think…" etc. Not being a psychologist I can't put a technical medical or psychological term to this. However, it's been my experience the ex may feel intimidated by your authority and strength, therefore speaking from an "I" point of view, doesn't bring enough to the table. Bringing the children into the argument is not a great thing, but helps her to add strength to her argument.

Should you experience this happening, it's best not to bring it to her attention, but rather to be mindful of your own strength, or dominance in your discussions. Perhaps if she's intimidated it may be best for the overall communication to listen a bit more and turn down your testosterone a bit. Once she's on comfortable ground in your discussions, she may be open to more discussion pertaining to the children and what will be best for all in your relationship. She may be a bit freer with providing extra time and privileges with the children. You don't want the children intimidated, when discussing important issues.

Next I met with Carrie, a 25-year-old single mother who recently gave birth to the most darling little girl. She has never been married, though the father of her child would still be considered an ex.

Carrie works a full time job, cares for her baby and maintains a household for her daughter. Her story is unfortunately all too common among young mothers that find themselves caring for a little one with no help from the father.

My ex hasn't been terribly involved in the life of my child. Though she is only a couple of months old, and is too young for him to be involved with activities, I do wish he would at least show more of an interest in her, and at least take as much of an interest in her well being, as he does for his own.

Working a full time job, leaves me with much less time than I'd like to spend with her, in these important first months of her life. The first several months is an important time for mother/child bonding, and I hate having other folks having to look out for her while I'm at work, but what else can I do to provide her with some stability in the home?

Since she is so young, and all of this motherhood is such a new thing to me, I enjoy spending time with her, talking to her, singing to her, and we watch cartoons! I'm not sure she gets the cartoons, but she definitely gets that we're together. Some of our best times are when I spend reading to her. She may not understand all of what's going on, but she hears my voice and knows that I am concentrating on her.

It's a big concern and leaves an ache in my heart that she is beginning her life basically without a dad. I can only hope that before long he will realize his responsibility, and the many things he may miss with his daughter growing up. She may be too young to take to the park and play, or to movies, dinner etc, she's not too young for him to begin a bonding process with. He will sit and talk with her and hold her on occasion, but has very little time for where his life seems to be.

Her Father has a good job, with a steady income and lives reasonably close. As yet, he has not paid child support, nor is he contributing to the care of his daughter.

Since learning of my pregnancy with my daughter, I've had to look at a lot of things in my life, and have come to understand the word compromise. *Unfortunately, her father doesn't seem to be aware of the definition.*

If my daughter were old enough to tell of her dad, I'm sure she would say he has a funny accent, has lots of scary tattoos and smells like yucky smoke all of the time!

The future relationship for my daughter and her dad is unsure at this time. As difficult as it is to say, I wish he would either be in or out of her life. Don't take a hesitant step forward into her life, and step out again. It's going to be very confusing for her, as she gets older.

I wish he could understand how difficult it is raising a daughter and maintaining a household. At the very least, provide me with some help, and not make things more difficult for us."

After having six children of my own, I understand all too well, in the first few days of a child's life, they bond indelibly with their mother. If you were to separate the mother and child after those first few days, a psychological imprint is left on that infant. Sure, they might get over it in time as they grow older, but it imprints upon the child this early in their life.

Carrie relates the understanding that while the ex's involvement in the baby's life may not be as intense as the mothers in the first few days, the first few months of an infant's life provides an opportunity for the father and baby to bond strongly. The bonding may still take place as the child gets older, but it's not the same as it is in these first precious months.

With my own children, my involvement with them definitely increased around the age of two years old. This is when they become a bit more mobile, had more of a personality that I could relate to and required less care than an infant. Things were missed in those important first two years. I generally wasn't home when they took their first steps, wasn't aware of when they went from baby food to solid food, or when they were first able to grasp a toy. Sadly, these are things I will never see again from my own children.

I met Vickie (W2) in 1988, and we were married soon after. It was a wonderful time for the most part. We had some great and loving times. Unfortunately, I don't think I was ready for a meaningful relationship, and it soon ended in our divorce. I had some sketchy details on her past marriage. I asked if she would share the story of her first marriage with all of us.

She consented. I respect her tremendously for going back and reliving the pain once again, of a wonderful love that took a terrible and tragic turn. One that none of them could foresee at the time, and one that she and her children have been paying a very high price for ever since.

Vickie writes:
This is a story of a good man, and a good love that went terribly wrong.

Steve and I met on a nude beach in California when I was 18 years old. He was tall and handsome, in a rugged way. He was gentle and had a good-natured humor. We were immediately taken with each other.

We were young, love was an exciting thing. For me the unique experience of the nude beach only heightened that excitement. We started seeing each other frequently, sometimes visiting the nude beach, sometimes normal dates as all young couples do, and we were a couple in a short time. We soon moved in together and had hopes of a wonderful life together. We were looking forward to beginning a family.

Steve and I were married a year later. I became pregnant with our firstborn son on our honeymoon. Steve and I had a great marriage for the first eight or nine years.

We had a Harley, and we worked on it together, taking road trips, the two of us. We were together in every sense of the word, we were young, and we were living our version of the American dream.

Early in our marriage, I learned that all was not as it seemed however. We both smoked pot together early in the marriage, but I soon started finding some drug paraphernalia that as far as I knew, was not a part of our life.

I confronted my husband, and we had some heated discussions. I attempted to see his side and tried some of it myself. I'd like to say I hated it, but I liked it! I could soon see though, this was not a road I wanted to be on, and it seemed to have a tremendous hold on his life.

Substance abuse and alcohol eventually took its toll on Steve. Ever so subtly, things began to get worse as the drugs crept into our lives. There was an episode of mild abuse a couple of years into the relationship, when I was pushed onto the waterbed, another at the ninth year that could have killed me. I decided at that moment, he would never hit me again, nor would any man for that matter.

Yet I still wasn't ready to throw away ten years of marriage without giving it one last try. The trying was going to be up to Steve though; I would support him in his effort.

The conditions to continue the relationship were my conditions. I left no leeway for mistakes, or a relapse. Maybe that was harsh, but I wasn't going to continue the cycle of being a battered woman. I still stand by that decision.

Steve checked into the VA Hospital for 60 days. Of "detoxing" and trying to learn to live without the alcohol and drugs. He did well for five months after his release. But relapsed.

He was high and drunk when he beat me up. I wasn't going to give him a second chance to do it again. I know he never wanted to hurt me again and felt he had failed me by relapsing. I told him I wanted a divorce, because I wouldn't let a man hit me twice.

A couple of weeks later, Steve was leaving for work one morning, and I noticed him putting a hose into the trunk of his car. This struck me as odd, but didn't think much of it.

It was only after he'd left for work that hose kept gnawing at me. My entire world crashed around me as I realized why he had put the hose in the car. I fought to drive such a horrible thought from my mind, but it wouldn't get out.

I had no car, and no phone. I immediately walked the few blocks to the nearest pay phone to call his work. His employer confirmed my nightmare had begun, he had not shown up for work that morning.

I called the police department and as best I could, tried to explain what I hoped could not be real. I asked that they begin looking for him and gave them as many ideas as I could on where he might be.

Not long after I had walked back home, a police officer knocked on my door to take an official report. I again gave him all of the details I could think of, trying to function with a mind that had become my worst enemy.

The officer left after taking the report and assuring me they would do all they could to find him as quickly as possible. I was left with nothing to do but wait, and wait, with every horrible thought that would spin out of my head.

I waited for what seemed like an eternity, but in reality was only a few hours. A knock at the door shook the very foundation of our home. It was the police officer. I knew before opening the door. I knew.

I don't remember what he said after "We found your husband," but I got the gist of "he has taken his life."

I immediately went numb all over, not wanting to face the reality. I wanted this man in the blue uniform to stop talking and go away, I wasn't hearing him. I wanted Steve to come home, I wanted to tell him "It's ok, we'll work this out," it was too late for that. That hadn't fully crept into my heaving lungs yet. He would never come home again.

As the words began to take hold, I was being told my husband had gone down to one of his favorite fishing holes by the river. He took the hose from the trunk, put it into the exhaust pipe of the car, in through the car window and went to sleep. It wouldn't have taken long. It took moments for his life to end, and those moments changed the life of my family, forever.

Steve took his own life. Why? Was it out of guilt or the fear of living alone or the pain of losing his children? I don't know what was going through his mind. I'll never know. All of the above and more I'm sure drove him to such a drastic conclusion. He chose a very long-term solution to a short-term problem.

I have always believed that if a person could look into the future and see the results of the choice to take one's life, they might find the courage to get help and decide on life.

My children ranged from eight years old to only a few months when Daddy went away. Watching the devastation our children have had to endure has been a constant ache in my heart. It never goes away.

We had four children. The oldest son, took it the hardest. He spent the first few months in or under his bed. He wouldn't go to school. This brilliant child was brought to his knees in sorrow and blame and has never recovered to this day, fifteen years later. I think the children were too young to remember going to his funeral, or they have blocked it out. I don't remember much of it myself. Many of the details from that period of my life now a distant blur, as if in a dream, or in another life.

It was many years until his six year old sister, came to terms with it. She was in and out of residential treatment programs from age twelve to fifteen, when she married, very pregnant, to an abusive husband.

The two younger boys have lived without a daddy and as they grew older noticed that their family was different. Other kids had fathers, why didn't we?

"Get us a daddy, Mom." I heard that a lot. They also grew up and got into their share of trouble. Numerous felonies put them into the youth corrections system. I think having the influence of a strong father figure in their lives might have made a difference. Maybe not, but they were deprived of that chance, and we will never know. Because of their past choices, and the choices of their father, they have a difficult road ahead of them, and they are still in their teens.

The pain and depression I have endured, was and still is at times, enormous. Being a single mom, trying to raise four messed up kids has been a challenge every day since Steve left us. Fifteen years later, I still cannot forgive, (almost but not quite) or get over my anger for how he changed our lives in that instant he decided to take his life.

I still keep Steve's picture on the wall. I want the kids to know their father in any small sense they may. I want them to know he was there, and I believe he still is. He loved them so very much.

I did eventually marry again. It was a short-lived marriage, but we had a wonderful, beautiful, and well-adjusted son who never ceases to amaze and entertain us. His father and I divorced and we have maintained a loving and close relationship. We have had our differences but work them out and move on. I wish my first husband had the wisdom to know that ending a relationship isn't the end of the world.

We can be single parents and still raise our children together. We can still be partners and friends. You have to let go of the anger, bitterness, and hurt and keep that loving relationship. The children benefit, the parents benefit. My youngest son is living proof.

I experienced two different marriages, two different ways to handle the end of a relationship. Don't stop loving the ex. Take your new road and enjoy it. Continue a different and enjoyable road with the children and ex-spouse.

What a tough story to read. What a difficult life to live. I have always admired Vickie's strength at always doing what needs to be done without exception. She's a survivor. She reminds me of the mother bear, ready to fight for her cubs at any hint of danger. How many of us would have given up, after one-tenth of the heartache she has been through! Yet her heart is still full of love.

Sacrifice though has taken its toll on her. She is a wonderful loving mother and has given all of her resources (literally) to raise her children. She is a living angel when it comes to her children and those around her. I wish her all of the blessings that the universe can bestow upon her. I know that one day she will find some special mate in her life. Few of us are blessed with more than one soul mate; I know she will find her second.

Being the ex, I know her other four children of course. And they are all wonderful children! Without the influence of a father though, they are doing what they know best, they are surviving. They haven't had the opportunity to see much else in their lives.

I could have been more of an influence in these children's lives than I have been. Though they are all grown, I can only hope that I can still make some difference in their lives. They deserve the love of a dad I can only be a substitute at best.

Nicole is the mother of two daughters, one in her mid teens, and the other pre-teen. Though she has been married to the same man for 15 years, her first daughter was born previous to this relationship from another man.

Through the years, Bryan, her ex, has been non-existent in his daughter's life. Her current husband is a wonderful provider, and together they have built a wonderful life with their family of four. Over the past couple of years, Bryan has been making an effort to begin to get to know his daughter, though he lived in another state. That is until a few months ago.

Since you mentioned this project you were working on, I've had to do some reflecting on my life, and I have to say, it hasn't been easy to face some things. Parts of the story, you may not be aware of.

Nicole was silent; her eyes were extremely deep, reflecting a regression to somewhere in her past.

Bryan and I were married at a young age, we were kids, we were in love, and it was a very strong and genuine love. We meant everything in the world to each other. At times, as if it were in another life, (smiling) I guess in a way it was. But the marriage resulted in the birth of my firstborn daughter, Chantal.

She meant the world to me, and to her father. Unfortunately, our marriage did not survive many years after that. We split and things were very distant for a couple of years. I eventually married my present husband, and we began to build our lives, and had another daughter after a few more years.

I hadn't seen Bryan over the next ten years, preferring not to go there again. He hadn't seen his little girl since she was five years old.

Bryan and I talked on the phone periodically throughout the years. Some things we said were good and some were that I was frustrated with him. I wanted him to realize that he was a parent and had a responsibility. Looking back, it's not the money I wanted. I wish he had fought me to see Chantal. Or that I was the bigger person and would have picked up the phone and said, "Hey, we are having Thanksgiving Dinner and you are invited." That would have been best of me to do.

He and Chantal had begun, over the past two years or so to develop a much closer relationship over the phone. I had hoped that one day he would be driving through our state, and they could get together so he could see her again. Their relationship grew amazingly strong over the phone.

Regardless of my situation, married or not, it should have mattered; he was after all, Chantal's father. I wish I had made him connect with her. I know he loved her so very much. He never felt good enough to be a part of her life. Talking to me, he must have heard that we were doing well and that he felt that he didn't have to be involved. That Chantal didn't need him, because we were not hurting for his money or him. In essence, I would have loved for her to know him, to see him laugh, and to be able to look into his deep green eyes. She will never see the twinkle in his eyes, nor the man that I fell deeply in love with which ended up with her being born.

My Mother has always talked with Chantal, and told her that she was a love child…. she was. We were two kids in love.

The last time he called in January, he talked with Chantal for a while, and I got on the phone. He told me he was driving truck through Texas on the way to Louisiana.

He always called me Nic and was always so kind and expressed his gratitude for doing well and working hard to take care of our daughter.

I hung up the phone with him with a simple "G'bye…." I looked out the window and noticed the snow was falling. I thought to myself of him, and thought I should have told him to be careful, and to watch out on the road. I thought he'd think I was nuts to call him back and tell him to be safe…. so I didn't. I went on with my business and next thing I know, he's left this earth.

A short three hours after talking with us, he had a heart attack and didn't survive long enough for an ambulance to reach him.

I found out later that he had been very sick. So sick his doctor had told him not to go back to driving truck again, he should have been home. I'm sure it took everything he had to climb into that truck and keep driving the way he did.

He had landed his latest job months before his death, and his life insurance had become active less than a month before his death. He left that to Chantal, a sign of his love and how important she was to him.

I know he would have loved to see her again, if he had only known how limited his opportunities were.

I'm so grateful that he had talked to Chantal on the phone, hours before going and seeing the Man up in the Sky. I know they love him up there, making them laugh as he always did. He was such a free spirit, always laughing and not worrying having a good time.

At the same time, I'm so frustrated with it all. I'm sad and mad and distraught that we have a daughter that will never feel his love. Only the real parent of the child can feel that unconditional love, or so I think.

Oh well, life teaches us many lessons; this is one that I have learned.... If only...

Well that reminds me, Chantal has some of his ashes that his sister mailed her. I'm going to order her a sterling silver cross to put the ashes into; it hangs on a silver necklace. This way she can always feel him with her. It's not much, but it's the best I can do.

If only…and as she says she is faced with only the choice of, "It's not much, but it's all that I can do."

Missed opportunities. How many of us have opportunities that we're not taking, because it doesn't appear to be our final opportunity? How many of us will one day find ourselves peering out the window, watching the falling snow…and thinking to ourselves, "If only…"

It doesn't matter what anyone else thinks, or if they suspect an ulterior motive. You may have things you want to say to your ex (lovingly) or to your parents; your children or other loved ones. You don't because they surely know how you feel. Perhaps they do…don't be faced with "If only…" Thank each of these loved ones for the part they have played in your life. Write a letter; make a phone call, or you can do it face to face. Make a difference in someone's life…and do it today. Today may be very short. You or your loved ones may not see tomorrow. No guarantees.

Another aspect to Nicole's story that so many of us find ourselves falling into. Like Bryan, many of us underestimate the impact of our involvement in our child's life. Sometimes we let our ex's determine our worth to our children. At times, when we are married, we let them dictate how we should act with our children. Well, it's not for them to decide. It's our decision, and ours alone.

You might be able to drag that stupid old mule out to the field. You might get him to stand still long enough to hook up the plow, you might get him to move…but until that mule makes up his mind, you won't get that stubborn knot head to plow a furrow.

Chantal knew all too well before her Father's passing, and as Nicole learned, that her Dad had a gift, that only he could provide.

Bryan was reluctant, because he doubted his importance or self worth. This child may have the opportunity to have a substitute father in her life, a favorite teacher or other male role models. It won't be the same. Unfortunately, her connection with her natural born father is lost.

I know, beyond a shadow of a doubt, her father is with her today, and every day. He is nearer to her than he was ever able to be in her life. As long as she holds this in her heart, she may yet experience a closeness she was denied with him in a physical life.

I can't help but ache, thinking of the years that Bryan missed his little girl, hearing only third hand what she looked like, of her radiant smile, the twinkle in her eye. She is growing into a beautiful young lady, and in part, it's because of the influence that her natural dad had in her life. I regret that I never had the opportunity to know him.

If only…

ASSIGNMENT

This one is so easy, and so rewarding!

All of us are so blessed, with the wonderful children in our lives. I challenge each of you to look around for the children in your neighborhood or town, whose families are broken and be aware of how you might make a difference. It may be volunteering as a sports coach as Naomi's ex has so many times. It may be as simple as letting them tag along on your next fishing or camping trip, when Dad isn't available to take them. It may be as simple as giving them a kind word of praise when they are out riding a bike, or throwing a football. Simple things can make a big difference to little ones with no Dad around to recognize their angelic talents.

Let's put single dads in their rightful place, as the neighborhood *hero*, to the children and the single mothers in our neighborhoods.

This can all be accomplished while you are growing closer to your own children.

CHAPTER 11
DARKNESS

The darkness begins to creep from the floor, up my legs moving higher until it engulfs my form. It chokes off the air I need to survive. It covers me entirely, removing all reason until I can no longer conceive of escape.

I have done all I can to avoid writing the following. In order to write this chapter, I must relive an experience. I do not want to step again into the choking darkness that descended upon the family of my dear friends, 15 years ago. Something more powerful than my fear prompts me to tell the story.

It is only appropriate to change the names of those involved.

As many horror stories begin, it was a cold winter's night, in November. It was a Sunday; I remember it all too vividly. The clock had just struck ten, someone knocked at my door. It was unusual for me to get a visitor this late at night. If I had known what stood beyond my front door, I may have chosen to eternally leave it closed. Opening that door on this night changed my life forever.

I opened the door. Standing in my darkened entryway was my good friend Ken, with tears in his eyes. I had to take a deep breath as I invited him in. Whatever the reason for his visit, my senses were screaming; this was not something I could fix. I couldn't know of the blackness he was carrying as he stepped into my home.

Ken was a single dad, one of my closest friends. He had four children, three daughters and a son. I had been fortunate enough to sit with him many times in the hospital while he and his wife at the time went through the birthing process. I had been blessed to see his little ones grow, to have dinner with his family, to read the little ones bedtime stories. He was like a brother.

Ken sat on my couch and began to sob. This was a strong man, a good family man. I had never seen him this way, nor could I imagine what must have crushed his heart to reduce this man to the emotional state I witnessed.

Ordinarily I would have offered my friend a beer. I didn't. I went to the kitchen and fetched glass of cold water for he and myself. I returned to the front room, placed his water in front of him taking the seat opposite. Neither of us could speak, I didn't know why.

I looked him over, trying to capture any clue as to what had happened. He looked smaller, his shoulders not as straight and forward as I had always remembered. His hair was disheveled, his cheeks glistening with tears and his eyes were bloodshot. He looked lost, seeking solace from any source of strength. The man was beaten and helpless. It was as though everything he had ever known had been taken from him.

"Did someone die?" I thought. I had been with him three years ago when his mother passed on; it was tough on him, but nothing like this.

I spoke "One of your children?" I immediately regretted the question. Perhaps if I had not asked, the darkness would have subsided. His children were his Achilles heals.

He nodded weakly as the tears began to come again. It was as if someone had punched me in the stomach, but it hurt more. I felt sick, nauseated, my head began to spin.

Ken began quietly through the sobs, searching for the words that wouldn't worsen the pain. He began to tell me what had happened to his daughter, Tara, then 11 years old.

Though it's been many years since, I've asked Ken to write his story in his own words.

Ken writes:

Things are in your life that you don't ever want to face, some that you never dream will happen to you. For me it began one calm November night; it was a Sunday. There was a knock at the door, as it was unusual for me to receive visitors unannounced, I was expecting, upon opening the door, some misdirected pizza driver, or perhaps a child selling whatever for his or her latest fundraiser at school, wanting to squeak in a few more sales at the last minute.

As I opened the door, I found my older brother Mark, with tears in his eyes. This came as a surprise since we had never had the best relationship. I immediately knew it must be important, or he wouldn't be imposing on my time. I invited him in. I had a guest over, and I asked if she would mind watching television in the other room, to give us a chance to talk. As she walked to the other room, he and I had a seat in my front room.

The things he began to tell me are all a blur, many years later. He proceeded to tell me he had been molesting my 11-year-old daughter for the past three years. I don't recall at this point what details he gave, or what he left out and I gleaned in the coming days. As I say, it's all a blur.

I don't remember much of my reactions at this point. I know it was not what I had ever expected when confronted with this situation. I didn't get furious nor angry. Stunned I guess would be the best description. How do you react when you are told something such as this? I know how we all think we would react, but when faced with reality, or the surrealism of it all, it's quite another story.

I guess our conversation lasted maybe an hour, maybe more, maybe two, I can't recall. That's not important. Then he left.

I do remember sitting on the couch alone, after he had gone. I had forgotten my company until she emerged from the back room. My head was swimming, trying to take it all in.

I remember calling one of my best friends later that evening, He also happened to be my boss. I shared with him what had happened. I told him I didn't know if I would be in to work the following day, or when. As any great friend would, much less an understanding boss, he was behind me, told me to take whatever time I needed. The friend in him showed when he told me to call, whenever, any time day or night if I needed to talk. And he urged me not to do anything rash.

Rash? What precisely would rash be in this situation? I remember at the time, not feeling anything. I was numb. Numb to the world around me. When someone would speak, it was as if silence took over. Sure the voice was there, but the silence was deafening. Silence would capture my mind, any voice no matter how loud reduced to a distant whisper.

I worked the next day and every day after. I needed to be in the normal world, to be around those that didn't know, those that couldn't understand this lunacy. I needed some sense of normalcy and routine in my life to understand that the world, through this would go on turning. The sun would rise tomorrow.

I called my ex wife, the mother of my precious daughter and asked if she was doing ok. She was as understanding as she could be under the circumstances. I felt I had betrayed her, allowing my own brother to do this to her daughter, this gift of a child we had both been blessed with. I didn't want any long drawn out conversation. I didn't want to offer any apologies or an attempt at an explanation. I had none. I had no concept of what the reality of the situation was. All I could do is to survive.

In the coming days, thoughts of revenge or perhaps avengement came into my mind. I had ways to kill him. I had been trained in the martial arts for many years. I knew how fragile the human body was and how quickly life could be terminated.

This was not a passing thought rather I gave it a lot of deep thought, a lot of analysis. I was not the least bit concerned with any consequences I might face. I knew only that someone had done me wrong, had wronged my daughter, a price must be paid.

When the thoughts penetrated I experienced rage. Such a simple four-letter word but what wrath it unleashed. I can't remember that I have ever felt such fury before or since. My sense of rational thought was beyond the borders of sanity, my serene life had been shattered in an instant, releasing vehemence inside of my soul I never knew existed. I felt the strength of a superhero and could sympathize with how Satan must feel when he's really pissed.

Through it all, some divinity was able to batter its way through the dark walls I had raised. I began to realize there was no "right" way to act in this situation. The definition of each person's actions when presented with a situation such as this was a choice of each individual. Reaching beyond my own hurt and pain, I began to understand the larger sense of it all.

I realized that my actions at this point in life might have far reaching consequences, for myself, my brother, more importantly my daughter and the rest of my children. I knew that if I caused harm to my brother, or killed him, it was likely to have devastating effects on my daughter. I could not be sure that she would not blame herself for my actions for her uncle being hurt, or killed, or her father going to prison. Would she resent that their little secret had been discovered? That she had ever spoken up and told the truth? How would this affect her in her future life? She was surely too young to know that I had choices, Mark had choices, and everyone else around her, their fate was in their own hands.

To this day, 15 years later, I still cannot explain my actions. I cannot explain why I stood beside my brother through court and therapy counseling. I can't explain why I had to support him. If I knew the reasons why, perhaps I would be more than just a man.

Did I do all of the right things? I can't answer that either. I did what I had to do to survive, to get through it, and to get everyone else through it, without making the situation worse.

This was the one time in my life, I can honestly say, that my needs came last. I knew that a time would come that I would be able to let loose, to grieve, to be enraged, but for the first few years, this was not the time.

I was not there for my daughter as much as I would have liked. I had no words to comfort her. I didn't know if the sight of a man, any man would bring back those horrible memories; serve as another trigger for her nightmares.

I wanted to hold her at night, when the darkness came. I wanted to take the pain away, to dry her tears, to put back some sense of security and safety that surely she must have had at one time.

But I didn't know how. I didn't know the first thing of how to deal with a little girl caught in this dreadful nightmare. I wasn't intelligent enough to know what to say, what not to say. I didn't know if the love I held in my heart would be enough for my little girl.

The years passed, and thoughts of the episode were pushed aside. The relationship with my daughter was distant. We both knew, but we didn't talk of it. I didn't have the courage to approach her, and year after year, she waited for me to introduce the subject, so she could unload all of those pent up emotions that she so wanted to release.

It was seven years I guess, before I was able to allow myself to feel the impact of those days. Everyone else seemed to be well on the way to healing, and it was my time to deal with the blackness that had held me for so long.

I spent many nights, crying, screaming, and drinking to numb the pain. At one of my deepest darkest moments, when I could hold onto the pain no longer, I sat down and wrote my daughter a letter. She had long since moved away, to begin life anew in another part of the country. I had always been better with written word, than I had been with voice. I was able to tell my little angel how sorry I was that I hadn't been enough of a Dad when she needed me most.

And life went on. The sun continued to rise every morning, bringing with it a new hope for a better life.

My daughter and my brother had no further contact. There has been no contact between my brother and my ex. My relationship with my ex has forever changed.

Life was simpler before November 1989. Life had a charmed quality that I don't know if we will ever experience again. Since, I have been much more aware of these same problems in the world that have affected so many close to me. I guess I had been blind to it, until it came knocking at my door on one arctic November night.

At the time, Ken's ex wife maintained a strength that was unequaled. She held her child that night, and many after. She did what she could to alleviate the pain, the suffering and dried countless tears, both her's, and her daughter's.

First and foremost, she was a mother. She would go on to raise all of her children. To fix them breakfast on this morning as she did every morning. She would do the laundry and clean the house. She would go to her office as she always did, and Tara would go to school. She wanted to provide some sense of a routine life, as their world crumbled around them. She could not be afforded the opportunity to hide from the world. It was up to her to contain the damage.

She looked at her ex-husband differently. They had been divorced several years. They were always "together" when it came to their children.

She could see his sense of helplessness. She could feel his pain, and know the guilt that he felt. This wonderful man was always in control and always had the answers. Now he was lost. He was much quieter. He wouldn't speak much. Her words seemed incapable of penetrating the wall around him. He kept his children at arms length, which made her furious at times. Each meal she fixed for the family felt incomplete. The house was never clean enough. The rooms wouldn't hold enough light.

She dreaded the coming of night, as she would climb into bed, in the darkness, and her mind would continue to work, bringing to her clear images of her daughter, held captive in the dark.

Ken had gone back to work, something that surprised me. He sought temporary escape from the hellish pit he was living in. He sat with his co-workers and let them know he was going through a very difficult time, but would prefer not to elaborate. He told them he had to work to get through this, and asked for their support. He admitted he was very unproductive at work, making many mistakes. His co-workers silently followed behind him, correcting any errors and showed all of the love and support they could.

The weeks and months that followed were filled with appointments with caseworkers and therapy for much of the family, though Ken refused to be involved.

Ken did something that surprised him; he stood by his brother in his therapy sessions and court dates. He admitted he felt as though he was torn between his love for his daughter, and the blood bond with his brother. He did his best to be sensitive to both when in reality he avoided his daughter. Not for any lack of love, but for a loss of his place in her world.

Mark had been cast out of his family for the most part, and Ken felt he was all he had to make certain he would survive this ordeal. He was careful not to let his daughter know what he was doing, for fear it would add to her confusion.

His relationship with his ex-wife was strained at best. They fought more than they had previously. The petty things that they argued over masked the deeper hurt inside. Love had taken on a different identity in the family. They seemed to be robots, taking steps forward, and performing menial tasks, to still appear human.

Tara took on a new personality of her own over time. She seemed to be freer with her words and emotions. She was soon playing again as she always had, though distrustful of most people around her, particularly men. She became bold in her ideas, and assertive in demanding fairness from others.

After a few years, I had several occasions to speak with Mark about the ordeal. It was difficult for us to get into a meaty conversation. Mark had been through several years of therapy, and I was grateful for his insight from the offender standpoint. I'm not certain anyone was ever able to answer the question of why this happened. Mark didn't seem to have an exact grasp on it. The closest he could describe it, he had mistaken sex for love. He had spent most of his life feeling unloved, as an outcast, and in some twisted way (his words) the perceived love that he felt during these encounters was a temporary fix for his pain.

Therapists had urged after a time, that the family should be reunited in order to work through this time of grief. Ken and Tara's mother disagreed vehemently with the experts. To this day, 15 years later, Mark has had no contact with the family again, with the exception of one of the younger siblings.

This child had been too young to understand the entire concept of what had happened, but understood only that Uncle Mark was gone, and could see no reason why they could not continue to see him. A meeting was arranged for a luncheon, away from the family between Mark, this child, and myself.

Mark and the child, under my watchful eye, spent a couple of hours catching up on all that was happening in each of their lives, and soon they again went their separate ways. I suspected this would be a step into reuniting the family (I had no opinion either way on this), but I was mistaken. After the meeting, the child has expressed no more desire to see Uncle Mark. It seemed to be a step in understanding that things were different perhaps his/her little way of saying "Goodbye?" I don't know.

The wounds have healed for the most part but the scars remain, as they will always. Mark continues to struggle over some legal issues with the offense, and in being labeled a child molester in the eyes of the law. A stigma is attached by anyone that finds out the truth of what he had done. Happily, he has married a wonderful woman, who knows his past and without reservation, she has forgiven him. No doubt Mark committed a senseless act directed toward a child, yet he deserves happiness in his life. The others have moved on in their lives, though the wound still bleeds for mother at times. Mark should be allowed to move on and rebuild a life.

Tara is happily married to a loving husband. They have moved far away and have two beautiful children. She maintains closeness with her mother and siblings; I get a call from her occasionally.

I won't claim understanding of the things Tara has gone through in her life, nor of the trials this may have brought to her husband. I can imagine he felt a great anger when she told him.

Tara is very headstrong when dealing with others. She has a very real sense of who she is, and she is not now, nor will she ever be a doormat. She is appropriately protective of her children and is a loving mother and wife.

A distance was created between Ken and his daughter that took many years to overcome. Perhaps it was from denial. It was years before Ken was able to face the emotions that had been brought by the darkness. He felt his time and emotions were spent in seeing the others heal. A large part of his time was spent in support of his brother. After a time, when he felt all were sufficiently stable and he could let himself fall apart, if that's what it took, it was time for his healing.

To begin healing one day, Ken took pen and paper, and wrote the letter to his daughter. Tara was kind enough to send me a copy of the letter, which she has saved, and agreed that it should be included.

A father's letter to his daughter:

My dearest daughter,

Only you and I know this letter has been long overdue. I have so many things to say, I don't know if I have enough paper and ink, nor the words to express.

It's been seven very long years since our lives changed forever. Seven years since I've been able to talk with you, as a father should talk with his daughter. Certainly not for anything you've done, rather that I could find no words.

I know there must be questions in your mind. The things that happened, the reason for my distance, and how it happened the way it did. I will do my best to answer any that I can.

Most importantly, know that you are and always have been, the most precious thing in the world to me. You were always the child that would play outside, in front of the picture window, so you could keep an eye on Dad. You were always the one to be the proudest of me when I would do something good, and the most understanding when I didn't. You were always "Daddy's little girl." Never doubt that.

Seven years ago, when it surfaced what your uncle had been doing to you, I cried. I cried tears that came from deep within my soul. I know you did too. And I wasn't there for you.

All of my life, I had never a doubt that I would kill anyone that would do such a thing to one of my children. When faced with the reality, this was the first thing on my mind. Only one thing stopped that rage, something I hadn't ever considered.

My love for a little girl calmed the fury. Not fear; or hesitation for any consequences I may have to suffer, but only the thought of how you might feel if I did such a thing. Would you perhaps blame yourself if I did anything to make our family situation worse than it had become?

I feared you would blame yourself for revealing your uncle's secret, and that your daddy had to go to jail, or to prison, or that your words had caused your daddy to do bad things to your uncle.

I felt I let you down, for not protecting you from this happening. I didn't want to let that happen again. I was wise in one respect

I should have been there for you. I should have been stronger, and wiser, been eloquent enough to be able to form the right words to comfort you. I know the words weren't important. I should have been there.

I was not, and I am so very sorry. I relied on your mother to do that, and as always she did it superbly. Mothers are truly God's Angels.

I am so glad that you have your mother's strength and have begun to build your life in a new state, with someone that loves you deeply.

I want you to know I love you more each day, a love that you will only understand when you are a mother of your own children one day. I am so very proud of you, and you are so special to me. You are very beautiful and so strong. You have grown into a very assertive young lady, and I know you will be successful at whatever you pursue.

Please find it in your heart to forgive me for being less of a father than I would like to be. I can't promise I will never fail you again, but I can promise I will try with all I have, to always be...Dad.

I love you VERY much,
Dad

The above is true, though the identities of the family involved have been changed as I mentioned. Regrettably the above story is also true in countless households throughout the world.

Over the years, I have encountered a great number of women that were sexually abused as children. I have also met many men sexually or physically abused in their childhood. I have seen statistics on this, though I don't recall what they are specifically. Whatever those statistics were, I sense they are extremely understated. If you don't know of any females in your life that have experienced this abuse, your eyes may be closed.

In the above situation, after the allegations were leveled against Mark, it came out that Ken and Mark's sister had also been a victim. Their own mother had been abused as a child, though neither of the boys had ever suspected it. This incident brought out a number of victims not only of Mark's but also of others dear to them, more so than anyone could have imagined. It was as if a gate had been opened; that others could walk through and speak their painful secrets.

I'm no psychologist, and I don't claim to understand what the hell is going on when someone forces himself or herself on a helpless child. I can't imagine what the hell they must be thinking. Never the less a serious problem exists in our country, and in many countries of the world. And sadly, the vast majority of the offenders are men.

Ken was a good father, like most of us like to think we are. He thought he was involved in the lives of his wife and children. It was a cold slap in the face to realize his brother was sexually assaulting for three years, and his daughter no less, and he had no clue that it was happening!

All too often the person that does this is close to the family, many times extremely close. They have the opportunity to know each of the children, and can judge from a child's personality which one is "safe" for them to approach. Which will be best at keeping a secret? Which do they feel closest to, that they can share this deceitful experience?

How can you prevent this from happening? How can you know if it *is* happening right now? Sadly, it's not guaranteed that you can. I've learned a few things you might do to be aware of unusual signs.

Mark had been a favorite uncle without a doubt. He had become extremely close with the mother and with all of the children. He had gained their complete trust (warning sign).

Whenever Tara was home sick, alone from school, Mark would come by to check on her, unknowing to the parents. Experience from this sadly comes from hindsight. Never allow a young child home alone from school. If they have been alone, ask questions, what they did, and whom they saw. The perpetrator of course will tell them not to tell, you can only hope for a slip on your child's part. If any unusual pattern appears, it's time to start asking some questions.

How did Mark know when she was home from school? Would he call the school guised as the parent to check? Or watch her as she walked to school each day? Would he drive by and randomly knock on the door hoping? Unfortunately all were true.

In Mark's particular instance, the last episode was on Tara's birthday. He had come by to take Tara and her friend for pizza. Of course this didn't raise any flags for the parents, as this wasn't unusual behavior. It was unusual however for a friend to be invited into this little web, not something the parents might have seen. This was his downfall.

Soon after leaving, Mark called to say he had left his wallet home, and that they were going to get pizza and have it in his apartment. (Warning sign) If he had left his wallet at the apartment, wouldn't they have to go out to get pizza anyway? Or would they have it delivered? What birthday was that for an 11 year old? Have it delivered to Tara's house so everyone can be involved in the party. Not something highly unusual that the parents might have picked up on that alone though.

The chink in his armor had been found. Tara had a friend to share her secret with. They would talk extensively. It only took once for older sister to overhear the conversation, she went to Mom. Mom called Uncle Mark in an incensed fury.

For some odd reason, Mark asked if Ken knew yet. In her anger, Ken's ex hadn't called him first; he was at his office for some weekend work. She said that Ken did not know. Mark asked if he could be the one to tell Ken. She agreed, as long as he did it before Ken got home. She wouldn't be able to contain her anger one moment longer.

I can't understand what would bring Mark to want to go to Ken and admit what he had done. It happened as I relate it. He had to know how distraught Ken would be. Perhaps he put his own life in danger to tell his brother what he had done. It was a cowardly act he had committed. Approaching his brother with this news took a courage I cannot fathom.

Knowing your child as closely as possible, and building a parent/child trust is key to avoiding such an incident. Not always, but it may help in many cases. As parents we all seem to have subjects we feel uncomfortable with when speaking to our children. Work towards eliminating those barriers in your home. Do it in an age appropriate manner. Some things you may not want to share with your children due to their age and maturity level, they should know that they can talk with either parent, ask any question and not be judged.

One clue that may bring things to light, watch your child when they are around older family members, friends etc. Watch the expression on their face when anyone, a male in the case above, comes too close, or touches your child even in an appropriate manner. Watch their eyes, you may get a clue that they are uncomfortable. This is extremely difficult for a child to hide. A wince, or an uncomfortable shy look in their eyes may tip you that something isn't as it should be. The person coming in contact may not be the perpetrator, but be mindful of the hint that someone may be making them terribly uncomfortable with physical contact. Don't wait until you have reason to suspect, watch them always!

If such a clue is discovered, take the opportunity to speak with your child alone. Hope that the child trusts you enough to confide. Don't ask specific questions (i.e.: is _______ molesting you?) this is more than a child can handle. But tell them, "I noticed you seemed uncomfortable when _______ asked you to sit on his/her lap. I hope you know that feeling uncomfortable with that is ok. You have the right to refuse any contact you are not comfortable with. And that if anyone else is making you uncomfortable in any way, and you would like to tell me, I will be here for you, *no matter what*."

If your child is being molested, your actions to this point will determine how much they trust you and how much they will reveal. Let any other spouse, ex spouse etc, know what you saw, perhaps their trust with that child will help uncover such a secret. It doesn't matter who finds out, it's imperative that this is stopped immediately.

Tara had ingrained in her mind by her uncle that she was very dear to him. That he loved her more than her parents did. He made her feel special, and loved, and wanted. At home she was one of four children, with him however, she was the only one. Other perpetrators will use fear as a tactic, threatening the safety of the child, her parents or siblings, should the secret ever be revealed. Apparently Uncle Mark didn't feel this approach would work with Tara. He pursued his most advantageous method.

If there can be a fortunate side of this story, it's that the abuse was stopped. Without the alertness of her older sister, this may have gone on for another number of years. People may have been hurt worse.

Know your children intimately. Know where they are and who they are with at all times. Of course if this is done in an interrogating manner, you will get nowhere. Be interested in what they do with their time. Share in their excitement, their joy, their sorrow, and their tears. Allow them to speak honestly, with no fear of reprisal. Tell them how special and dear they are to your entire family.

Sexual abuse is not confined to young girls.

I recently met my young friend Paul who is 14 years old. Paul has never known his biological father but was raised with a stepfather, until his mother divorced the man for physical abuse. A distance was apparent between Paul and his stepfather for a number of years after the divorce, but this child sorely missed a male role model, weak, as this man may have been.

Through Paul's urging and phone calls to his dad (stepfather), they began to get together occasionally to get to know one another, and to spend some time together. Step dad was remarried to a young girl (far too young in some states), and they had two children together. Paul delighted in his new siblings and took the opportunity at every chance to baby sit them while his dad and their mother went out. Soon he found he was taking care of the children, much more than he was seeing his step father.

This relationship continued on until young Paul had decided he would rather die than let his father continue the abuse he was having to endure.

Paul had been raped several times by his father, and forced to endure and perform oral sex for many months. Physical evidence on his body backed his story.

The police were called. Dad was picked up and arrested, did his time in court. I don't know all of the details, but he has not spent time in jail or in prison. This family is not well off financially, so it makes me wonder how the system failed this young man.

Was the father innocent of these crimes? The father never claimed innocence. Is he going to counseling or some type of rehabilitation? No. He continues to live in the same town as young Paul, though he has a restraining order against him, to prevent any contact with Paul. He still has access to his younger children. Unfortunately, this is not the end of the story, it hasn't ended yet. I refuse to think of what his younger children may be experiencing.

Days ago in our city, a little girl who had been kidnaped nine months ago, was returned to her family. The little girl had been abducted from her home at knife point last year, in the predawn hours of a summer morning. She has been found alive and well, 20 miles from her home, with her abductors. This little girl is doing well and no apparent harm has befallen her, beyond the abduction. The city is still in exuberant celebration. We all feel we are witnessing a miracle that is much more than anything we dared hoped for. I had given up hope of her ever being found alive. I lost my faith when her parents and siblings refused.

Some words in her story continue to haunt me.

This family lives in a predominant neighborhood in our city, and it sits at the edge of the mountains of Utah. From this girl's story, she was taken out of her home, and into the foothills behind her home, a few miles up, and lived in the hills with her abductor and his wife, camping for two months.

When news of her abduction hit the community, several thousand volunteers turned out, combing every inch of the city, and of course, the foothills. They searched for weeks. Some never stopped always alert to anyone suspicious that might be the latest suspect as reported by the News Media.

Posters and billboards were predominantly displayed with this little girls picture on it, everywhere in Utah. Whenever we would see one, it was my children that spotted it first. "There's Elizabeth!" they would yell. They were well aware of what had happened to her, and they were concerned, as though it were their own sister. They felt they knew her intimately.

Thousands of searchers turned out, I was convinced she must have been put into a car, and whisked out of the city, and probably the state, before anyone was aware she was gone.

I was so wrapped up in my little life and troubles, and they had so many volunteers, that I was sure I couldn't be of much help. I may be wrong.

I have spent many years in the forests and particularly the mountains. It's not unlike me to be up, and follow that little inner voice, to explore some very remote places in the Wilderness areas of Utah. Yet I never get lost. I've got a very strong inner compass that always guides me home. My explorations have led to many interesting things; man no doubt has probably never seen.

Knowing that she had been taken a few miles into those foothills camping for two months, I have to think of what if. What if I hadn't underestimated any small contribution I might have made? What if I had decided, if nothing else, I will get in a good hike, and gone up to the area to do some exploring as I searched. Would it have made any difference in this little girl's life? Sadly, we'll never know. But for me, it is a missed opportunity that might have made a difference.

When the news report came across the radio that the little girl had been found, I heard it while driving on my way for a haircut. As I stepped into the barbershop (ok, so it was a salon) some of the girls were talking, they had heard. I told them as much as I knew, that she was alive and well. Two children watching their mother receive a hair cut overheard the conversation. Intensely inquisitive as children are they kept coming over and asking what I'd heard. Their interest was in whether they had caught the man that took her. I hadn't heard any of that yet as the story was only moments old. But I was aware that they, like my own children felt very close to her and were concerned for not only her, but also for all children subjected to such a predator.

When my own children heard the miraculous news, they called me immediately. They were so excited they were bouncing off the walls. They not only recognized the miracle, it seemed as though they expected it! Did I miss something with my adult logic?

Bottom line, I disappoint myself for not trying to help, when I was no more involved with my life than anyone else. Hopefully at your next opportunity, you won't do the same. I know I won't make that mistake again.

This child and her abductors were spotted due to an alert citizen, a normal, everyday individual that was aware. She was aware due to the media reports and the Rachael Alert system in our State. This individual contacted police immediately, alerting the officials of the person's location. Thanks to this one aware individual, this child was brought home. A miracle happened that day.

In rare cases a female sexually abuses or abducts a young male or female child in cases such as the above. No one is safe from this sickness, and it has no apparent pattern in its victims.

ASSIGNMENT

List 20 females, adult and children, first names only. Once you have the list compiled, put a check mark by the first three names, skip the next two, check the next three, skip the next two, etc.

When finished, look at your list. By at least one study I've read, three of five females have been sexually molested or raped in their childhood. By these statistics, the number of checks you see on your paper would fit a national average. How many of the 20 on your list have had to live with this secret their entire lives?

It may not be your place to question what happened in these people's lives. It *is* your place to realize how prevalent this crime is, and be mindful of how you might prevent it from happening to any one you encounter.

If it's something that interests you, volunteer in a troubled boys home (or girls home, as appropriate) in your area. Look into organizations like Big Brother in many communities that could greatly benefit from your experiences as a loving Father. After all, our responsibility is to protect *all* children. If this is not something that interests you, I challenge you to at least go speak with the personnel in one of these organizations, if for nothing else, the educational experience.

CHAPTER 12
BEYOND SURVIVAL

As I walk along my path in life, I look at my feet, or the path directly ahead to avoid any obstacle seeking to trip me up. It has never before occurred to me, to raise my eyes and focus my gaze on where I want to be.

Of course we all want to *survive* the situation we find ourselves in after a breakup. We all want to rebuild our lives, *re*-build our lives better than it was before. In order to do that maybe we should take another look at *life itself.*

If life is merely survival, I for one will welcome the eternal sleep with open arms. Surely life has more to offer.

When we were children, we had dreams of careers as a policeman, fireman, Air Force pilot, and a myriad of others. Few of us envisioned a vocation that seemed an exercise in futility, barely making ends meet only to perform the same mundane task day after day, after lonely day. When did we lose sight of our dreams?

The advantage in this wonderful country we call America is in the great diversity of peoples and cultures within our borders. We have the opportunity to experience virtually every culture from around the globe. However, in all of this melting pot process, we have become a country with citizens that appear to have no passion, other than our *drive to succeed* in life.

Many other countries have their culture and heritage steeped in traditions for many thousands of years. They have an advantage in that *they* know who they are, they know who the neighbors are, and they know who the people in the same town are. They are all born of their same culture and heritage, and they *celebrate* their very being!

If you have the opportunity to join wonderful Italian families for a traditional dinner, you will experience the family at all stages of their lives. The grandmothers, mothers, daughters down to the wee ones will gather and begin cooking early in the morning. The men, again from grandfather down to the smallest of gentleman will involve themselves in chores as well as games, tales of all sorts while the women prepare a feast fit for a king, or many kings! Their passion for cooking is unequaled. Their speech habits are vibrant even titillating. They express not only with words but intonation, hand gestures, fiery expressive eyes, and a whole smorgasbord of body language. They are passionate in their life and their heritage!

The goal is not the obvious feast in which all contribute rather it is the act of being together as family, and allowing each of them to express who they are.

Take the opportunity sometime to visit a celebration of the Cinquo de Mayo (the Fifth of May) with our Latino neighbors to the south. They are equally expressive and vibrant as the Italians in their speaking as well as their zest for life. The passion of the cultural celebration will energize you for weeks!

We come back to our own little world, to see these wonderful American brothers and sisters, buzzing around like busy little bees, concerned only with making more dollars. Buying more things to live in bigger homes. All without *passion*! Buy the things, build the bigger home, but do it while you are pursuing your passions! When you have this wonderful home built, invite a family of Italians or Latinos (or a myriad of other cultures,) in to show you how to celebrate it!

Celebrations of our country heritage, the Fourth of July, or our Christian holidays such as Christmas, pale in comparison to the passion expressed by other cultures. It's something we do and have commercialized attempting to put the passion back into our lives. So far, for me at least, it's not working.

One of my favorite people, whom I have yet to meet, is Steve Irwin. Some of you may know him as the "Crocodile Hunter" on television. This man has *passion* for life! So much so that I laugh when I see him on his shows. This man is exciting; he loves what he does; he adores his wife (God be with you, Terry), and it shows in every word he speaks, every move that he makes. We all have the ability to be as passionate with life as Steve does. We may add our own little quirks and forms of enthusiasm, as he does. The man should be patented! (Maybe he is?)

Our children bring to us many blessings. One of which is to remind us of the dreams we once shared with only our closest friends, or to the entire world, at least anyone that would listen, if we were one of *those* children, the ones with an endless supply of energy. They too have a passion for life. If you've lived with a child from the time they begin to creep and explore their world, heaven forbid they begin to speak. The endless array of questions can make you want to scream!

I once read that a child from the time they learn to speak until they enter kindergarten will have asked over a million questions. If they continued to learn at this rate, they would learn everything there is to know by a mere ten years of age. And we tell them to stop asking so many questions! I can attest that my first daughter was WAY over a million questions before we happily carted her off to school.

She is into her 20s and while she's no child prodigy, we managed to keep her mind open that she appreciates and accepts many beliefs and different cultures. But if we'd had the patience to answer all of her questions, what could have been? She's an amazing gift to the world as she is (as are all of my children), but she may have been the first woman president, a brilliant scientist, or scholar. Who knows, I may have learned some things in researching the answers to her questions too!

We look at children, while we listen to their dreams and want our words to be encouraging. We tell them they can be anything they want to be when they grow up. Not often do we assist them in finding what they want, much less assist them realizing the dream. If we were to be truthful, we're thinking, "Yea, wait until *you* grow up and live in the real world." More likely, they will repeat the pattern we are setting so clearly for them to follow.

Well, perhaps it's time to shut up and listen to them, rather than be cynical. Perhaps it's time for *us* to relive those days as a child, and assist them in seeing how they can accomplish what we had once dreamed, by *showing* them how it's done. We can walk hand in hand on this path with our little ones. We can help them begin on the road to their dreams, while we do the exact same thing ourselves.

We all know children's dreams can change from week to week. As they get older, it takes a bit longer before they flip flop. Oddly enough, the reason they flip flop on career choices is it's not progressing! They don't see themselves coming any closer to their dream, and being logical as we are as adults, they alter their plans. If something isn't working, I'll try something else! Rather than keeping the goal, they (and we) lose sight of the goal and change it, rather than our approach to meeting that goal!

The difference between a dream and a passion is slight. Simply put, a dream is something we would *like* to do. A passion is something we *like* to do! Dreams are for the future a passion is *now*.

No age is too young to begin dreaming, nor to begin on the path to making that dream a reality. No age is so advanced that we cannot make dreams come true. After all, how do you know how long you are going to live? *Your life's length is often determined by your passion for living.* Certainly if you enjoy your life, you are going to want to stick around as long as possible. It will be so much more fulfilled that it will at least seem longer!

As an example of how to get a child on their chosen path, and fuel their dreams, let's say your little princess decides at age six she wants to be a fireman.

To help nourish your child's dream to be a fire*woman,* contact the local fire department. Inquire when you and your daughter might visit for a tour of the firehouse. Many of the firehouses welcome the public, especially the children. If yours does not have such an option, try another until you find one that will. Before going, you and your daughter can bake some cookies, brownies, or a cake for the firemen to enjoy. For recipe suggestions see Appetizers and Fun Snacks in Chapter 21 of this book. Your daughter will find this as a means of establishing her own bond with her heroes.

Your child will experience a firehouse and all the excitement first hand. She will be able to bring her dream a bit closer and bring delight in the eyes of the professionals working in the firehouse. After all, many of them are *dad's* too. We all want to feel what we do for a living is exciting to others, and it's a bonus if children think so too.

One visit need not be the end of it. Certainly don't overstay your welcome, but visiting monthly, or every couple of months, even briefly to bring more treats and to say hi will help keep her dream alive and in the forefront. If she decides after a time she wants to do something else, that also is to be encouraged in the same way. It will keep her choices real, and she will live a small part of her dream with each visit, and with each preparation in the kitchen before hand. Maybe along the way, *you* will also see the ways to begin living your dreams.

On one of your visits to the firehouse, watch her. Notice the joy in her smile, the magical energy in her step, the gleam in her eye. Remember what it was like when your dreams were *real.*

Your dreams are *still* real. You've put them on the shelf for a bit. Bring them back to the forefront. Take them from the shelf, dust them off, and shine them up. Take a good look at them. Identify the first step in making this dream a passion, take it no matter how small.

A friend of mine, Tom, was diagnosed with cancer a number of years ago. Sadly, his cancer was well advanced and his prognosis was bleak at best. The doctors had given him 6-18 months to live. Tom has never been one to be kept down. Of course it took a few days of adjusting to this tragic news.

My friend was extremely resilient, as he always had been. He knew that resiliency was a choice, not a gift he was born with.

It wasn't long before he was pulling out all of the stops. He had always wanted to scuba dive in the Caribbean, so he did. He had always wanted to salmon fish in Canada, and to catch a 600-pound halibut in Alaska. He did. He had always wanted to make a difference in his life so he began to visit the retirement homes and present slide shows of his adventures, when he would take time to be in town for his cancer treatments. He brought much joy to the shut-ins, allowing some of them, through his slides and his dreams to relive some old memories or at least many of their dreams. He brought new life to some dear folks in the twilight years of their lives. He made a difference in many wonderful ways.

Tom had always wanted to visit the Taj Mahal, he did. He had always wanted a photo safari to Africa. He went. Tom had always wanted to spend more time with his young daughter. He did.

They built his daughter, Amanda, a giant dollhouse together that brought a light to her eyes that was simply adorable. Undoubtedly this wonderful doll house will be an heirloom for many years as Amanda will hand it down to her daughter, and her daughter's daughter, accompanied with many tales of the wonderful man she had come to know as Dad.

Needless to say, Tom long outlived the doctor's prognosis. The doctors had given him 6-18 months. Spirit had other ideas. Tom lived almost four years to the day from receiving the prognosis. He had lived many life times in those four years.

The last ten days of life, Tom was bedridden in a cancer clinic. I took the occasion to visit with him a few times in his last days. His body was sick and degrading. I had the wonderful opportunity to catch up on things he had experienced in those four years. I joked with him that the cancer hadn't gotten his body; he had worn it out! Laughingly he told me the last four years had been wonderful to him, above all it had taught him to live, and experience adventure. He *appeared* to be dying. He was merely setting preparations for another adventure, one that would top everything he had experienced thus far in his *life*.

Tom spoke of the cancer as though he were grateful for the affliction.

"Kev," he said, "At least I was given a sense early enough that my life wouldn't last forever, and had the opportunity to live my life before it ended. Not in spite of the cancer, but because of it! Up until that first diagnosis, in many ways I considered myself immortal. I thought I'd always have time to accomplish the things I wanted in my life. I had always envisioned my life as I got old, had grandkids and would have the time to do all of the things I wanted. In one short instant, I was awakened to reality. It was time to revise that vision.

"Who knows how long any of us may live? It may be years; it may be months, or it may happen in the next few minutes. I would have some great regrets, if my life unexpectedly ended, and I had done nothing but the day-to-day grind. While that may be fine for some, that's not life to me!

"If it took cancer to give me the wonderful life I've had over the last four years, so be it!"

One cold wintry evening, Tom set out on his new adventure, leaving all of the wonderful things in this life behind, perhaps taking the memories with him, but leaving the photographs behind. After all, he wanted to travel *light* for this trip. He didn't want to be burdened with extra baggage; he would be prepared for anything.

When you lose a gift such as Tom in this world, you sense a great loss. More however, I celebrated the chance to know him, the chance to witness second hand, what life was.

Memorial services were held in the rest homes he had visited many times. The residences relived the tales he had told and shared the slides once again, the highlights of his adventures. A sense of peace came in knowing when their time came to leave, Tom would greet them, as he had so many times before in the recreational rooms. No doubt he would have more tales to share of the things they were to experience.

Sitting in a doctor's office, four years previously, Tom had been presented with a situation that most of us would look at as the end of our life. Tom chose his own way. He knew his plans had forever been altered. He may have a limited time to do what he had set out to accomplish in his life, but nevertheless he was going to do as much as he possibly could.

As we all know, going through a serious breakup in our lives can be as difficult for us to survive as the loss of a loved one. How we choose to *survive* this situation is entirely up to us.

For those that pass to another world, they are beginning a wonderful adventure (at least if *we* believe in an afterlife). As we pass from one relationship, we have the opportunity to begin a new adventure. A time to reflect on the wonderful times we'd had but more importantly to refocus again on where we are going.

Please take the time to write out the answers to these questions:

What is important in my life?
What are my dreams, what can I make passions?
Am I excited in life? Why or why not?
What can I do to make my life more fulfilled?
What can I do to make a difference?
What is my next step toward fulfilling this?
Which day this month will I take that step?

As the old adage goes, "A journey of a thousand miles begins with the first step." As you take that first step, and another, your past life will grow more and more distant, until only the wonderful memories will remain. You will also take with you on your journey those that have become dear to you. Your children will delight in who you are becoming. Children love unconditionally, but the more of you that you are, the more they will love the real you.

You will also leave behind those people and thoughts that hold you back and have kept you from your dreams. They would prefer you stay home with them in their *non-life*. They are still stuck in *survival* mode. Misery loves company. Let them find someone else to keep them company. Perhaps the best thing you can give to them is to be *you* and to show them how it's done.

Looking ahead you see many new and wonderful things. You will be presented with many stimulating opportunities, things that may have never occurred to you. You will find that the journey itself is presenting you with so many unexpected gifts. Opening yourself up to this journey will provide all of the resources needed to complete it. It is the *way* of the Universe. It's the *way* things happen.

Contrarily, if we sit home, few of those opportunities ever present themselves to us. We are too hard to find!

Cherish the dreams of your child. In doing so, allow your dreams to live again. You once may have lost sight of them. Know that this was also a choice. Vow that you will not lose sight of them again. The simplest way to not lose sight of a dream is to live it.

The real danger to not living out our dreams is that we may be destined to repeat what we have been doing in our past. *Living* once again puts us in contact with people and energy that aligns with who we are. You will meet many special people, you may meet *that* special person, and many of her dreams and ideals will be more closely aligned with yours. This can be the beginning of a world you have never dreamed existed. If we seek to *rebuild* a life the way we always have, we will live in a life we have always had.

Sometimes in order to have the life of passion, we need to step out of our comfort zone. A new pair of shoes will feel uncomfortable for a while. Any old cowpoke will tell you, when he gets a new pair of boots, the first thing he's going to do is get them wet. He'll take them to the nearest stream or pond and wade until they are completely soaked. He will never take them off, until they've dried and they fit right. Once the leather in the boot is thoroughly drenched and then dries to form his unique foot, it's a comfortable pair of boots. We enjoy our comfortable boots, and they serve us well. And after a time we wear those out! It is time once again to get a new pair of uncomfortable shoes!

Take your life out and get it wet! Let it experience all of the things you've not done previously. Take yourself to a new height. It will be uncomfortable for a time, as it should be. After all it's new! It will take time to form this life to your needs. Once it is comfortable, enjoy it. Use that time to relax and recharge. Relish in the accomplishment. Recharge yourself to approach the *next* level. No *law* says you can't abandon a pair of boots before you have worn them out! Wear them as long as they suit you and you have an open path to another, something that will suit you better.

Each time you approach a new intensity, naturally you will want to take some of the things you have learned with you. In approaching any new venture, the slate is wiped clean. Taking a look at things from a fresh perspective many of the old rules and ways of doing things may not apply. It is completely for *you* to decide how to write the new rules of your life.

If you *used to be* one that stayed home on Sunday afternoon watching the ball games, you may choose to abandon that tradition in favor of playing a game of afternoon football with *the guys*. You may take an entirely different approach and use those few hours a week to visit a museum or see an opera, something, and anything to pursue your passion in life.

A passion is a wonderful thing, however it need not always be the same thing you are passionate for. You have plenty of time in your life for more than one passion!

All of my life, I've been marveled by things that anyone does well. It doesn't matter if it's Amish women making a quilt, a cliff diver in Mexico timing his leap with the waves as he jumps to begin his aerial ballet, or a

Mozart hopeful letting his energy speak through the ivories of a grand piano. As I have so often experienced, it may be a skilled chef, who *passionately* loves his trade, creating a masterpiece for his guests to enjoy. Beauty lies in all these, and so many more. When someone is doing something enjoyable, it cannot help be anything short of miraculous. It is an expression of who they are. Years of tradition are demonstrated in the skills they've learned. *This is history expressed and history in the making.*

The very expressions they release contribute something *good* to the world. No matter how small and insignificant, or how grand and wonderful, they are making a difference. The very flow of energy is something wonderful to experience. Be open to it. It's all around.

It's no great secret that one of my passions is cooking. Walking into a comfortable, well-equipped kitchen is like an artist approaching a canvas. I take stock of the ingredients on hand and begin to formulate a design for my painting. If needed, I visit the local grocery store, or whenever possible, the local farmers markets to obtain only the freshest ingredients.

Whatever the dish, it will be a one of a kind. It doesn't matter if it's some idea I'd heard of, a recipe I have found on the internet or one out of a cookbook, or maybe one that I've decided to create originally, it will be something unique. It will never taste the same again. In the kitchen I'm allowed to be creative in my own way, as long as I can keep people out of my way! But the joy in trying to move around some little one, as they attempt to pour a glass of juice, is something to be cherished. It's not the juice they are wanting but rather to be a part of what's going on!

Cooking also allows me to be focused on one particular task, for however long it takes. (Also a reason I golf!) Total attention must be paid in the preparation of a dish, especially when using a sharp knife! Browning meat, or sautéing vegetables demands a meticulous eye, they must be *just so* to give the perfect flavor and texture to a dish. *I* get to decide what is *just so*.

If I didn't know how to cook but wanted to, how would I learn? Many of my dear friends have learned to cook in my kitchen, preparing for dinner parties. This process is mutual, as I've learned many things from them as well! A mind that wants to learn should also be approached as the painter approaches his fresh canvas. Both the teacher and student should question all rules. Some great new dishes (and paintings!) have been borne from this method of thinking.

If I wanted to learn to cook different cultural cuisines, I would take a cooking class. These are inexpensive, don't require a great deal of time commitment, and are a wonderful social outlet. I will also meet many people who have the same interests as I, and all will be at different levels in their learning process. This allows me to not only teach when appropriate but to learn as well. Some people would refer to this as interacting, which can be a great deal of fun! (Or so I've heard.)

I had a wonderful, beautiful, and tall friend named Kristy a few years ago. Kristy was engaged to a wonderful man. She had many hopes and dreams for the future. In a conversation one day, she expressed that her life had no passion outside of her relationship with her fiancé.

I asked her a few questions. What were her interests and what would she like to do? She struggled for a bit as we often do, until she confessed with some embarrassment that one of her dreams had always been to learn to ballroom dance. Getting her to bring that idea off of the shelf and dust it off for presentation was the most difficult part of the process!

We quickly did a bit of research on the Internet for dance classes offering ballroom in our area. The search provided several options. The phone numbers were all advertised on the websites (and in the yellow pages of the phone book), and she made a few quick calls. She chose three or four that she seemed to like, and took the opportunity over the next few days to visit each one to view their facilities and get the price and schedule details. In the first few minutes after she had identified her passion, she had a plan well formulated and was quickly running to meet her goal.

She approached her fiancé with the idea, and being the loving man he was, he was more than happy to step out of his comfort zone, to join her in meeting her passion head on.

I spoke with her again a few months later and asked how it was going. Her eyes immediately lit up, as she began to tell me what a wonderful experience it had been for both of them! They loved the teacher and the people in her class, and they were soon to be attending their first formal dance at the studio, complete with fine tuxedos and ballroom gowns. She had an excitement for life again! Kristy and her fiancé were married not long after and now a few years later, are very happy in their marriage *together*. No doubt they would have married anyway, but this gift of dance helped them do it *passionately*.

Whatever your passions, take them off the shelf, identify them, dust them off, and do something *today* to get started. It may be as simple as it was for Kristy by picking up the phone book or searching the Internet. It may be as simple as going to the local bookstore and finding a book on the subject. Do *something* today. Information is power, the more information you can put in front of you on *how* to meet your passion, the more powerful you will be in obtaining it.

ASSIGNMENT

Make a list of things you have always dreamed of doing. Items can range from simple (planting a garden) to the flamboyant (visiting Mt. Olympus in Greece).

Pick one, take the first step, and make it become a reality.

CHAPTER 13
BELIEFS

I have mastered all fear in my life except one. When I lay on my final bed as my breath slips away, I fear I will realize I do not have a single passionate belief...my anguish to be my last emotion.

I don't want to impose my beliefs or morals on anyone. That would ruin the tremendous fun of living in this world of diverse peoples. However, I encourage you to know what you believe, evaluate what you believe, and be wholeheartedly committed to those beliefs.

We get so caught up in day-to-day living or surviving, we lose sight of the beliefs we have been raised with, or have worked out for ourselves. It may be time to once again evaluate what we believe in and how our actions are following those beliefs.

Following are some ideas you may or may not believe in, or wish to use. I urge you to use what you wish and leave the rest. Write down, type, and print whatever what you believe in specifically. Read it daily; re-commit yourself to your ideals daily. It will only take a month or two until these become second nature again and you may only need to refer to your list occasionally.

Give an honest day's work for an honest day's pay.

This is tremendously important. We must *believe* in our work, to be successful. If you do not, it may be time to reevaluate your chosen profession. Your employer will show faithfulness as you do to your employer. You will be successful, which will open a tremendous amount of possibilities for your success in the future.

Your word is your bond.

Keeping one's word earns respect quickly. Always, with no questions or excuses fulfill your promise; whether this is a promise, a date, a commitment, or a contract with the utility company, your word is *law*.

Believe in something.

You may meet people in your life that don't seem to have an opinion concerning anything. They may have no strong commitment to any issue. What a boring way to go through life! You will also meet folks that believe in *something* so strongly that they insist you must believe also. What a boring way to go through life! Believe what you believe and believe it passionately. Don't impose your beliefs on others, (even your children). Leave yourself open to other possibilities. What an interesting way to go through life!

Have a passion.

Think of something you love to do, or are committed to. Find a cause, a charity, and a hobby, *something* that allows *you* to be *you.* Anything that you are good at, or have a drive to be good at, can be your passion. Passionate people are stimulating to be around! We are passionate in our work, NO! Find something that *isn't* work. We all need a distraction from our work, something that excites us and recharges us *for* work! And for life! Oh! Simply talking about it excites me!

Everything in moderation.

Crap! See above! experiencing everything in moderation is a successful way to live a moderate life. Who wants that?

If something is worth doing, it's worth doing well.

Set aside the proper amount of time for any project. If you need to reevaluate the time on the project, do it. Don't reevaluate the project to fit the time. We spend *so* much time in our lives; redoing things we didn't do right the *first* time. This can apply to *everything* you do.

Set aside your "tithing."

10% of everything you earn belongs to *you.* It comes out *before taxes* and belongs to you and you alone. It is not to be used for emergencies, vacations, or anything else you *have* to have. Budget so you have those other things provided for. 10% belongs to *you.* This may take a bit of time to rearrange your budget. Do it. You deserve to be paid for your labors.

You are successful at what you are doing.

No matter what you are doing, you are doing it better than anyone else. If this isn't the success you desire, be successful doing something else.

Laugh.

Laugh every chance you get. If you don't get a chance, laugh anyway. Watch the smiles it brings.

Giggle.

When you aren't laughing.

Look people in the eye.

My dear friend Kelly reminds me that I rarely look people in the eye when I speak to them. I only do it to her because it makes her crazy. Look everyone squarely in the eye, whether engaged in conversation or passing on the street. This conveys honesty, confidence, and integrity. All of these are qualities that you have.

Walk in the rain.

Few, simpler ways are available to be in touch with the wonderful comfort of our lives than to feel the rain against our skin, feel its cleansing touch. When things get tough, realize it has been raining for *millions* of years and it will rain for a *million* more. Feel special?

Enjoy sunshine on your skin.

This will quickly bring you back to the comfort mentioned above, after walking in the rain.

Seek to know unconditional love.

Practice on your children.

Boys don't hit girls.

No one has the right to hit anyone. Hitting is one of the most obvious attempts at control that can be expressed. I think most from healthy families have learned that hitting is not an option unless it involves our own physical safety. I cannot imagine the terror of a woman, who has no semblance of a male's strength, being hit or physically abused by someone she loves dearly. The helplessness of that is something I hope I never experience. Yet some women live through this, time and again. If you have an issue with physical abuse, get some help, get past it, you will be wonderfully free. Sincere apologies *will* be in order. Yet no apology is good enough, until you have put forth the *effort* and the *time* to overcome being abusive.

Finish what you start.

This is self-explanatory. Finish every project you start. (I'm making this commitment!)

Be kind to animals.

While this may not be the greatest analogy, I've had the opportunity to train several dogs in my life, mostly hunting dogs. Dogs, like children, are extremely intelligent. As long as you explain things *clearly, consistently* and *patiently*, they *will* learn. *Consistency* is a huge key. Always teach the same way, with the same consequences. Dogs and children can understand and appreciate *consistency.* Have you ever been in the situation someone was trying to explain something, perhaps in your employment, and no matter how much they explained it didn't make sense? No matter how hard you tried, you didn't *get it.* Being inconsistent with both dogs and children will result in the same frustration you experienced. Children and dogs *want* to please. They would like nothing more than for you to be proud.

Dogs are as loyal as children. Your kindness to animals of all kinds weighs heavily on your children. I've not yet met a child that was abusive to animals that didn't in some way learn it from an adult. Make no excuse for neglecting or abusing an animal *or* a child in any fashion.

We don't kill spiders or bees in our house. If I find a hornet, trapped behind a window, trying to get out, I will find a cup or a glass and place it over it. The children will bring a piece of paper to slip under to trap them inside. I will take it outside and let it go. Sarah in particular has a great fear of bees, but she respects that I respect the bee's life enough not to kill them. Spiders are treated the same way. Any insect or animal deserves the same respect.

Celebrate life.

You have been given a gift of this life. Realize the richness and the beauty of your life. You evolved when an egg and a sperm merged to create life. You began this journey with nothing more than a simple, single cell that began to grow, against all odds. You have accomplished much in your life. You have coordinated a network of friends and family that is nothing short of miraculous. As a single dad at times you will be brilliant, other times you will be an imbecile. It's all part of life and each moment is to be celebrated, and appreciated. You can laugh at yourself, or be proud of yourself (humbly of course). The following biblical verse describes it well:

"To everything there is a season, and a time to every purpose under heaven: A time to be born, and a time to die; a time to plant, and a time to pluck up that which has been planted; A time to kill, and a time to heal; a time to break down, and a time to build up; A time to weep, and a time to laugh; a time to mourn, and a time to dance."

Ecclesiastes 3:1-4

The most important thing we forget is that we are all on this earth together. We are all undertaking a journey that has its ups and downs. How we choose to support each other on this journey not only determines our end results, but also determines the very fiber of our character. It matters not if you know the person you are interacting with, we are to help each other on our particular journey, please try to remember this. Our purpose in this life is to be loved. We all want the same thing.

Say, "I love you" often.

Say I love you often, especially to your children. In the family I grew up in "I love you" was rarely spoken, and always understood. My children have broken me of this habit, and I make certain to tell them often, "I love you." Don't let doubt invade their minds of their importance in your life.

It's not cool to date your ex's sister or best friend.

I don't care how *right* it feels for both of you, this isn't normal. If you were meant to be, you would have been with her in the first place and not with your ex. If your ex fixes you up, you can consider it. There are plenty of other fish in the sea, it's time to bait the hook and go fishin'. Likewise, dating married women can only bring hurt and pain to all involved. Avoid it. Go fishin' in another hole.

A dog don't shit where he eats.

Dating in the workplace, or any other person, such as a landlady, neighbor's wife etc, should be considered very carefully. You will experience a double whammy when any of these relationships go sour. If you break up with someone at work, you may lose your job, she hers, or at the very least, lose the respect of your co-workers. If you date your landlady or a neighbor, neighbor's wife etc, remember after the relationship comes crashing down, you still need a place to live! If this is something you feel you need to do, proceed with extreme caution. Don't do it out of convenience, it may become terribly inconvenient down the road.

Don't get involved with a cheater.

Dating a married woman that is cheating on her husband, or a woman cheating on her boyfriend is asking for trouble. Certainly people have the ability to change. An old saying goes, "once a cheater, always a cheater," or "You can't teach an old dog new tricks," or "a leopard will never change his (her) spots."

If you think a cheating woman can love you so much that she'd never cheat on you, go to Las Vegas, you'll get better odds on any house bet. "Changing" requires changing some core beliefs, not merely the behavior itself. Get involved with someone of a higher moral character.

Don't look like a geek.

Whether your children admit it to you or not, your appearance is very important to them. When they are seen in public with you, they want to be proud of you; they don't want to feel they are taking some poor homeless guy to McDonalds to buy him a meal. They don't want to have you at a school function embarrassed to introduce you to their friends or be seen with you. Clean up your act. Clean clothes, a good haircut, and some aftershave or cologne can go a long way.

Dependencies.

We all know dependence on cigarettes; chewing tobacco, and alcohol are unhealthy. I have them and am committed to quitting for my children. We can always find justification for such actions. You will also find justification for leading a healthy life style. It depends on which side of the fence you choose to do your looking.

Make only promises you can keep. Keep your promises.

This applies to all people you come in contact with of course, your children and your ex are especially important. *Most importantly, keep the promises you make to yourself.* Each year, most of us make New Year's Resolutions (promises) or we commit to quit smoking, drinking, living a healthier lifestyle, dieting, the list goes on and on.

If you were to make a promise to another person and break that promise, it would probably be overlooked, at least once or twice. However, if you were to make a habit of breaking your promises to that person, you would be seen as unreliable, and probably a liar.

So why do we allow ourselves to break the promises we make to ourselves, and think nothing of it? Consider this as unacceptable behavior, as you would if another were continuously breaking promises to you. The great thing is, unlike trying to make someone else keep their promises, you *can* control keeping your promises to yourself!

ASSIGNMENT

List your basic beliefs in life, on who you are and who you want to become. Note one example of how you've used that belief in the recent past.

Evaluate that list and determine if these beliefs are taking you places you want to be. If they are not working, make adjustments as necessary.

CHAPTER 14
KIDS WORDS

No sword cuts deeper than the words of an angry or hurt child. Nay, it cuts deeper than any bone or vital organ. It cuts a parent into his or her very being.

My oldest daughter Shiloh writes:

Going through the divorce between my parents at the young age of five doesn't seem to have left me with many vivid memories. I am sure that I did have feelings stirring and many questions to ask as we had a long drive from Colorado to Utah.

My sisters and I saw our father a couple of times a year at the most. My father was not good at sending birthday cards or presents, or keeping in contact over the phone.

These are the little things that count in a child's life. It left me feeling like I was forgotten.

It was emotionally hard and as I got older, with the "Daddy/Daughter dates" (authors note: this is a big thing in Utah for daughters to take part in activities with their dads) *having to find someone within the community to take me. As a result of my dad not being able to attend it put dents in my self-esteem that would not be repaired for quite some time.*

I wanted my dad to dance with, laugh with, and to feel secure with by my side. I played soccer for five years, and didn't have my father cheering me on down the sidelines for a couple of years.

At Parent-Teacher conferences my mother went alone. I would wish that my father had been able to go so that he could tell me how proud he was of me, or to guide me in some other areas I needed improvement in.

It is crucial for a child to feel important. If they don't feel important at home, they won't feel important when they walk out the door to school, a party where there is peer pressure, or with friends.

My dad had girlfriends that I felt were more important than I was in his life. I, at times, felt like I was put second. I had a hard time feeling close relationships with girlfriends because I felt I had to compete with these women in my father's life and saw women as a threat. I know now that it has affected my relationships with men in my life also.

I didn't feel that I was good enough, so in return I would settle for anyone who told me what I wanted to hear.

I want to tell all the divorced fathers (and mothers) that the one *major thing that can save heartache and emotional scars is to keep the unkind words to themselves. This is my blessing that my parents gave to me in allowing me to have my own relationship with each of them. I do not remember either of them saying a negative thing about the other. I never felt like I was in the middle of them.*

I am sure you would not want to hurt the child, and the other parent is a part of who your child is, so do respect that.

I would always comment that I had the best-divorced *parents a child could have.*

My father moved back to Utah when I was 12. It was nice to have him close again. This started the healing process for me. I was so glad to have him come to my soccer games and to see him every other weekend. We started to build memories together.

My dad didn't have a lot of money, so we would create memories by going fishing, watching a movie, or playing video games.

As a child it doesn't matter how much *money wise, but the* time spent. *Even if it is a simple phone call to say how did your day go? Happy Birthday, I miss you, or just thinking of you.*

SURVIVING THE SINGLE DAD SYNDROME

As I have become an adult and able to put words with my emotions a lot of healing has been completed. My father has listened to how I felt, that I was affected by his choices in life. Him listening felt great. I know that he did the best that he could at the time with the circumstances he was in. I love him for who he is!

Be involved in your children's lives, it's the best *thing you can do for them.*

Sometimes we as the adults attempt to remember our childhood, and I think to a certain extent, we see it through rose colored glasses, or those of us with very unhappy childhoods, through glasses that may be much darker. We don't want our children to grow up too quickly and take on adult responsibilities, and a view of life they may not be ready for. It may behoove us as adults to attempt to view our world through the eyes of a child again.

Our planet earth is a very diverse place, with many cultures and beliefs; many different economic and social classes are present in our many countries. Finding the opportunity to show this wonderful world to our children, as well as to put it in front of our own eyes will generate a life changing experience for all of us.

Plenty of organizations provide an opportunity for you and your children to take a working vacation. These organizations provide the opportunity, at your expense, to volunteer in various parts of the country, and in other countries of the world, to help with different projects for needy children and their parents. You may be involved in building a home, or a hut, or farming crops, helping harvest, as well as a variety of other projects.

This may be an expensive vacation if you are on a tight budget, but if you are not, it will provide you, and your children the experience of a lifetime. Think outside the box, if this is something that interests you, look into it further. We are so involved in our own culture and way of life, and we raise our children the same. A look into another culture for a few days, a week or longer, will leave an indelible memory that you will share for a lifetime.

As a human race, we've done things the same for thousands of years, we grow, we conquer, we rule. Isn't it time we listen to the children, and perhaps try another approach? I'd never considered myself a pacifist in the real sense of the word. I think it's time I may have to reconsider this war thing. Thank you children, for opening my eyes.

It must be very confusing for children when we as adults cannot see the innocence and divine beauty in each person. As the protectors we must make certain we rid the world of evil, for the sake of our children. It gives me pause to wonder though, are they not smarter than we are? With our vast technologies, and the tremendous minds we have in the world, can we not find a way other than military force and killing thousands of innocent people?

Hear the tremendous wisdom brought out when a child speaks honestly from the heart in the coming chapter. When a child speaks without fear of correction or discipline, many lessons are taught to those more experienced. The project of writing this book, has forced me, through many questions to children, to look at myself honestly, and face things I did not want to face. I had to realize, I was not all I thought I was. Sometimes this was a horrifying experience.

ASSIGNMENT

You will play a game of 20 questions with each of your children, one on one. Let them know you will give them a free pass; no answer they give will have any ramifications now or in the future. A lot of this is going to depend on the amount of trust you have established with them in the past. They also get to ask 20 questions.

Do not ask your child any question they may be uncomfortable with. They may ask you any question they wish. Each of you may decide not to answer if you choose.

As you list your questions and think you know the answer, write it down. You may be surprised (that was my boyfriend last week Dad!).

The goal is not to see how many questions you get right, but rather to learn more from your child, and to provide an opening for more communication.

I'd suggest starting your questions off simple (favorite color, favorite food etc) and move to the harder ones. (Boyfriend/girlfriend, happiest/saddest?) Make your last two questions fun to help lighten the mood (What is the grossest thing you've ever eaten?)

Following is a list of questions to use as a guide to get you and your child started:

Questions either might ask:

1) What is your favorite color?
2) What is your favorite food?
3) What is the grossest thing you have ever eaten?
4) What is the best thing that's happened this week?
5) What is the best thing that's happened in your life?
6) Who is your best friend?
7) Who do you admire most in the world, other than your parents? Why?
8) What is your favorite animal? Why?
9) Who is your favorite musician?
10) What is your favorite song?
11) If we could go anywhere in the world, or in space together, where would it be?
12) What is your favorite movie?

13) If you could develop a talent that you feel you don't have, what would it be? (Painting, sculpting, music, singing, daredevil, etc)
14) What is the scariest thing that's ever happened to you?
15) What is the most embarrassing thing that's ever happened to you?
16) When was the last time you cried? Why?
17) What is your favorite scary movie?
18) If you had 1 million dollars, how would you spend it?
19) If you could make the world a better place, what would you change?
20) If you had only 1 month left to live, what would you do with your time?
21) What makes you happiest?
22) What is the saddest thing you can think of?
23) What is the best thing we have ever done together?

Questions you might ask:
1) Who is your boyfriend/girlfriend?
2) Who is your favorite teacher? Why?
3) What is your favorite subject in school? Why?
4) Who would you like to be your boyfriend or girlfriend? Why?
5) What do you want to be when you grow up?
6) What is your favorite sport?
7) Do you want to go to college? Where?

Questions your child might ask:
1) What do you do for work?
2) What do you like most at work?
3) What do you like least at work?
4) Do you like your boss?
5) How much money do you make?
6) If you could do another thing for work, what would it be?
7) What did you want to be when you grew up?
8) Who was your first girlfriend? First kiss?

CHAPTER 15
IT'S ALL ABOUT THE CHILDREN

I adore the pictures of angels I see in paintings, religious writings, and on the walls of churches. They have a divine countenance, dressed in beautiful silken robes with halos above. They bear no resemblance to my angels, with spaghetti on their faces, chocolate on their fingers and toes, and their clothes are soiled with my front yard!

None-the-less, the halo remains in tact.

I recently received the following email that's been circulating on the Internet.

The Cost of Raising a Child

The government recently calculated the cost of raising a child from birth to 18 and came up with $160,140 for a middle- income family.

Talk about sticker shock! That doesn't even touch college tuition.

But $160,140 isn't so bad if you break it down. It translates into $8896.66 per year, $741.38 per month or $171.00 a week. That's a mere $24.24 per day. A little over a dollar an hour.

Still you might think the best financial advice says don't have children if you want to be rich. It is the opposite.

What do you get for your $160,140?

Naming rights, first middle and last!

Glimpses of God every day.

Giggles under the covers every night.

More love than your heart can hold.

Butterfly kisses and Velcro hugs.

Endless wonders over rocks, ants, clouds, and warm cookies.

A hand to hold usually covered with jam.

A partner for blowing bubbles, flying kites, building sand castles, and skipping down the sidewalk in the pouring rain.

Someone to laugh yourself silly with no matter what the boss said or how your stocks performed that day.

For $160,140 you never have to grow up.

You get to finger-paint, carve pumpkins, play hide-and-seek, catch lightening bugs, and never stop believing in Santa Claus.

You have an excuse to keep reading adventures of Piglet and Pooh, watching Saturday morning cartoons, going to Disney movies, and wishing on stars.

You get to frame rainbows, hearts, and flowers under refrigerator magnets and collect spray painted noodle wreaths for Christmas, hand prints set in clay for Mother's Day (or Father's Day), and cards with backwards letters for Father's Day (or Mother's Day).

For $160,140 there is no greater bang for your buck.

You get to be a hero for retrieving a Frisbee off the garage roof, taking the training wheels off the bike, removing a splinter, filling a wading pool, coaxing a wad of gum out of bangs, and coaching a baseball team that never wins but always gets treated to ice cream regardless.

You get a front row seat to history to witness the first step, first word, first bra, first date, and first time behind the wheel.

You get to be immortal.

You get another branch added to your family tree, and if you are really lucky, a long list of limbs in your obituary called grandchildren.

You get an education in psychology, nursing, criminal justice, communications, and human sexuality that no college can match.

In the eyes of a child, you rank right up there with God.

You have all the power to heal a boo-boo, scare away the monsters under the bed, patch a broken heart, police a slumber party, ground them forever and love them without limits, so one day they will like you, love without counting the cost.

Enjoy your kids and grandkids.
Author Unknown

By this stage in your life, you know how you would like to be a dad. I challenge you to take that idea and put it back on the shelf. Might as well throw it out the window; you're not going to need it. In the same sense, we think we would like to be the dad we had, or we had always wanted, right out the window with that one too. *Your task is to be the dad your child wants and needs you to be.* Anything less is not acceptable.

We become so involved in our dad role, we are generally distanced from what is happening in our child's life.

I stand and applaud the mothers, at least many of the mothers. Mothers realize it's all about the children. I have experienced so many mothers that sacrifice their goals, dreams, time, and in some cases their health for their children. This may be an instinctual thing, propagation of the species and all that. Whatever the reason, it's a difficult and selfless thing they do constantly, when they don't feel well or when they're hungry; their number one concern is always for the children.

I've had the opportunity, especially over the last couple of years to spend a great deal of time with children, others and mine. I eavesdrop on their conversations, or instigate a conversation of my own with them. I was surprised to learn that what we as parents think they are concerned with isn't always the case. It helped me reflect back to when I was their age, and the things that concerned me most. I can't recall that I had the concerns that worry my kids today. It's interesting how we lose this perspective over time.

One of my favorite movies of all time is *The Medicine Man* with Sean Connery and Lorraine Bracco. In that movie, a line is delivered at different times by both stars, "Have you ever lost something? Your purse, your car keys? Well it's rather like that! Now you have it now you don't!"

Well it seems I've lost something, as much time as I've spent with children, I cannot recapture the true innocence of my youth. I've been to the seminars that teach me to get in touch with my inner child, and I run around doing all sorts of goofy things, but something is missing. My mind cannot seem to reach through the thick curtain of crap raised in my mind through adulthood. I cannot pierce that quagmire and feel again the light innocent playfulness I knew as a child.

Sure many of the memories remain. I remember the ball games in the local vacant lot. The hours upon hours of summertime fishing spent with my closest buddies. The smell of home cooked bread as I entered the house after a long day of playing.

I cannot recall however the wonderful excitement of my first hit at bat, the various school awards for musical or sports accomplishments. Nor am I able to conjure up the heart pounding experiences of *The Blob*, the *Thing from the Black Lagoon*, or King Kong meeting Godzilla, when those creatures still existed.

I've tried to spend time with the kids, doing child things, romping in a mud puddle, playing ball in the park, swinging on the swings. Always this little adult thing in my mind is watching the children to make certain they are playing safely, much more safely than I did as a child of course.

It's sad to have lost this. I know I had it once, but it is gone. It's kind of like my car keys or wallet. Yet if I had lost something material, it wouldn't have taken me 38 years to realize I had lost them. Perhaps those secrets are best left to those who enjoy them most, to the children. Even so, I continue to pursue the elusive butterfly.

Some of the children I've spoken with are concerned with popularity in school and with their friends. This is a major concern for them, to be popular. We all look forward every year to the weeks before school opening (August on my children's schedule) when it's time to do the annual School Shopping. For many of us men, this is August, for the mother doing the shopping this is sometimes referred to as "Hell month."

This is the time when every concerned parent knows by way of their child, what is in and what is out this year. The name brand clothing that they all must have is outrageously priced, and it will run you a bundle. If you have boys, you may not be subjected to this very heavily, though they still have their name brand requirements. If you have female children and they are striving to be popular with school friends, hold onto your wallet. It's going to cost you *big*.

The need to be popular can be an intense driving force in your child. In order for them to feel they are going to get all of the breaks in life, be involved in the cool activities at school, meet the best boys or girls to have as boyfriends and girlfriends, they have to be active with the "in crowd." This was important when I was a child, but I think for various reasons, that drive for popularity in our children is more intense today. Sadly in some of our schools, not being a part of the popular crowd may cost a child his or her very life!

The schools today are much different than my childhood. Some of them can be downright scary places! If you have not visited your child's school during a regular school day, when classes are in session, I would encourage you to do so. The child's words cannot express some of the things you may experience. You may come away with a whole new understanding, and perhaps a fear for what they are going through.

One of my biggest concerns is a child that is being bullied. To my knowledge, I don't have a child that is being bullied, and it can be hard to detect. Yet, make no mistake it is very prevalent in our school systems. It's not only boys doing it. Girls can be more ruthless on another female child than any boy would ever dream of being. Girls can be much subtler, a mental and emotional bullying takes place that can be much more damaging than physical bullying.

The other girls may sneer at your daughter, because of how she dresses, what she brings for lunch, or the way she wears her hair. Nothing will be ignored, and your child cannot prevent it. Imagine the darkness and fear that must accompany a child on a walk to school when they know they are going to go through their own version of hell today, and every day. This plays heavily on your child's self esteem, and it will have lasting affects for many years, in some cases for the rest of their life.

If you have a child being bullied, it will be difficult to detect. Pay attention to your child's mood both when they leave for school and when they arrive home. Listen for the clues that they may be having difficulty with classmates. Pay attention that they mention a number of friends. A child with a good number of friends may not be subjected to such bullying.

Bullies are cowards; they travel in groups. They have a pack mentality and hunt in these packs, as wolves do. You won't find the typical school bully we knew as a child, the loner, and the one that did things for his own satisfaction. They are out to impress their friends by instilling fear and terror in the child that travels alone, the one not as strong as they are.

If you have a child that is being bullied, my heart aches for you and your child. Our first instinct when we find our child is being subjected to such behavior is to call the *other* parents. This is a viable option. Don't confront the bully yourself unless you witness things first hand. Having you stand up for your child will generally serve to increase the punishment they receive and may get you in legal trouble.

Should you contact the bully's parents, have a bit of understanding for them also. The bully is as hard to detect as the bullied child. A bully will rarely act out when parents are around, nor any other adult or teacher for that matter. They hide their crimes well, in darkened hallways or classrooms, behind the school, or in isolated parts of the neighborhood. The parents of this child should be aware that this is a concern.

Work to instill a value system into your child of not only bullies but also any unkind behavior.

If you are a parent whose child is not being bullied, your child can help. They can help by understanding how the bullied child feels. They can be empowered to make a difference.

Your child may avoid confronting the bully, or being involved with the bullied child. They don't want to be subjected to the torture. This is the kiss of social death. Your child and their friends can make a difference. They can become friendly with the bullied child and hang out with them. If a child is being bullied and your child with 12 or 15 friends shows up to eat lunch with them, the behavior is going to stop. At least while they are around. When the bullies see no convenient opportunity to torment this child any longer, they will move to another. And your child and their friends should move on to protect this other child. Let these bullies know this behavior will *not* be tolerated in our school!

Your children will understand that by eliminating bullies in their school, they are protecting themselves and their friends from ever having to be the target themselves.

Children understand well when protecting other children. This is especially strong if they have brothers and sisters.

I think one of the reasons I was never bullied in school was because of my older brother. He was a cool kid, and he was extremely tough. If anyone had picked on me, they would have answered to him. Bringing in an older brother and sister, not to bully, but to protect may also be another option in the above case. Sometimes though, this can also escalate if the bully has older brothers or sisters. We don't want any fight that's what we're trying to avoid. Generally if you let your child handle it with friends, they will get it worked out.

One of the concerns on my son's mind is a mean teacher. Prevalent in his thoughts when he begins school every year, and by the end of the season, he loved the teacher, and the teacher loved him!

Remembering my days in high school, each year would bring rumors of the teacher you did *not* want! I had many of them. They were highly overrated! Any teacher appreciates a good student. I tell my son, "Just get in, work hard (like he always does), and be yourself. You will get along with this teacher fine, like you have others before." So far it has always worked for him.

A couple of years ago, my son and I took some time off from school to travel across the country to visit my parents and family for the holidays. We had a wonderful time and didn't give much thought to school, since he was always an exceptional student.

When we returned however, he had several days he was too sick to go to school. He was vomiting and of course we thought it was the flu, and would soon pass. After a few days his teacher called and asked if he was all right, and would he return soon? We assured the teacher that he was sick and would get better soon.

Fortunately this teacher was very in-touch and fond of our son. She said that while gone on vacation he had missed some new things they began studying and wondered, since he is always the perfect student, if his missing out on this could be a factor. She asked that he come to the school and talk with her. We agreed.

Well, as it turned out, she was right. He had always been one of the best in his class, and for some reason he couldn't grasp this new subject, because he had not been present when they explained it! He was very frustrated and upset; it's like they were speaking a foreign language! He had worried himself so badly; he did make himself sick to the stomach. After a short time with his teacher, going through the new subject, he had it well in hand and was back to school, performing to his usual high standards.

As a parent, I realized what high expectations we had put on this boy! At our next opportunity driving in the mountains, I explained to him some of the smartest people in the world ask the most questions. No one knows it all. Even though he thought Dad was the smartest man in the world, (jokingly) I am one that asked a lot of questions and not good at bluffing my way through anything. He should never be ashamed to seek out help when he didn't understand something. I will have to admit to some of the blame, as I'm not always the most patient when it comes to all of his questions. I've resolved to correct that.

Since 9-11, our children are very concerned with war, as many of us are. For those of you that are military families (Mom or Dad in the military) I think those parents provide for their children better at handling rumors of war, and the consequences of a conflict. Many other children however don't equate the distance of a war in Iraq or Afghanistan and how far away it all will be. They sympathize and relate to the children of those countries when they see them on television or in any news media. Our children have a very deep understanding of peace, deeper than we may realize.

Sitting down with a child and speaking with them in an age appropriate manner will help alleviate some of their fears. A war on our soil of course would be very terrifying, and the chances of that happening are small. A war in any part of the world is not a good thing, but their subjection to the horrors of war will be minimal in most cases. If you have a child nearing draft age, you'll certainly want to help prepare him or her with as much information as they are prepared to deal with.

Hopefully by the time this book is done, this whole Iraq war will have come to a peaceful ending. But looming on the horizon is North Korea, Iran, and perhaps other countries. It's time to talk with your child and explain the reasons for war. Spend more time listening than talking. Listen to their fears and concerns. Ask them, "If you were President Bush, what would you do differently?" Their insight may surprise you.

More so, it gives them a chance to speak honestly about fears. Allow them feelings without judgment. Encourage writing any thoughts to their congressman and the President. Teach them that their voice is important. This goes a long way in their future.

My youngest daughters had a tremendous fear of dogs when they were younger. I don't know where they got it from, but it was *real, intense* fear. If a dog came around us, they would literally climb up my legs, up my torso and nest around my head, circling to keep an eye on the animal, like a treed bear cub. They were absolutely terrified! How did their mother solve this problem? She bought them a dog!

You might be saying, "Well that was a stupid thing to do!" You would be incorrect. She bought them a puppy, one that wouldn't grow into a dog for a few months at least, and he is tiny. His name is Sammy, and he's one of the cutest little pugs I've ever seen. He's so ugly he's cute!

This immediately removed any fear of dogs. They love to hurry home to play with him. They will chase down any dog in the park, or at a football game to pet it. I have taught them to always ask the owner first if they might pet their dog, trusting the owner's judgment on the safety of the animal.

My girls went from fearing and hating animals to passionately loving every dog or cat that they lay eyes or hands on. The lack of fear is in *understanding* animals. This is a real sense of *power*.

My oldest daughter (of the three younger ones) has a fear of bees. This one is a bit tougher to tackle. I have tried all of the talks on bees, and explained to them they aren't the least bit interested in stinging her, and that when they sting they die. This doesn't help the fear any at all trust me.

A friend wisely suggested I get her a bracelet or necklace with multi colored stones on it. I did. I explained to her that the colors on this bracelet would make the bees think she is a Queen Bee, and of course they would not harm their Queen. So far it's working, she'll still hold up the bracelet and race by the bush in front of my house that is infested with hornets in the summer months. The fear seems to be pretty much gone.

This is a *false* sense of power. But to her it is power nonetheless and does not put her in a harmful situation. Hopefully she will soon lose that fear and won't need the bracelet any longer. Kids have a way of working these things out.

Kids have their own sense of logic. My children grew up in the Church of Jesus Christ of Latter Day Saints (The Mormons). In my first marriage, we were active in "The Church." One of their beliefs is that before you come to earth, you are in heaven and pick your parents before coming to earth. As all Christians believe, after you die, you go back to heaven.

Sitting at the dinner table one night, my young daughters all had friends in the apartment complex we lived in. Since many of their friends' moms were single, several of them were getting new dads. My oldest Shiloh, six at the time approached the subject "Mom, can we get a new dad?" After we were able to close our mouths and put our eyes back in our sockets, Mom asked her, "What makes you ask that?"

"Well, a lot of our friends are getting new dads." Shiloh replied.

Her Mom laughed, (thankfully) and asked, "What would we do with your old Dad?"

After giving it a great deal of thought, with furrowed brow, she replied, "We could send him back to Heaven!"

I'm sure in times since my ex wishes she had taken her up on the idea.

Recently, my son came to me and said Sarah was in the bedroom crying as she was missing her great grandfather. This hit me as odd, since her great grandfather had passed away precisely one week before she was born. For some reason though, she's always felt closeness to him.

Nevertheless, it was an opportunity for a talk. I went to her and rubbed her back, stroked her hair as I told her what little I knew of her great grandfather. I explained that he is her guardian angel and is with her always. I encouraged her to talk with her grandparents and great grandmother to find out more of her grandfather. The only thing she knew was of his passing prior to her birth.

Who knows what worries our children? When it's something that concerns them, stop everything you are doing, take the time to learn what makes them tick. This will increase your bond faster than any time spent in playgrounds and pizza parlors.

My son has been involved in sports since he was quite young. I make it a point to go to his practices, and I don't believe I've ever missed one of his games. He is finishing his basketball season.

I'm concerned when I see the news stories of parents that get out of control during the sporting events for the children. Parents are so competitive! Many children are embarrassed by their parents' behavior when they act out at the games.

As I was growing up and actively involved in sports, things seemed very competitive to me. If we lost a game, it was tough. Our parents though, were not involved as actively as parents today. Maybe they were. *Maybe* they had the ability to keep things more in perspective.

Occasionally you will see a mom or dad living vicariously through their children at these events. Mom or dad may not have been the star player on their team or perhaps they were and are missing those glory days. They see an opportunity in their child to be a professional baseball, basketball, or football player. They so desperately want to give their child a life that perhaps they never had.

Is this why children play sports? Their only goal is to become rich and famous on a basketball court, football field, or hockey rink? That's not why my son plays. My son plays because he loves to play.

I've learned over the last season in particular when they won only one football game, and only one basketball game the whole season, that *winning is secondary*. I have seen him come off the court or field, game after game. The expression on his face attitude provides no clue if they won or lost! Imagine that! *My son has no understanding that winning is everything!* And his abhorrent behavior extends to his teammates! They come to play because they love the game! They love the competition. The final score means nothing to them! What lesson are these kids being taught?

It took a lot of self-examination to understand his way of thinking and why it was so opposed to mine.

I think back to one important wrestling meet I had as a senior in high school. This was the final match of the season, against our neighboring and rival town in Ohio. This promised to be an exciting match as it always was. The teams were both great, mostly seniors for their last high school match of the season before the end of year tournaments began. This was the last chance for most of us to hone our skills in competition before the big matches began. The tournament matches coming up would surely influence our sports careers for the rest of our lives.

I remember the crowd was enormous, and they were loud. Many exciting matches proved to come down to the final buzzer. I remember my opponent who I had met before was a seasoned competitor, and we were well matched.

Being creative I gave every ounce of strength I had. I remember the crowds stomping feet, the roar was deafening as our match ended. I remember the camaraderie of our team, and theirs. I remember clearly the smell of sweat and blood. I remember looking up at the crowd cheering and yelling as I left the mat. I remember they were whipped into frenzy. Why? I have no idea, I can't remember if I had won the match or not. Nor can I remember what the final score was of the team match; oddly these details escape me.

The final score wasn't that important. If it were, I would surely remember it. The *score* of that match, to my recollection has had no bearing on that which I've become in my life. It certainly didn't determine my career in sports, as I chose other professions. If I had been outstanding in my wrestling career, would I have made different choices? I had many friends who were state champions, the best of the best. None of them to my knowledge ever went on to become sports stars.

My son and his teammates are very aware that the *score* has little bearing. The important lesson is the competition, the sportsmanship, the individual and team efforts they put out. My son will learn in his approach to his career life, that as long as you are doing something you enjoy, and you do it well individually, as well as with a team, the work itself is its own reward. No doubt he will be very successful at whatever he attempts in life. No matter what he is doing, he will be enjoying it. If he is not enjoying it, he will not be doing it.

I try to project myself into the future to view this apparent unimportance of the final score and how it may serve my son in his working career. I see him in a large corporate boardroom, making a presentation he has worked hard with in an attempt to win over a client's business. It's apparent from his demeanor that he has pride in his work. He has performed the task because he loves doing it. He is only concerned with the client's opinion on his work, not for the sake of winning a large contract for his company, rather because he has put his heart and soul into his work. He carefully weighed the client's needs, and their determination of what they want to accomplish with their money. He has put himself into his work, because he loves the work, not because he wanted to win the contract. The client senses his love for his work, and it has a heavy weight on his decision over the competition that may be more concerned with winning the contract. This client has no doubt he would like my son working for him, because he loves what he does!

One important tip I learned through my children is in use at bath time. I hated giving my little girls a bath, or letting them take one, because after the bath or shower, it was time to fix their hair. Through various girlfriends over the years I learned the basics of braiding, but I am inept when it comes to this talent. But more important, brushing or combing a little girl's hair after a bath is a battle! We don't like to hurt our little children, but brushing that tangled mess is far more difficult than untangling a backlash on any fishing reel I've owned. Some children's heads are tenderer than others, and this can be a very trying experience.

Through necessity I hit on the idea of using conditioner. This isn't something I use on myself, I'm blessed with hair that doesn't seem to need it. Most men are! So before they finish their bath or shower, I help them shampoo their hair. After shampooing, I condition their hair and lightly rinse it. I then get a comb with large teeth, and gently comb out the tangles. The lubrication from the conditioner helps those tangles come right out painlessly. We rinse again and another comb, and out they come to some nice fluffy towels. Find a spray on conditioner product that you can leave in which makes things simple. Before the hair is completely dry, comb or brush again, and braid it if that's the style she'll want that day. Braiding isn't too bad, but our large fingers are not built for it. Most any female can show you how. The rest is practice! Keep lots of little hair "thingy's" in the house, it makes things much easier.

If you are lucky, as I am when the children are gone, whether they've grown and gone, or have returned to Mom's for the week, you'll find your house is trashed. I get so frustrated with the constant cleaning. That is until I begin to look through the rubble that was once my home and begin to find the love notes left by my angels. They're not notes in the traditional sense of the word. Rather they come in the form of a ribbon tied around a doorknob from my six-year-old, a carefully drawn heart with the words "I love you, Dad," scrawled ornately from my eight-year-old. Perhaps it's a controller from the video game machine, carelessly tossed in an unlikely spot by my eleven-year-old. I'll find a tiny hand print of finger paint on the wall, or a spot of peanut butter left on the coffee table. I clean incessantly but some of the loving reminders I choose to leave. It helps with the loneliness.

ASSIGNMENT

When attending your children's activities, begin to see it through *their* eyes. Don't pay so much attention to the score of the game, or the perfection of the dance performance. Look into the intensity in their eyes as they perform. Look around particularly at the other parents and note their behavior. Watch the pride in each parent as his or her child performs, or scores an important goal on the field, court or rink. Make a point of congratulating one or more of them. Give a word of encouragement to your children and the others as they come off of the stage, or the court. This is what their life is, learning, performing, growing in ways we may have forgotten.

Most of these children will one day become parents. A simple word from a parent may have a profound influence on how they see their youngsters perform in the future.

CHAPTER 16
INTERVIEW WITH KIDS

I spend a great deal of time seeking to understand the type of dad I want to be to my children. The answer comes when I realize it's not what I want, but rather that I must be the dad my children want and need. So I asked them.

Recently I had the opportunity to sit down with two of my children Sarah (age eight) and Camden (age eleven) and one of their friends Kendra (age thirteen) to hear what it was to be a child of single parents. This was a great experience, to sit down and see the world again through a child's eyes. Some comments surprised me since I thought I knew my children well.

Sarah and Camden are from two different mothers. I've worked hard to keep them together as brother and sister. Most of our visitations are together, though Camden visits more frequently, due to his mother's work schedule and the relationship his mother and I have maintained.

Kendra was eight years old when her mother, sister, and she left their dad. She remembered more about the breakup and their life together than the other two had with their families, since they were much younger.

Kendra's mom and dad are both friends of mine. I had more insight than normal concerning the parents' separation.

They expressed misunderstanding as to their parents' separation. As parents, we shield the children from any gory details of separating. Our response to a question when raised is purposely vague. This can cause some confusion in a child's mind.

What they remembered ranged from arguments over a piece of paper, or a pack of cigarettes, to Mom dumping a glass of orange juice on Dad while he slept, and brought up memories of violent physical fights. None of them remembered or probably ever had known the real reasons behind the separations. And perhaps that's best until they are much older. It is important when they ask to stress that you still love their mother very much, that she is a wonderful woman, and she is a part of them, literally. When you criticize their mother, you are criticizing a part of that which they are. This is to be avoided. It's important that they understand "Mom and I look at things very differently, and it's better if we don't live together." If we have one thing in common, we both love our children very much, and want the best for them.

Children from the youngest ages will always remember the bad times, the violence, and any angry arguments. This is human nature. The best way for them to not witness these things of course is if they don't ever happen. Unfortunately in many marriages on the brink of separation, this isn't always realistic, though I think it *could* be. At the very least, we as parents should be responsible enough to make certain the children are not witness to our angry or violent moments with anyone, especially their mother.

Some might argue that this doesn't give a child a very realistic view of the world. Children will observe enough violence in their lives, through movies, television, video games, or real life situations. They don't need to see it from their parents to understand it.

When the couple first separates, it's not unusual for the children to be more than a bit confused. They sense life has become unstable. As these three children expressed, they didn't know from one moment to the next, what their future family life held for them.

When Dad didn't call, or visit, they felt unloved, forgotten, and unwanted. In some cases, they lost touch with their father for long periods of time. This brought fear that Dad was on drugs again or dead, and they weren't being told. The children unfortunately don't have the verbal faculties at young ages to express these emotions and fears. This may result in acting out, performing poorly in academics or sports events, and essentially disconnecting from the family as a whole. They may fear losing their mother and siblings and be left alone. After all, it happened to Dad, the strongest and most stable person in their lives, why not everyone else also?

Dad had been one of their best friends, a protector and comforter. Now Dad was nowhere it seemed, on the face of the planet. This will cause fear! They feel Dad doesn't love them; he doesn't want them or doesn't care. Children don't have a switch to turn their love on and off, as they perceive we might.

When Dad was around, they never remembered Mom's financial worries. Mom may share her fears with the children out of frustration or because she no longer has the ear of her husband. Kids shouldn't be concerned with the family finances until they become much older, if at all.

Since they are dear to their mothers, it hurts deeply when she cries. It is scary when they don't understand why she is crying.

Some of the children are aware that Dad (or Mom) pays child support. Often though, except in more mature children, they misunderstand the reason for child support.

They get some sense that Dad pays support so he can see his children. I was shocked when I heard this from my own children. It's important that they (and you) understand the commitment made, between you and their mother, before they were born, that you *both* would be responsible financially. Paying child support *consistently* is your responsibility in their care and upbringing. Hopefully, depending on your ex's views, your ability to see them has nothing to do with your child support payments. If you do your part in taking care of your responsibilities, this should never be an issue.

Thoughts they expressed were on step dads or that potential step dads could be in their lives. All expressed they were very happy with the significant others in their mothers lives, with few reservations. They were happier when Mom was happy. Of course they liked it when this step dad (or potential) was nice and fun to be with. They were more afraid if he was not, more so than when Dad wasn't nice, this was a stranger in their home, and it held an unknown factor.

Overall though, their mother's loneliness is a great burden to them. They see their mother shine when she is happy and loved. Depression puts a dark cloud on the home and they don't want to see her unhappy. When their mother is happy and loved, they see a future again. Instinctively they see themselves and their family moving forward.

Kids worries are more than I remember as a child. Children in our generation seem to be more involved in the world around them, than I certainly was in my little hometown.

Some of their fears were the same as when I was young, it scares them when people die. They may be touched by the death of a family member, grandfather, uncles, aunts, grandmother etc. Things that are a part of the circle of life, and of course they will be affected and have concerns. Suicide in younger children is on the rise. If this has touched them, it can be very disconcerting.

With our nations constant Terror Alerts, they may be a bit clouded as to what a terrorist is. They fear men in long beards in pickup trucks afraid they may have a gun beside them and will start shooting. Children are more aware of people that may speak with a foreign accent; they wouldn't have knowledge of which dialect this accent might come from. Many of these fears perhaps unknowingly are passed down from parents, other family members or friends.

While it's important to have conversations with your children regarding bad people, war, and terrorism, don't let them get overloaded.

When September 11th struck, many of us adults were glued to our televisions, radios, or computers, wanting every bit of information. Our young children were caught on the periphery of this tragedy. If they were very young, each time they would see the World Trade Center towers collapsing, they may have been thinking these weren't the same buildings over and over, they thought each time they saw it, it was happening, somewhere again. The entire world seemed to be collapsing, with millions of people being killed. If they are seeing these things over and over, make certain they understand it is the same film being played again and again. And turn off the television! Let them have some escape from these tragic scenes. They are much more impressionable to these images than our hard hearts as adults.

They know what it felt like when Grandpa or Grandma died, seeing thousands of people crushed by a giant building is overwhelming to them. They may not have the faculties to express this. They will talk to their friends though, over and over and over.

When parents are unhappy, whether it's from a September 11th scale incident, or merely financial or family problems, their tendency is to think they aren't being told everything. When that happens they tend to think the worst. "Are we going to be out in the street?" Or, "Did someone die?" It's human nature, as it is with us. Communicate with them, of course you won't tell them everything! But make certain they at least understand what the issue is; it will help ease their minds.

Kids have a lot of worries in their lives. Gangs, drugs, and the violence these bring were unheard of when I was young. Chances are, depending on your location your children are having some contact with those that use drugs or are involved in gangs. Don't think if you are affluent and your children attend the most prestigious schools they are not subjected to such things. Gangs, drugs, and violence have left few untouched areas in this country. Listen to your child when it comes to what they see at school, they may enlighten your thinking.

The children talked of things their parents do. Things they don't like. Their parents should take care of themselves. No smoking, chewing tobacco, or alcohol abuse. It bothers them to see parents worrying constantly, or angry. We don't realize the affect when Mom or Dad yells. I've been known to raise my voice more than I should. At times this is the only way to get my point across! I have committed myself to finding a more peaceful method of getting their attention.

After the serious talk was out of the way, I took the opportunity to ask what they like to do. What are their happiest memories and things that make them feel good?

The things most important to them, depending on age of course, was sports and performances such as dance, plays, and school social activities. They expressed the importance of their parents attending these events, to share in their happy times. They want their parents to be proud of them when they do well, and it's not possible for a parent to do that if they aren't in attendance!

Kendra is of the age that boys become more important. This is an important part of a child's social life and acceptance into the popular crowd. Though she was quick to add, "They are important, but not as important to me as family and friends." I told her to wait a couple of years and get back to me on that. Her opinion, like most teenaged children, may change.

I was surprised to hear one of the most important things to all three of them was picture day at school. This is a big event for them! They seem to understand the importance of these pictures, how they will have many of them through their entire lives. They want to look their best in them. I had no clue when I was in school, that I would still have many of these pictures taken of me as a child. And in many of them, I looked like a dork of course.

Both parents being involved in Parent/Teacher conference was mentioned. They feel that school is such a big part of their life, it is only fitting that both parents should be involved in the conferences regularly, and to praise them, to help them in the things they need help with. I have attended only a few and I learned how others see them, which I hadn't thought of. I am making a commitment to be more involved.

The world has changed greatly since many of us grew up. In our day-to-day race to keep up, we may lose sight of the world as our children see it. We want to do all of the things required of us, to make our children happy and healthy in this world. We work hard; we do our best for our employers, hoping for advancements.

We do our best to give our family nice homes and nice furniture, so their friends won't be embarrassed when they visit. We want to give them all the high tech toys they ask for, the video games, hand held games, televisions, and stereos, not to mention the latest popular music CDs to go with it.

Remember in your game of running around; to give your child the greatest gift you can, their dad. You are and always will be more important to them than you may realize.

CHAPTER 17
RAISING CHILDREN WITH HEALTHY IDEALS

It is nothing less than humbling, to take my new borne babe in my arms, as the heavenly glow begins to lift, to realize I stare into my own eyes, glimpsing both my mortality and immortality. I see the beginning and the end.

What a wonderful opportunity we have been given in this gift called fatherhood. No matter if you are dirt poor, or tremendously successful in your career. If you have children, they want two things from you, which we all have the same amount of, love and time. Time to get to know us, time to learn to love us, time to create memories with a person that can contribute a tremendous value to a child's life.

I've spent many years in the company of women without children, and women that have children. A subtle difference exists between the two. A love is conveyed in a woman's touch that has children, over one that has no such blessing. They convey a warmth and security that cannot be felt from anyone else.

Should you think for one moment if you have the custody of your children, that you might replace the love and warmth provided by a child's mother, you are sorely mistaken. You cannot replace that love; you can only do what you can do.

In the same respect, the love and strength offered by a gentle, tender father is unmatched by anyone in the world. You alone can provide things to your children that no other can. This love is not fleeting, nor temporary, it lasts an eternity. Your influence on your child carries through generation after generation.

I've been blessed with a son that is wise beyond his years. I'm proud to say most of the time he refers to me as Dad. At times if I'm out of line in his opinion, or being a bit of a jerk, he will respond to my discipline or comments with, "Yes, Father."

He reminds me (much too often for my taste) of the difference between a dad and a father.

My preschool aged granddaughter also can convey the same message. I had a conversation with her this past weekend, and she was speaking of her "BF Father," her mother interjected so that I would understand "Her Biological Father." How insightful is this little child?

She has an understanding that she has a biological father, one who was at least 50% responsible for her conception. He believed his responsibility ended. She also has a dad who is no blood relation or biological. He is the only dad she has ever known. He will unselfishly give of himself, his time and his financial resources, tempered with loving discipline to assure this child has as normal a childhood as possible. She repays him with unconditional love. My thanks to my son-in-law Tyler for all he does for my little granddaughter.

Our commitment to fatherhood begins with conception. How we proceed on our path to dad is forever in our hands. And varying degrees of fathers or dads exist. I know we all want to be a loving dad, but unfortunately, for a variety of *excuses*, we fall short.

For as many families that have ever existed, you will find different methods of doing things. You are fortunate that you get to choose your method.

Many years ago, our great ancestors spent a great deal of time as a family unit. They hunted together, built shelter together, and as they evolved, farmed together. As the years passed, the family unit remained strong, settling this wonderful country of ours, and homesteading together. Modern technology not yet a dream; any down time was spent with family, around the hearth, fixing meals, doing chores. When I was growing up, as early as 40 years ago, it was uncommon for most wives to work.

It was a much simpler time. We always scraped by, never wanted for material things. Many things I experience in our modern culture, was little more than a dream.

The bicycle was the main mode of transportation for a child, and we went everywhere on our two-wheeled machine. A simple day of fishing with my friends at a local pond or lake would occupy us from sun up to sun down. Playing baseball or football at the local vacant lot was equally satisfying. We were convinced we had the best climbing trees in the entire world, or at least our corner of it.

How many children are allowed to climb trees as I did when I was a child? We seem more concerned with the trees than we do with a child's healthy growth.

I would bet if I went back to that little town today, many of the trees would still stand healthy and strong, nonetheless worn with the remains of my foot and hand prints on the trunk and branches. Sadly, many were cut down for progress, but the memories remain. If the tree was destroyed years later what difference would it have made if I had spent countless hours in its branches, spying on those yucky girls. It would have made a difference to the tree to hear my giggles I would bet.

In the good old days men brought home the bacon, and they did it well. Mom could stay home and raise the family. It wasn't the best of circumstances, but it was in my opinion more family oriented than things in our over scheduled world.

Today, it's pretty much the norm for both Mother and Dad to work and have their own careers. Children are so over scheduled with sports, clubs, or crafts they have limited time. The children go from morning until well after dark with their own activities, and it may be a struggle for Mom and Dad to schedule, so at least one of them can attend to support their activities. A true family time may be limited to a few hours a week at best. How would a single parent find the time?

Mom and Dad become involved in their work life to make ends meet. As they work hard at what they do, they meet a great variety of people and they develop talents completely separate from their partner. This in and of itself can be a great thing. However, without the time as family to share what both are involved in, as well as the many activities the children are involved in, we find ourselves being pulled in completely different directions.

It is a blessing when one of the parents are offered a big promotion, yet sometimes it's in another city or state. At this time, the parents must come to a realization as to what is important. No matter what the decision, whether to go or stay, it's a no win situation, someone's priorities will be placed second to the other partner and to the family.

It's unnatural for us to begin to grow apart in this world, but we set ourselves up for it! We work separately; we develop different interests; our goals grow apart and without proper communication, the inevitable sneaks up on us until we feel we don't know who our partner is any longer. Sooner or later, the marriage breaks up, and it's a mad scramble to save what scraps of the family we can before it's completely destroyed.

When the separation comes, Mom is going to have her way of doing things, and you will yours. If you have been together for quite some time, hopefully many of the rules have been established. Change the ones you are not comfortable with but allow your ex to use her method.

Teach the children the difference in their two worlds. Give them the reasons why if it's age appropriate. Let them know that if they should happen to visit other countries when they are older, those countries also have different rules and customs. We show respect to the citizens of those countries by following their laws and rules. You can seek the children's advice in naming your world. You can name it "Dad's World" or "Kids World" or something they will have fun with. Paint a mental picture for them, "The sky is a rather pleasant shade of mauve," (red, guys), "not boring blue! Kool Aid flows from the faucets, and the refrigerator is stocked with chocolate." Show you are going to be fun and can be creative. You will have many hours of enjoyment telling them of the world you live in.

Though the children may have two sets of rules and two places they live, *consistency* when they are in your home is critically important. Set a time for bed, a time for brushing teeth; draw up a schedule on the calendar. The kids will know what to expect when they are in your home, and it will become their home as well.

Discipline is important. As the fun dad we don't like to think of disciplining a child. Say yes as often as possible. Say no when necessary. Things may be a bit lighter than they were when you were all one family, but that's ok, that's one of the perks.

As married dads, we don't think enough before disciplining children. When they get to the last raw nerve, and you're about to explode, it's sometimes difficult to take ten calming breaths, "Center yourself" and speak lovingly to the children. Yea RIGHT!

Keep it in perspective. The children are still at a learning stage. Sitting and speaking *with* them, is very beneficial. Being the larger individual in our homes, we stand over the child, towering, shaking fingers and scolding. We've all mastered the technique of letting the veins bulge out on our temples; it has that added terror when we want our way. It's not that much different than the tantrum of a small child is it?

When you discipline the children, don't tower over them. Imagine you are ten years old; 80 pounds soaking wet, and you have Karl Malone (a 6' 9" muscular basketball player) towering over you in rage. You don't know what this person is going to do. When angry, it sounds as if he is speaking a foreign language! All you want to do is agree, to *whatever* it is he is trying to say! Your life may well end right here and now. "For gosh sakes, they won't need to bury me, he's going to pound me into the ground!" Kids can feel this same fear when you are angry with them.

Rather than towering over the child, if age appropriate, get down on one knee at least. Put yourself at their level when you speak with them. Put an arm around them and speak slowly and calmly. We have our personal space, but we love being with our children. We don't respect that space around them. We want to be *in it* with them. If they seem nervous or uncomfortable with you in their space, respect that. Allow them room to breathe as you administer the discipline. I've often told my kids they are lucky I allow them to breathe, but I'm only kidding!

My contention has always been that our world may be in such a sad state of affairs because spankings have been outlawed. I'm not so certain I was right on this one. I don't spank, or at least haven't had a need in years. But, if you feel you absolutely *must* spank, follow an old adage I heard once. One swat on the seat of the pants is discipline, anything more than that is for the adult. It's not necessary to injure a child; you merely need to get their attention *when all other methods fail*. Do this *only* when you are calm and have your temper at ease. If you have developed a relationship, as you will find outlined in this book, spanking will not be necessary.

From the time my son Camden was young enough to understand spoken words, if he was getting a bit wild or out of hand, all I would do was calmly say, "Cam," and as he looked at me, I would shake my head subtly. He would get the message and my perceived inappropriate actions would immediately stop. This was the bond we had developed.

Excessive discipline is not only illegal but is also child abuse. It squashes their self-esteem, kills their creative thinking process, destroys their spirit, and is completely counter productive to raising a responsible open-minded child. On the other hand, a child with *no discipline* will find life in the real world very difficult. *Consistency* again is critical. It can be very confusing for the children when we send mixed signals. We think we are consistent, as married parents. Having an open and honest discussion with children, when not in a disciplinary situation may convince you that you are not seeing things the way they do.

In my years training both horses and dogs, the secret to training either was to manage them but not break their spirit. A horse or dog with no spirit was nothing more than a flesh and blood robot without a mind. All that is required to training a horse or dog is to understand what they are thinking. They instinctively *know* what to do. Getting them to understand what *you* wanted them to do sparks the conflict.

To ride a horse that is manageable, yet still be able to feel his wild spirit as his muscles twitch beneath is an exciting ride for anyone! I hunted on my horses for weeks at a time in areas deep in the wilderness areas, usually alone. A horse with no spirit would have never survived if I had been injured in the remote country. I depended on him to get me out!

Children are no different. They need to understand rules, and rules are also made to be broken. The desire to be creative and spread their wings is strong. They will test your limits to see what is allowed and what is not. They know right from wrong, but getting them to do what you want, when you want is a challenge. Be clear, precise, and consistent. This will help them in their future lives, working, building their own families as well as allow them the freedom to think outside of the box. They may surprise you with their accomplishments at a young age.

In my personal experience, I get grouchy, snappy, etc *not* from what the children are doing, but because of outside pressures at work, financially, with the ex, etc. The child is the trigger that sets off the bomb. Keep it in perspective when you feel that tension building. This is a good time to get out of the house for an outdoor activity. Getting into nature is very calming and you will see an immediate change in the children's temperament.

You also have the opportunity to express your personal beliefs concerning all things. It's important if you are spiritual to let them know what your spiritual beliefs are and why.

In recent years, The Dalai Llama toured the United States. Those attending his appearances asked if they should quit their religion and join his, he would always say, "No," understanding that their religion worked for them. When asked for the most beneficial spiritual advice he could give to people, with all of his wealth of spiritual knowledge and experience, his reply was simply, "Be a good person."

Certainly no matter what our spiritual beliefs, I think we all want our children to grow to be a good person. The Dalai Llama in his first reply taught tolerance for other beliefs and religions. There was more than one right way to believe. In his second, he expressed the simplicity of true spirituality and the desired result. "Be a good person" can be taken to so many levels and is something we can all work toward for the rest of our lives.

Your children (hopefully) *are* good people. It's your duty not to screw that up! That would be the thing a bad dad would do. Shame, shame…

Assuming we don't want to be the bad dad, how do we *keep* our children good people? A lot of what children learn is taught by example. They will learn to speak from love and kindness, even when they are angry, when they see you do it, and repeat that example *consistently.*

They will learn *honesty* from you, honesty in all of your dealings. When you do something honest if you are presented with a choice of being dishonest, don't make a big deal of it. Explain you were given one choice, the honest one. We all like to think we are honest, make certain in your child's mind it's always that way. I learned this in the same way, by example. My father is as honest a man as can be found. I've learned it from him, and I will pass that legacy to my children. I don't doubt he learned it from his father. Grandfather was also a wonderful man and a grandfather.

You *are* building a legacy with your young ones. The things learned in your home together are memories to last their entire lives. Make no compromise for poor ideals. Be clear they have choices throughout their lives and you will do your best to help them to make the best choices.

Never miss an opportunity to talk with your children when it comes to *big* things. If we are always going on and on with something trivial, soon they develop the tune out and finely tuned out mode. You will know when it's happening, the eyes become glazed, the head cocks to one side. A little drool trickles from the corner of the mouth. Hey, you *know* this look! Speak with honesty, integrity, and always keep your word. They'll be in the moment with you. Children learn from your words, they learn more from your example. Don't think they will miss a thing! They will catch it all.

If you should you find yourself in a situation of making a wrong choice (and your children know it), make every effort to rectify the situation immediately. Make them aware the situation shouldn't have happened and you have done all you can to correct it.

Next we're going to discuss something we shouldn't have to discuss, but we are in case anyone has missed it, that's visitation.

Have regularly scheduled visitation with your children. And stick to it with great commitment! Again, children learn by example. Your word is your bond to them. It doesn't work like, "My word is my bond when it's convenient for me." Your word is your bond period.

If you do not have regularly scheduled visitation, get it. If the court does not allow it for some reason, do *everything* in your power to get it, no matter how long it takes. I cannot stress the importance of this enough. Do whatever you must to see your children regularly. It may mean cleaning up your act, it may mean some life changes for some, it may be as simple as scheduling it with the ex, but do it. Do it now.

When you have regular visitation with your children—do it. Be at your appointed time *on time*. Waiting a few extra minutes for someone they love, to a young child will seem like an eternity.

Ever notice as you and I get older, a year isn't as long as it used to be? I have a theory on this that I think is very interesting, even if no one else does. When you are ten years old, one year is equivalent to one tenth of your life. When you are 20, one year is only equal to one twentieth of your life. When you are 30, one thirtieth of your life etc. When you get to be my age, almost 50, one year is a small fraction (one fiftieth) of your life. Time goes very quickly. Forget one day, gee whiz, I can go through a day, blink and completely miss it. For you youngsters this is what you have to look forward to!

So if a child has to wait an extra ten minutes, let's not discuss an hour or two, waiting for you to show up, and you are a fun dad so they get excited, time passes s o s l o w l y.

Don't keep them waiting. Let them learn from your example, when you say you are going to do something, that you are dependable, that you will be there for them, not only when it counts but *always*.

Being there for them when it counts is going to mean nothing if you aren't there for them when *they* feel like it counts.

Family time is important. Your family may be a bit smaller, but you still have family. Set aside these times and let nothing, not work, not previous engagements, not commitments to anyone else, get in the way of your family time. Sure, emergencies are unavoidable, a car accident for instance. Your children will understand, and they will know if you are a person that *always* has emergencies or if you are a man of your word.

I grew up in a small town many years ago obviously, and in the old days we literally would make a deal, for a car or a home with nothing more than a handshake. This was law as far as we were concerned. I'm not discussing only children's deals. This was the law in the adult world too. You could count on the fact that if something was promised on a handshake; it was as good as done. No excuses, no "outs" or "do-over" it just *was*.

Your little ones expect to see the same from you in your dealings, with them and with everyone. My father is *still* from this old school I'm proud to say. If he tells you he is going to do something, it is done. Never have I known him to go back on his word or a promise, and I never expect I shall. It's completely against his nature. It would be his undoing to break his word. Give your children the same and teach them that you expect the same from them. You will not be disappointed. They will have much more wonderful lives for having this one quality.

And of course your word is your bond with your ex also, if you tell her it's going to be done, do it. Avoid arguments and excuses. See that it's done. She will gain a great respect for you, for this at least.

Children are being raised in a different world than we were. The roles today between men and women are much closer today than we have ever known them. Teach them to live in this world. Communicate they can do anything and be anything they want when they grow up. Perhaps they will meet their goals before they grow up. Labels for men's jobs or women's jobs don't exist; they are only jobs.

When the children help in the kitchen, have them set the table. Teach each child to cook, and do dishes with you. The girls can be the servers for the meal; the boys can bus and scrape the dishes. Switch these roles often. Simple tasks like this will instill the non-separation of roles deep in their minds.

I certainly wouldn't want my daughter turning down the CEO position of a company because she was taught to serve the dinner rather than clear the table! Now is when you teach this.

You are not alone in raising your children! In many cultures the belief remains, "It takes a village to raise a child," and it's very true. Everyone in your town may not directly assist in raising your children, yet countless family members and friends, teachers, grocers, employers, doctors, and clergymen play a very direct role in the raising of your child.

From the bakery worker who rises in the wee hours of the morning baking doughnuts and breads to the police officer patrolling your neighborhood late at night, the commercial fisherman setting his lines at sea, and the farmer planting his crops in the field as he peeks at the sky, for signs of rain, all will have an indirect hand in caring for your child. They also help provide you with the necessities of life! In our day-to-day pursuit of our dreams, we may lose sight of how connected we are as a society.

We as a people have decided to form societies as a very sophisticated form of division of labor. This is a great thing! Your children will be subjected to a diversity of opinions and cultures as you were, when you were raised (and still are today!). You will make it through this, learn to look for those resources in other people and in positions that will directly affect your children, they will be highly beneficial.

Along with the police officer, one of your responsibilities of course is to be a protector to your children. The newspapers and media have been filled in recent years with child abductions, and some horrible tragedies brought upon our innocent wee ones. It makes me physically and emotionally ill when I see these reports. Sadly, the majority of these perpetrators are males.

Your job as a dad, and as a member of your community is to also be a protector for *all* children. Should you witness an injustice being committed against a helpless child, it's your responsibility to intervene. Hopefully, you won't have to prevent some child's parents from committing an injustice, but it does happen.

Be mindful of children when you are at the park, make sure they are safely playing, hopefully with their parents nearby. A male presence will deter predators. Be watchful and vigilant to all adults in the area. Play a game in your mind, matching up parents with children, by their actions and communications.

Be smart; don't judge discipline as wrong, unless it is beyond the bounds of safety. At the same time, don't be overly concerned with the legal ramifications of stepping in where you don't belong. Too many people do not want to get involved. Predators rely on this fear, and they prey on it. It's better to have a few legal hassles, than have someone's child missing or dead. Should you act prudently and non-violently, I think you will find most courtroom judges will weigh heavily in your favor. Use your best judgment when your intervention would be appropriate. When a child is in danger, be prepared to act, if only a simple cell phone call to the authorities.

Twenty years ago, when Danica, one of my older three girls was two years old, they had come to visit at my home in a neighboring state. I was uneducated when it came to young children. I was a dolt, but I was willing to learn. I only hoped one of them wouldn't be seriously injured while I was on my learning curve.

We had gone to the swimming pool in our apartment complex; it was a nice sized outdoor pool. I took the opportunity to sit and relax while they played in the water. These water wings the little ones wear were not very well known at the time, and I hadn't taken the care to buy the little one a flotation device.

No, I didn't toss her into the deep end and go have a seat in the lawn chair. I could see she had a healthy respect for the water, so I let her play on the steps, which weren't terribly large, and splash her feet. I delighted, as she became a bit more confident with the water as she would take another step down, and as I was getting up, she would see me, and plop her little bottom on the step and continue to play. It was as if she was thinking, "Uh oh, here he comes to stop my fun." So it went one step at a time. As I sat chatting with one of the mothers, I was watching her, but probably not as intently registering what she was doing, as I should have been.

She did it; she took the final step into water that was over her head. I bolted from my chair and ran to her aid as she desperately tried to keep her mouth above water. It was odd though at the same time, she seemed to be thinking, "If I could touch the bottom with my hand, I could push myself up." So she was reaching for the bottom and trying to get a breath at the same time.

This all took place in only seconds, but I remember it so vividly it seemed longer. It struck me as I was making my mad dash she made no noise! No splashing, no crying out, nothing that would have drawn my attention to this babe in trouble, if I had not watched it happen. She was so tiny, and so fully submerged, she was not able to reach the surface to splash, and her mouth was so occupied trying to get some air, she wasn't going to call out!

Watch your little ones carefully. They do some things without thinking of their own safety. After all, my daughter had never been in this predicament before, and Dad hadn't cautioned her, how was she to know she couldn't breathe under water?

I've never claimed I was the sharpest tool in the chest, and you would have thought I would have learned my lesson from this episode, but I didn't.

Different day, but on the same visitation, the kids wanted to go out and play. The two older ones weren't old enough to watch their younger sister, but it was a safe neighborhood. The pool had a fence around it and how much trouble could she get into? Those are the thoughts of a dolt. I let them out to play. I was lazy, doing something unimportant around the house. I did go check on them a couple of times.

Soon the older one, Shiloh, came in. I asked, "Where is your sister?"

"She's with Kiley," (her other sister) came the reply.

So in came Kiley not long after. "Where's your sister?"

"Oh, she's with Shiloh."

Alarms went off. As I said, I may not be the sharpest tool in the chest, but I'd like to think I have a higher IQ than a can of fishin' worms.

Out I went as I encouraged Kiley to find her older sister and begin searching. I headed straight for the pool of course, thinking the worst. I got to the pool and it was quiet, I took a good look all over the bottom of the pool.

I found only one middle-aged gentleman and I asked if he had seen a toddler come by, dressed only in big brown eyes and a diaper.

He pointed off toward my apartment and said, "Well she still has the brown eyes, but I think she lost the diaper." That would be her! She hated wearing that diaper! I thanked him as I hurried off and asked if she came back by, to grab her, if I couldn't catch up with her, I'd be back to check with him. Not too smart I'll admit, but I wasn't thinking clearly. Approaching the IQ of the can of worms.

I ran back to the apartment, no kid. I found the other two, but only two. They couldn't find her. Ok, it was time for some rational thought. Some two-year-old rational thought.

I thought, *Ok, if I were a two-year-old, where would I head? The pool?* Checked that… We had no playground, I had checked everywhere else I could think of, at least everywhere except where she was.

I lived in a complex of apartments you would go into the entryway, to the first level of apartments, and upstairs to the other two levels. The thing was, all of the entryways, and stairs, and doors looked the same. My apartment was on the end one. A two-year-old may not put that together.

I ran to the entryway next door, up the stairs to where my apartment would be, if I lived inside of that entryway. There she was with her little fist, banging on the door-yelling "Dad!"

"Dan!" I exclaimed. We always have called her Dan for short.

As she turned to see me bounding up the stairs, she looked confused and scared. She didn't seem to understand what I was doing on that side of the door! I picked her into my arms and carried her home. She held me oh so tightly.

If God forbid some child should be abducted or missing in your community, do all you can to assist in a search for that child. Time is of the essence in bringing these children back to their parents safely.

As the children get older and they reach that puberty age, it's time for the "sex talk." It's best to have the ex do the talk with the female children as the child will be more comfortable, and so will you. If the ex is not available to do this for any reason, certainly another grown female that is close to the child may be appropriate.

You have the privilege of doing this with your male children. *NO, I'm not going to tell you what the talk involves! Other* resources exist for that. Keep in mind your sexual actions in the past are going to speak volumes over the words you will express. Be discreet.

A few guidelines that may help the talk go much more comfortably. How do you know when it's time for the talk? When a child begins to understand the differences between the male and female body, it may be time for the talk. It's important to find out what they know, before you will know how much you want to reveal. Certainly their age and maturity level needs to be taken into account.

When it comes time, prepare with a comfortable setting. A place the two of you can be alone and reasonably undisturbed. The child's room may be the most comfortable for them. If they share a room, your bedroom may have to do. The atmosphere is tremendously important.

The tone of the conversation is also going to have a lot to do with your child's level of receptivity. Make it serious but still a bit lighthearted. Making it too serious may frighten your child away from any form of intimacy in the future, and certainly into having any serious talks with you in the future! Let them know that when the time is right, it's one of the most wonderful things that they can experience. If it's not the "right" time, it can cause a lot of trouble!

Explaining things to your six-year-old for example, the details of course may be very sketchy. explaining the difference between boys and girls, and the most basic physical differences may be enough to satisfy their curiosity, and paves the way for future discussions of the subject. When your child reaches nine or ten, it may be time to go into more detail. When you see them a bit red-faced and embarrassed, lighten up a bit. You may be giving them more than they want to hear, you may be giving them what they need to hear. Be sensitive to what they are feeling.

A bit of humor is certainly ok and helps to lighten the mood. explain it all clearly use the proper terminology, but don't get into medical terms if you can avoid them. Clarifying some of the slang or profane terminology used by some of the friends he may one-day experience, may also help to clarify things. Help him understand why such derogatory terms are inappropriate.

Take the word *bitch* for example. Explaining that a bitch is the proper term for a female dog that has had puppies, and is not an appropriate term for a female acting out of the norm. The term is disrespectful to all females and reflects more on the person's intelligence using the term than it does on the female.

The word *fuck* is another example. It refers to what should be a very beautiful act, and degrades it to something less than an animal act. Something I ran across on the Internet said the word originated from an old English term

"Fornication under Consent of the King." Whether this is true or not, I don't know, but it's an interesting interpretation. Since we have no Kings, the word certainly has no place in our vernacular.

Like it or not, these are the terms your son will one day be presented with, and it might be best that he get your interpretation up front.

Hopefully, you will one day let other females come into your life (shudder, I know). Sooner or later you will *want* this to happen. How do you best know when to introduce *her* to the children?

First, when you begin to date, speak freely of your children and your relationship with the person you are interested in. You may save yourself a lot of time with some women that may not be interested in having other children involved in her life. This is their right, and it's certainly ok. Don't play it up though, or use the kids as a bargaining chip for the female that loves kids. It is what it is with your children. Leave it at that.

As for when to introduce them, that's entirely up to you. It may be difficult for children to have other people constantly coming into and out of their lives. Children can become attached very easily, particularly when they may have lost mother all together. Be mindful of how any changes in your relationships may affect your children. Several dates may be in order before considering the introduction. Others may want to wait until engagement for marriage is being considered. Personally I wouldn't wait beyond that. What if the new woman and the children didn't get along at all? This could save you a lot of heartache and expense later.

The first few times you may want to speak of this new person as a friend, but you can only continue this so long before the kids get wise. Their little brains work very quickly and have an uninhibited imagination. You may want to begin with a fun activity for everyone when you bring your new friend into this world. Keep it discreet, be close but *sucking face* is a dead give away. If she has children, getting them all together for an outing can be fun. It can also be hectic, so consider this carefully.

After the initial introductions, don't overload the children with your newfound friend right away. Let your relationship with her grow independently as well as together with the children. If the kids take to her, let it grow at it's own pace. When *she* is present, it's essential that your children receive a great deal of your time and attention. They will feel slighted and may get jealous of your new friend if they seem to not exist when she's around. Keep that relationship centered around the children when they are present. After all, *she* is also going to be a big part of their lives if things go well.

If, on the other hand, the children can't stand her, respect this. Take *her* out of that world for a while and pursue the relationship independently. The children will resent time away from you that they feel they are not getting when *she* is around. It may not be anything personal against her. If they have valid reasons they don't like her, pay particular attention to those reasons. Warning! Danger Will Robinson! Danger! Danger!

Kids are very intuitive. If you have always been open with your children, hopefully by the time this situation appears they will be open with you. I trust my children's intuition tremendously. They have never been wrong yet (Of course I'm still *single*…hmmm…). This may be the opportune time to let your children know their feelings are valid, and they are important. How they feel they fit into this whole *family* is essential to the way everyone is going to get along. It may also be the appropriate time to ask the reasons they feel the way they do, without making them feel those emotions aren't valid, ask if they feel they have given the other person a fair chance.

When this situation arises, it's not necessary to dump the potential SO or W. Perhaps things were a bit too fast for the children. Again, take that relationship away from the children for a time. Let it grow, or you may find it ends, end of problem! Given enough time your children will usually adapt to the idea. The children want you to be happy, and once they come to the realization that you and W aren't going to make it, they will generally come around.

Children may hold hope that you and their mother may reunite. They may also simply be jealous of your time. Aside from these, if those opinions persist you may want to take a serious look at that relationship with the other woman. I had one ex girlfriend that seemed to think my daughters were her personal slaves when I wasn't around. Sadly, it took me too long to find out, when it came to light, that relationship ended immediately. It may have taken me too long to find out because my daughters didn't realize how important they were to me. They hadn't told me because they felt it would have only gotten worse for them. And I'll have to admit; my actions to that point may have left that question. The best thing I ever did for them and for me (and for the ex) was to end that relationship in no uncertain terms.

Keep in mind, their feelings may be valid and with an honest look at the other person, the children may be right and you couldn't see it! We all fall into the trap of having someone around that thinks we're special, and compliment us, make us feel good (let's *not* take this any further).

If you are one of the unfortunate ones, and it's not uncommon, the child may want the other person out only because they want to be selfish with your time, or your potential relationship with their mother. If this is the case relax, obviously work needs to be done with your relationship with the child. Time and understanding will usually take care of it. It's an opportunity to reiterate with your child that you still love their mom, but things aren't meant to be for the two of you. Let it sit for a time (weeks or months). Don't drag someone else into this situation when she and the children may end up resenting each other.

Don't try and force two opposing forces on a magnet together! It won't work! You will waste a lot of time and energy and may lose a lot of trust from your children. Let it work itself out (or not) in time. After all, we've always had people in our lives we do not like! We can't put our finger on why, but that is real as well. It simply *is*. Chemistry between two people is very real, no matter how many times you put sodium in water; a violent reaction will always result.

As a parent, another of the serious responsibilities we are endowed with is that of the *protector*. How seriously we take this role as dad runs from far right to left on the spectrum. We are given this responsibility because we are adults, and children put themselves in situations, or *we* put them in situations that are not always safe. Remember back when you were a kid, we did some things when our folks weren't watching that we wouldn't think of doing since we've become smarter!

It's up to you to protect your children in every way possible, and make certain they are safe. Let's take driving as one example. When I was young, growing up in my small town, it wasn't unusual for us to ride in the back of a pickup truck. No seatbelts, or seats, we rode in the back. Forty years ago, we didn't have all of the knowledge we have now, this was an extremely unsafe situation! Still, it gave me some wonderful memories, I don't know what the big deal was, but we always enjoyed it.

My children want to do this, and I've denied them this childhood pleasure by being *adult* and explaining the dangers involved. Not to be one to refuse my children completely of pleasures such as this, I'll choose to change the situation, to allow them this pleasure and do it as safely as possible. The next time we're camping, way back in the mountains by the old logging roads; I will put them in the back of the truck and drive very slowly and carefully. I'll also put a responsible adult in the back to supervise.

When I put my child in the car, certainly I've come to know a few of the safety concerns. If they are young enough, they have a suitable car seat, and it is installed on the seats per the manufacturer direction. My vehicle does not have a passenger side air bag, but that is also a concern with young children. An air bag currently is designed for adults. Should a child be hit with an inflating air bag, they may be seriously injured, possibly killed from the air bag alone. Little necks are not strong enough to withstand the blow. Manufacturers are working on a design that will be safe for both adults and children. Follow those design improvements closely.

Always buckle the children into safety belts. Have them in their seats and be sure they are buckled in properly so the seat belt can do the job it's designed to do. My children know it's standard procedure to get into the car and buckle seatbelts. They know the car will not move until this task has been done.

Kids can get restless in the car, which will always be the case I'm sure. You may want to entertain them by singing songs (one of my kids favorite things to do) or have coloring books to keep them busy if the drive is going to be a longer duration.

When I was younger, it seemed I drove much faster and was in more of a hurry to get to my destination. I was trying to get where I was going quickly, so I could relax! This doesn't make much sense as I look back on it.

As I've gotten older, I've decided it's not worth the rise in my blood pressure to be in such a hurry that I'll speed, or get upset with other drivers. Road rage is a big issue in many cities, and it can make us do some stupid things. I've been known to get upset when I was younger, calling other another driver a moron and worse. When my oldest was three years old, I had another driver cut me off as I expressed a big sigh of frustration. My daughter inquired, "Is that guy a moron, Dad?" I'd been mouthing off when I shouldn't have. They watch everything you do, everything you say, and they remember! This is the time to relax, try to arrive safely, and don't be distracted by other drivers.

We see some silly, stupid things on the road. Consider that you have thousands upon thousands of people living in your city and county, all on the roads, and we all have this little map in our head to guide us. It's absolutely amazing that all of these drivers, operating these several ton *weapons* at various speeds, and we don't have more accidents than we do! Patience is always required especially when our children are in the car. You can also practice when they are not in the car!

Consider if you get into some stupid argument with another driver, and maybe give him/her the one finger salutation. If the person has upset you enough to do this, what is your reaction going to be when he/she responds in kind? It's time to stop it before it starts. You do *not* want to be in a situation of trying to protect these little ones when some mentally unbalanced person decides to escalate a small situation far beyond a normal person's limit. It would be *scary* for you; it would be *traumatic* for a child.

I don't want to stereotype all women, but many mothers have a sense of *reality* when they have children in the car. They are not as territorial as we are. They don't do stupid things simply to protect their *pride*. It may require that you lose a little pride when another driver cuts you off or makes a left turn in front of you. Keep your head; make certain you all arrive safely. After all, that's the *real* goal when you are in your car, with or without the children, to reach your destination *safely*.

If losing face or some pride in front of your children worries you, don't let it. They know who you are. They won't give it a second thought. It may pay off when they become teens and begin to drive. They will know how to drive from your example. Your example in any of the above situations may save your child's life when they are driving and you are not around. Keep the big picture in perspective.

Driving is one of many examples that we are entrusted to keep children safe. I am not one to try and protect my child from every bump and bruise. I don't want to raise children that are sissies so I allow some things that might let get them bumped up a bit, if they think it's going to be fun to try. After all, they are growing up in a real world, one that is not always safe. They also learn to take responsibility for their own actions. If they climb a tree and fall out of it, they won't blame it on me or on the tree. They accept it and are not afraid to try again.

When I start getting a bit bored with my life, or am in a rut, I like to energize myself by doing something, anything, for the first time. Whether it's something as simple as going to a new restaurant, hiking in a new area, taking a skydiving lesson or taking a trip to a new part of the world, it gets the juices flowing again!

Because children are children, their lives are filled with firsts. Firsts are what being a kid is all about. From their first breath of air at birth, they begin a journey of new experiences. So many things excite them in those early years. The first time they roll over, the first time they crawl, things begin to take off with those first baby steps! Hopefully we have been present to experience those wonderful few "first" moments of any feat they've accomplished.

It's so important when your child experiences anything for the first time. The first day of school, their first puppy love, first sporting event, or first school performance. How sad must it be for the child that goes through these, time after time, with no parent present? I can't imagine the loneliness a child must experience, as they look out on the audience, or the crowd in the stands, seeing their friends parents and loved ones cheering them on, and not see a single familiar face to offer support.

By being as involved as possible in your child's life you will experience many new things with them. Share in their excitement, feel their energy of accomplishment. Let them know how proud you are of them. Much more will be "said" in that you experienced it with them.

When your child first learns to ride a bike, keep them in a safe environment. No rule says those first few turns of the bike wheels can't be in the safety of your own home. Let them become comfortable with the feel of the balance and coordination. Take them outside, to a place that's safe and coach them along, helping them become more adept at this new skill. Project forward, seeing all the places this new mode of transportation will take them in the coming years.

When they crash and fall, pick them up. Encourage them. This is what life is, falling down and getting back up, with renewed confidence!

Attend Parent/Teacher conferences, especially the first, but all of them are important. Your child wants you to be proud of them, and they also want you to hear from their teacher the areas you can help them with. They depend on you as their number one teacher. In our busy worlds, we sometimes rely on the schoolteachers much more than we should. The teachers have plenty to teach with school subjects, it's still up to us to teach the child basic life skills.

The child's first sleepover away from home is tremendously important. Sure they will spend nights with you, but the first night at friends, without Mom or Dad around can be a scary experience. Let them know you are available by phone to come get them if they need you. This is a great way to begin the process of teaching independence that is so important when they leave the nest. None of us would think of our toddler taking their first step, without our outstretched hands in a safety net, to catch them if they fall. So it will be with all of their firsts. As they grow, we will expand that safety net to allow them to test their wings, but we will always pick them up when they fall. We will always to help them up, dust them off, and send them on again with a word of encouragement.

Overprotection is the other end of the spectrum. Allow your children to experience, to "do" on their own, you must tolerate questions and offer support. As they come to rely on your shadow in the background, they will be confident in trying new things, in stepping out of the sandbox, exploring the world around them. Your child will learn a life without limits.

You may choose one day to expand your family by presenting your child with his or her first pet. Pets can be a pain to care for, but the trade off in teaching your child responsibility, gentleness for animals and nature, and the true love a pet will offer is well worth any price. A boy being trailed by his faithful dog is one of God's great joys. Such loyalty from both of them! And the things they must experience!

Pets offer another blessing many of us take for granted until we lose one of them so dear to us. One day a child's favorite pet may pass on. This is an example of the microcosm we all live in. Your child may have their first experience with death through the loss of a pet.

Psychologists and veterinarians agree it's essential to have a waiting period before purchasing the replacement kitten or puppy. The child needs that time to grieve, to feel the loss, to pay some humble final tribute to one they loved so dearly. Replacing the pet in the first few days or weeks does an injustice to your child and the new pet in your home. Give it a few months and let them have their time with their memories. You will know when it's time for another pet to come into their lives.

As parents sometimes we are in a big hurry to make their hurt go away. This doesn't teach them reality! "But they're only children!" Of course they are. Children will experience hurt, teach them to embrace that feeling, to appreciate the emotion of it all. It's perfectly normal to miss someone or something they love so much. But life will go on, and they will love again.

When another person in their life passes on, a grandparent perhaps, or god forbid one of their parents, they will be much more familiar with a sense of loss. They will understand it, and it's much easier to deal with a feeling they understand, than one that is foreign and appears so very tragic. If you get well into your life before you have to deal with this type of loss, it can be devastating.

When the child experiences their first funeral, know that funerals are for the living not for the dead. When I'm laid in that casket, I'm not going to give a cat's damn what's going on. I'm going to be too busy experiencing my new adventure! But the folks that knew me well, or anyone that passes away, need that time to grieve, to say goodbye. Studies show people that deal with loss well and quickly, live longer than those that don't.

I was privileged to have many years without having any relatives pass on, no one near to me died prematurely, or at all. Many years ago, I had one of my best friends take his life. He lived in a state other than where his family was. While I never met any of this man's family, I had heard they were not real pleased with where he was and the lifestyle he was living. He had a great life! But in all fairness they had no way of knowing that. Not long after he passed, his family flew to town, picked up his remains and left the state, with not so much as a "by your leave" for so many friends he had come to love.

I was a bit taken aback. I was accustomed to the fact that when one dies, we attend a funeral. We were left without that. I had a tough time dealing with that, and I didn't understand why. One night, it had become too much to bear. I opened two beers, as he and I had so many times, set a lawn chair out on the deck under the blanket of stars on a warm June night and I had a talk with him. I took the opportunity to say goodbye and relive the memories we had experienced together. This was my "funeral" for John, one of my best friends. It was all I could do, and all I needed. Do you think he cared? I don't know, but I imagine he pretty much had his hands full with his new journey. He never was one to sit around, to stew in his own juices; life was full of new things to experience.

We all have a need to say "goodbye" in our own personal way to someone or some pet that we loved dearly. Life is too short to grieve for long, but we need to remember all of the joy and love we had, then we may move on.

When your child is experiencing their firsts, take pictures where appropriate. Take a picture of your child with that first missing tooth, or performing in the first school play or Songfest. These memories only come once, get a record for their scrapbook.

Children can't be completely afraid of situations that are out of their comfort zone. I want them to evaluate what their limitations are. It's not unusual for my 11-year-old son to walk across a felled tree that may be eight or ten feet off the ground. If he falls, he may get a bit scraped or bruised, but how will he know if he can do it if I don't allow him to try? My daughters have no desire to cross that same tree yet and that's perfectly fine. They may one day, they may not, I *can* leave some decisions up to them.

One of my greatest rewards is when I'm taking the children back to their mother, and I hear, "This has been a good day." That warms my heart, knowing I'm at least making a difference. What greater reward than making a difference in a child's life?

ASSIGNMENT

Make a schedule for bed times, teeth brushing, etc. Have the children help with the schedule. They will have a sense of ownership and will be more likely to follow it.

Have a child safety seat for each child where it's appropriate. Have it examined or inspected if necessary. Your local law enforcement is more than happy to do this.

CHAPTER 18
FUN PROJECTS FOR KIDS

I long to be a child once again, to splash in puddles, to run in the rain and make castles in the sand. Not the adult castles I pursue most of my life. Rather a simple one that will wash away with the gentle surf on a summer's eve, wiping the beach, ready to build anew.

Walking on a beach one sunny afternoon, I happened across three beautiful children, building an ornate sand castle. The ocean was approaching high tide, and the waves crept closer to their construction as they worked feverishly to finish before the tides would surely wash away what they had spent so many hours building. I thought to myself, *Foolish children, what an exercise in futility!* I was none-the-less captivated by their attention to detail. I sat myself on the sand not far away to watch. Perhaps it was some hidden sadistic quality in me, perhaps it was my desire to observe life, and not interfere.

As the waves reached the sand castle, the children stood up, giggling, watching as the timeless cycle of the waves made a ruin of all they had built, soon smoothing it out leaving no trace of their efforts. I was surprised at their seeming acceptance of what was happening. They were not disturbed in the least that their beautiful creation was gone. Rather, they ran off, talking and laughing, up the beach, dropped to their knees in the sand, and began building again. They seemed none the worse for the experience.

I realized, these wonderful innocents saw something in the world that I did not. They saw the world as it is, not as it should be. They lacked the experience to know, that things could be different, if they only wished hard enough, or had worked their sand castle in a different place. Perhaps if they had built channels to divert the water away from their labors, their efforts would not have been in vain.

But I pondered, *Was my viewpoint more realistic than theirs? Did I spend entirely too much time in my life, trying to change the world, to fit my way of thinking? How wonderful if I could be as accepting of the world as it is, as they were?*

Realizing that some day in the not so distant future, everything I was building in my life would also be washed away, as the waves cleaned the sand of all human trace. How much more stress free my life would be, if I were to accept the ageless cycles of the universe! What an exercise in futility my life is, when trying to change the laws of nature! I witnessed, in that fleeting instant a flow to things, learning to work with that flow, rather than spending years of my life, trying to resist the inevitable. These marvelous children in their innocence had taught me a Universal Law.

Knowing the girls would be leaving the state with their mother soon, Michele and I planted some lemon seeds that we'd been drying a few weeks ago. She loves to do anything with Dad, when the other kids aren't involved. If dirt is included, so much the better!

This past week, my youngest daughters had come to visit me for their last weekend visit, before moving away with their mother, to start a new life, in another state. It was difficult for me emotionally, to accept this flow, though I did my best to be supportive of them and their mother, knowing that this could be a wonderful opportunity for all of us. As I dropped them off at home, and gave them last hugs and kisses, speaking words of love, hoping they would not forget me, they headed off up the drive to find their grandparents.

Michele, as always, skipped her way up the drive, carrying the last treasures I had left with her, including a piece of cornbread she had brought for the short drive home. As she saw the neighbor's goat, bleating a greeting to her through the fence. Squealing with delight, she dropped all of the precious gifts, grabbed the cornbread and began feeding him through the fence. Talking and laughing, she was completely in the moment. My heartstrings tugged a bit, knowing she had moved on, typical for her my little angel. Perhaps she hadn't grasped the entire concept yet?

On the contrary, Michele grasped the world "as it is" and took full advantage of every opportunity. Life is for playing, and nothing will cut into her time to enjoy every moment of it.

My attention was drawn to Sarah, older by three years, trudging up the drive, carrying their suitcase and jackets. She seemed to have the weight of the world on her shoulders, not having time for such trivial things as feeding cornbread to a goat. She, as I, was not "in the moment," she felt she was leaving her dad, she knew the work ahead of moving to another state, leaving so much of her family, friends, school, and church behind. How I wish I had taken more time to explain to her, the wonderful magic of finding new friends, making new "family" and all of the blessings it would entail!

Somewhere between the ages of six and nine, she had lost the innocence. Lost the mystical talent of seeing the world as it is, and gained the adult wisdom of attempting to swim against the flow of the Universal tide.

We had spent three days together camping in the mountains, laughing, floating inner tubes down the stream, fishing and splashing in the water. We sat up late by the fire, telling ghost stories, some silly, some terrifying, and some stupid. Each night Michele would curl up on my lap, and drift off to sleep, content with the way of the world. It was "our time" together, and it seemed more precious than the last several years with them, because I knew it was changing. Hell it had changed.

All but the memories seemed to fade, as I drove away, ever so slowly, peering in my rear view mirror, wanting to keep them in sight as long as possible. The tears and the ache in my heart faded the reflection in the mirror as I focused my gaze to the road ahead, and the long drive home.

After being involved in my children's lives so actively for 27 years, I knew my life was different. I would have more free time, yet I knew I faced hours and days of melancholy remembering the good times, longing again to hear their laughter, and feel their warm hugs and chocolate milk kisses. They would do a lot of growing up in their time away. I would miss the things I had grown accustomed to.

A few days later, the morning arrived when they would be packing the truck and leaving the state. I woke in my bed my first thoughts were of them, wondering where they might be. After rising, I poured myself a glass of juice and walked out on my rear deck needing the comforting embrace of the morning sun. As I sat sipping my juice, my eyes wandered to the flowerpot that Michele had planted the lemon seeds in. Peeking out of the soil was the first sprout of the little lemon tree. A tear came to my eye as I remembered her tiny little hands planting the seed with such care in the soil. How appropriate that it should sprout on this day of new beginnings.

Every morning I go out to my deck and check on her little lemon tree. A second has sprouted. I look at it as Sarah's tree, even though Michele planted it for her sister. It brings peace knowing they have left a little something for me, other than the wonderful memories.

I have some hair bands that they'd left and I promised to send them. I've changed my mind as they hang on the mirror of my truck, right over a little stuffed animal that Michele carelessly left on the dashboard of my truck. Maybe one day I'll return them, along with the lemon trees, but for now, I'll keep them.

Over the past few years, I had attempted to be as creative as possible with the kids, beyond the everyday routine, and spend some unique time with them. Many of the ideas I'll share with you, were of their own making. This unique way of thinking became ingrained in all of us, though I think it came easier to them, than to myself.

If your kids are younger, buy a pack of licorice, black, blue and red, and any other color that may be available in your area. Plant them in the garden. If you don't have a garden, use a screwdriver, poke holes in the lawn and plant them. Or do it in a planter box, or several planting pots. Invite a friend or neighbor over and have them take a picture of you and the kids in front or behind of your Licorice garden. Take it to the local film developer, have it blown up into an 8 X 10 (color glossy) and frame it. This isn't expensive; it's around $5 if they have one of those photo-enlarging machines plus the cost of a frame. If you are bold, have it blown up poster size to hang on your wall.

Let that photo serve as a reminder to you and the kids that life is crazy! Nothing is out of bounds when they come to Dad's house!

You will have serious times in your life, generally when the kids visit that's not the time. It *is* the time to be a kid again but be reasonably responsible regarding their health and safety. Use your imagination and have some fun. Invent your life together.

By the way, you may want to make a copy of the above photo for each of the kids. This may be passed through generations after they are grown and you are dead and gone, but will always be a reminder to them of the fun that Dad was.

Other fun projects: You can decide what is age appropriate:

For the young ones, gather the stuffed animals in the house and any other toy animals, take them out on the lawn and construct a zoo. You can use grass clippings, leaves, or sticks to pile up to make sections for the cages, walkways etc.

Find elephants and kiss them.

Bang on pots and pans, use different spoons, spatula's etc to make different sounds (no glass!).

Hug trees together, before and after you climb them.

Build a debris hut in the yard or in a nearby wooded area. A debris hunt is a tent built by survivalists to use as a shelter. It can be built anywhere, with any materials at hand. If you enjoy the outdoors, chances are your kids will also. Purchase *Tom Brown's Field guide for Children* at your local bookstore or online at www.trackerschool.com, it has a wealth of information for the children.

Build an igloo in the wintertime. Milk cartons with the tops cut off make great molds for blocks.

Walk in the woods, or by a river. Walk very slowly, check out everything, every bug, every bush, every flower, smell the flowers, taste the appropriate ones. You will be teaching your children a love of nature that will last a lifetime. And when you are walking and looking, watch what *they* look at. You may find you are missing things that they are not. They are very observant.

Buy a magnifying glass. It's great for the walks in the woods and by the river. It's great in the house or in the yard to examine the bugs up close. I once watched two ants for an hour with my kids, as the ants were trying to move a small rock out of their ant hole. The ants succeeded but were exhausted.

Teach them how to walk quietly when looking for game. Let them teach you how to walk with the maximum amount of noise when you don't want to see game. My kids like to run up ahead and hide to jump out at the appropriate time to scare me. They're not great at hiding; I can always spy them poking their little heads out to see how close I am. One of these days I'm going to sneak around behind them and give them a good scare!

Giggle often.

Take them to a nearby area, yard, park, river, or woods and gather things for a centerpiece for your dinner table or coffee table. Let them decide what is appropriate. You have veto power on dead animals.

Let them play dress up and go through your closet and dress as you, as they see you. Teach them to re-hang the clothes later. Good luck with this!

When my oldest girls were younger, it was a practice in their church to have "Daddy Daughter" dates as a church social function. When Kiley invited me to hers, it was a Halloween dress up affair. She had decided she wanted to go dressed as Daddy and Daughter with the roles reversed. I was of course mortified at the thought of dressing as a female, but I stepped out of my comfort zone, and with her help, put on a dress, panty hose, high heels and wig. Try *not* to get a visual on this! With my beard and mustache, I was one butt ugly woman. Off we went to her church social.

This took place in January, and it's cold in Utah. I learned a great respect for any woman that dresses in a dress, as my butt hit the cold vinyl seats of my pickup. Arriving at the church, we were greeted with much laughter, but it was all in good fun. We played several games with the kids and I also learned the impossibility of toppling backwards off of a chair and trying to keep one's knees together.

This date is still one of my daughter's most memorable times for us together.

Take lots of pictures.

Teach the boys how to pee in the snow. Teach the girls how *not* to tell Mom. I'm kidding! Just seeing if you were paying attention.

When outside walking, turn over a leaf or a flower petal, show children the intricacies of the details and how hard it must have been for God to create this. Show them and let them find for you, all of the wonderful complexities of nature, bee's nests, bird's nests, bird feathers, and the small details involved in each. A scavenger hunt can be fun and exciting.

Look on the ground and the trees for the tiny creatures we all overlook. The magnifying glass is useful for this.

Throw rocks in the stream or a pond. Learn to skip rocks.

Invent the family victory dance or shuffle to be performed at the end of each activity that was the best!

Make play dough (see recipes).

Support your children and encourage them in their activities. My son loves sports and particularly football. We've gone to most practices and all games together for the past two years. This is important to him and to me. The girls enjoy going along and playing with other kids, walking the dogs, and cheering for their brother. No matter what the activity, encourage them as they learn and grow.

Edette writes:

It can be financially hard to be a single parent, whether you are the one with the children or not. There are many activities you can do that don't cost anything or costs very little

You can put a blanket on the floor and have a picnic.
You can read stories.
You can turn on music and dance with your child.
You can go to the park.
You can go to the mountains, ocean, lake, etc.
You can visit free museums.
You can put a tent up in the back yard and sleep out.
You can move furniture around and lay blankets over chairs etc.
You can paint, color, and draw.
You could make cookies and give them to a neighbor
Rent a video and make popcorn.
Play house with them.
Play trucks with them.
Play hide-and-go seek.
Go for bike rides.
Go see Christmas lights.
Talk a lot to your children. Get to know them. Find out what they are doing.
Ask them how they feel about things.
If you have a video camera, make your own video.
Tape-record your children talking.
Run through the sprinklers.

Naomi writes:

Build an alien spacecraft out of pillows and blankets. Use kitchenware to create a command post for the ship.

Golfing. dads love to golf to relieve stress and to bond with the guys. Golfing with the kids while bonding is very rewarding. For children too young for the course, try miniature golf, they love it. Or try the driving range my children at ages five and six have enjoyed getting out and hitting a bucket of balls. You'll find a bucket can go a long way with a couple of children. Take the time to teach them the basics of the stance and the swing. My 11-year old son competed in our family golf tournament at the age of nine, the youngest ever and he held his own! He had a couple of drives that when we found the ball, I mistook it for mine! He can hit! Ok, so I suck at golf.

Some of the golf courses will allow young ones to play with you. Get a golf-cart as that is a long walk for a little one. If you have a par three course in your area, this is a perfect place to get them started and won't wear them out like the longer courses.

Take the time to have lunch at the clubhouse with them. The burgers or hot dogs are right up the alley for young ones, and spending time eating in something as exclusive as a golf club is a real treat for them.

Buy one of those little putting cups (electric ones) and leave the putter and a couple of balls out. Let them putt in the hallway or living room. This is a great indoor activity on a cold and rainy day. They'll enjoy themselves tremendously, and they'll soon be putting like pro's with a little of your guidance. Don't expect them to be perfect, let them have fun and enjoy something you do.

Going to the park is a great activity. Some tips, take water and maybe a lunch to have a picnic.

If I were to play with them at the park as long as they'd like to stay, I'd be exhausted! I'll generally spend some time playing with them, but will also take a chair and a favorite book along to read while watching them. This gives me some relaxation time, and allows them to spend more time playing than I would allow if I had to chase them around the whole time.

My philosophy is if they're grumpy, put them in water. I don't know if it's an instinctual thing with children, but most of them love water. Some of the best times with my children have been at the river in the wintertime. The water doesn't freeze in the river. They dress appropriately in heavy boots and snowsuits, gloves, hats etc, and are allowed to wade in water shallower than the tops of their boots. This never works, but it's part of the fun. We're close to home, and they can come warm up with hot chocolate when we're done. Kids are used to being in water in the summer time, my children think this is extra special because no one goes in the water in winter! Bathtubs are also great. In the summer go running through the sprinklers; get in the kid's pool yourself! Water parks are excellent if you want something more commercial.

I had the occasion to walk with my daughter (then six years old) down by the river after a snowfall. It was a beautiful sunny day. I had been explaining animal tracks when we came across tracks from one of the neighborhood cats, likely out hunting breakfast that morning. Sarah decided this would be fun to track the kitty. Off we went.

Cats don't concern themselves with going where humans are comfortable, and my little girl could duck into places I couldn't, but she kept right on that cat's trail. She followed him for over an hour and a half while Dad tagged along. We'd stop in the areas the cat chased some thing, as tracks would be all over the place. We would try and guess what it had been after, and whether it had caught the prey. We'd pick up the trail again, and off we'd go.

This is an excellent activity. It gets them outdoors and teaches them to be more aware of what's going on in their world, and perhaps you too! Of course we also ran across other types of tracks that we would try to identify, mice, birds, one great blue heron with huge tracks, a bobcat, several dogs, pheasants, deer, rabbits, and squirrels. If you're not familiar with the types of tracks, there are great books on them, but it's as much fun to guess with your child on what it might be, and how long ago it had passed by.

Given the electrical power problems we've had over the last couple of years in the west, it's not unusual for the power to go out, sometimes for several hours. This can be a scary time for children since it's something other than what they are used to. My children have come to get very excited when the lights go out. They know that it's time for a different kind of fun!

My children will go around and collect every candle in the house. They will come up with many more candles than I thought I owned! How do they find them all?

We light a lot of candles and out comes the book of fairy tales. This is essential equipment for the single dad. I use *A Treasury of Children's Literature* edited by Armand Eisan Copyright 1992, which we enjoy. You will find many in your bookstore I'm sure.

I'll light one tall candle to sit beside me, get out my reading glasses and begin to read the fairy tales. It's *so* important to do the voices! They laugh and giggle, and I enjoy this time so much. It is much too tempting when the power is on, to watch television or play the stereo. When the lights go out, it's time for us.

After the stories are read, we'll light one candle place it on a blanket in the center of the room and tell ghost stories. It's always a good idea to have some snacks around that don't require cooking such as cookies and milk, Kool Aid and cupcakes, chips etc. Save some for your emergency rations. If possible, make it something like smoked almonds or peanuts, that the children don't get every day. This makes the entire experience all the more cool.

Shut off the lights some night, light some candles, and get out the book. This is good old-fashioned fun, practiced by our parents or grandparents before electricity, radios and televisions.

We like playing games on the computer or video games together. When I first moved back from Colorado to be closer to my children, I had been away from them for a few years, only seeing them a couple of times a year usually. This is not something I'm proud of. We had grown apart in many ways.

I did one intelligent thing however, not knowing the importance of purchasing a video game player. I spent a lot of my time with the children, particularly my oldest who was ten at the time, playing video games. We had a particular game, one of those treasure seeking, puzzle solving games that we would play from the time we got up in the morning, until midnight many nights. The littler ones would join in the fun by going around and collecting the money for us when our funds ran low in the game. While this was a simple thing, (we ordered in lots of pizza and fast food) it provided a unique bonding experience while we were trying to become reacquainted.

We would work on a particular puzzle until we were exhausted. We would turn it off and go to bed. I remember on more than one occasion I could see the main character, running around every time I would close my eyes. I would sit and analyze everything we had done, and things we might have missed. I could stand it no longer, "Shiloh? You awake?" I'd ask.

"Yes," she'd reply.

"Maybe if we tried this and this and?" I'd ask.

"I was just thinking that Dad! Want to?" She'd answer, and we'd sneak back out to the front room while the others were sleeping and play some more. After all, Mom wasn't around to tell us no!

Nickelcade—In our town, Nickelcade is a place you can take the kids and has hundreds of video games. They all take nickels! The kids gather tickets and can turn them in for prizes. It's not terribly expensive, and the kids have great fun and so does Dad!

Some other ideas for your children follow. Some are expensive (i.e. Disneyland) others require little or no money (i.e. going to the park or walking in nature)

Disneyland

Lagoon (a local amusement park)

Fishing, we also trap crawdads while fishing

Hang out at the mall.

Play with friends by this I'm sure they meant their friends not mine

Circus

Concerts

Library

Hopscotch—let them teach you!

Snowboarding or skiing

Football

Basketball

Baseball

Jump rope

Singing, find a book of silly songs!

Taking pictures

Swimming at the local pool. If possible, find a favorite swimming hole in a river or pond. This is something I miss from my childhood. Swimming pools aren't the same!

Parades, car shows, fireworks, car derby's, mud drags

Going to the car wash. They tell me they love it.

Children's Museum

Art Galleries, some have children's areas.

Visit a Cattle/Dairy Farm. Horse ranches are also good.

Commercial Fish Farms are a great place to take little ones fishing. This doesn't require much skill for the little ones to catch fish, and they won't become impatient waiting for a fish to bite, as they come fast and furious! They will clean or filet your fish for you on site for a fee, and it is a great healthy way to stock your freezer with fresh fish. Licenses are not required for these in many states, the fish farm will be aware of the requirements.

By nature, kids love animals. If they don't, it's generally from a lack of experience with them. Anything you can do that involves animals, kids will usually take to immediately. These would include petting zoo's, the Zoo, Cattle farms, Dairy farms, Horse Ranches, Aquariums, Fish Farms, even the dog pound can enlighten your child, and you!

Jumping on a trampoline

Cheerleading (you *can* too!)

Dance

Tumbling

Making crafts (paper, glue and string)

Paintball in the woods

Use leftover photographs to cut out faces. Cut out coats, pants, shoes etc from magazines and glue them on cardboard. Attach refrigerator magnets to the back with glue and stick them on the refrigerator.

Christmas shopping (for dad) Traditionally, I will give my children $100, so they can shop for Dad. My extended family is a long ways away, and my tree is generally pretty bare. I will usually take them to a store that has a fast food restaurant inside, so I can eat while they shop, and I'm not far away, but out of their sight so they can shop in secret. I have been extremely impressed with some of the gifts they've purchased.

Christmas shopping (for each other) our folks used to turn us loose in a store before Christmas with a small amount of money to buy presents for our brothers and sisters. It taught me to stretch a dollar and to think of gifts my siblings would like.

Putting up Christmas tree and decorations. Make some of your own decorations, string popcorn, make ornaments, Santa's etc.

Make candles

Make chocolate covered bananas

Telescopes (magnifying glass)

Pillow fights

Play with pets

Lay a blanket on the lawn, watch the clouds and pick out the figures of animals, etc.

At night spread out the blanket and look at the stars. A simple book on constellations will provide a wonderful evening of star gazing for all of you. Telescopes are becoming less expensive along with guidebooks on the different stars, if this is something you and the children are interested in.

Have dinner parties! I have a lot of dinner parties for my single friends, some with children and some without. The children have the benefit of making new friends as well as having some of their old ones over regularly. It's a great social event in my house.

Achievement days are something that comes from my daughter's school. They will pick up trash, visit old people in homes, take cookies to the residents, etc.

Theaters. We don't go out to the movies but opt to rent movies. Going to a theater once in awhile is a great activity for a kid.

Christmas caroling

Growing crystals. Put sea salt in water, put it in walnut shells, let it evaporate, takes three days or more for crystals to form, depending on the humidity in your area. (Alum also makes good crystals.)

Grow avocado tree-—one simple plant to grow is an avocado tree. Take the pit and clean it off, put it in water for a few days. If you begin to see a little fuzz growing on the seed, take it out of the water (replace the water with clean) and use a soft paper towel or napkin to gently wipe off any gunk on the outside. Put it back in water. After as long as a month, you will see the brown skin begin to split. Once the outer skin comes off, you will see the seed split and a root and stem begin to grow. This can take another month or more. This is the time to place it in a pot with potting soil and water and let it grow. Water it as you would any other houseplant. My ex informs me however I won't get any avocados; apparently you would need both a male and female plant to produce avocados. How does one tell what sex a tree is?

Grow herbs for cooking.

Take children to your work to show them what you do. They tell me this is important.

Hunting

Horseback riding

Hay rides, remember these when you were a child! What a wonderful fall or winter experience!

Zoo

Play dress up. Make a video.

Watching videos, put blanket on the floor, make popcorn and snacks. Suggested viewing list
(My children are ages six-eleven, we all enjoy these.)

Shrek
Old Yeller
Finding Nemo
Beauty and the Beast
Treasure Island (the old Disney one)
Grease
Ice Age
Xanadu
Barney (my youngest one enjoys them all)
The Sandlot (this brings back some old memories of my childhood)
The Santa Clause (with Tim Allen)
The Water Boy (Adam Sandler, age appropriate)
Big Daddy (Adam Sandler, age appropriate)
Spirit (animated)
The Bear
Lilo and Stitch
Blues Clues (Ok the older ones don't enjoy this, but the youngest is addicted.)
Where the Red Fern Grows
Treasure Planet, a remake of Treasure Island
Return to Atlantis

Dumb and Dumber
The Prince of Egypt (animated)
Nature movies are great, *National Geographic* etc.

After picking the kids up for their Wednesday evening visit, I was driving down the road with my three young ones. The following conversation took place:

Dad: "Michele! Guess what surprise I have for you?"
Michele: (unimpressed) "What?"
Dad: "The movie *Spirit*."
Michele: "I don't want to watch it."
Dad: "Why not?"
Michele: "Because it's scary."
Dad: (laughing) "No honey, Spirit is the horse, the cartoon horse?"
Michele: "The one with ribbons on it?"
Dad: "No, he doesn't have ribbons."
Michele: "I don't want to watch it…I'll watch it when I'm eight."
I was laughing so hard I had to pull off the road.

Make a house out of Popsicle sticks and match sticks (glue) plant grass around it.

Blowing bubbles

Karaoke machine

A few weeks ago, while a friend's children were visiting, we saw the movie *Signs* on DVD in our house. For those of you that haven't seen it, one favorite scene in the movie is when the children make tall pointed hats from tin foil "so the aliens can't read our minds." My kids saw that and laughed and laughed. We had to pause the movie, break out the tin foil, make our own hats so we could wear them without fear of alien mind reading, while we ate popcorn and finished the movie. Before the movie ended, my friend (whose children were visiting) stopped in on her way to a party, she insisted she have a hat also to wear to the party she was to attend. She hadn't finished cracking up before she left for her party.

A few days ago, I received a new friend in the mail. For those of you, who received visions of a blow up doll, shame on you!

My grandson Braxton sent my new friend and his name is Flat Stanley. Braxton lives a long way away, and we don't communicate much, he may be trying to con me into a letter with this technique of Flat Stanley, but I'll let you be the judge. Braxton is seven years old. Following is his letter.

Grandpa Kevin,

I am doing a project at school studying regions of the U.S. I was hoping you would help me. I am sending Flat Stanley to stay with you for a while. Would you show him around and send him back to me dressed in an outfit that shows what activities he did.

If you could please take pictures of what he does and where he goes. Thank you very much for your help. I'll be excited to get Stanley back and find out what he did at your house. We'll put him up at school.

Love,
Braxton

Enclosed was a cutout of Flat Stanley dressed in shirt and tie, with black colored dress shoes. Included was a letter of introduction from Flat Stanley.

Hi! I am Flat Stanley. You will never believe what happened to me. During the night, the bulletin board in my bedroom fell on me and lo and behold, I was flat! I was even flatter than a pancake. This proved to be very interesting to me. I could slide under doors, catch art thieves, be a kite and be rolled up into a tube.

One day my dom and Dad sent me to California to visit friends. Airplane and train tickets were too expensive so I went by mail. I am now coming through the mail to visit you!

After I have visited with you for a couple of weeks, please send me back home with a note telling what I have been doing. If you go on any trips while I am visiting you, I would like to go along. If I do something special while I am at your house, could you please put an outfit on me to show what I have done or where I have been? Otherwise would you give my clothes some color please.

Please send me back to—
Name
Address
Etc.

Sincerely,
Flat Stanley

I'm not *completely* convinced I'm being conned into writing, but after all it's been awhile since I've written anyone a letter, and if he goes to this much trouble to con me into a letter, I guess I can go to some effort.

This weekend the kids and I will take Flat Stanley out to the Golden Spike monument, not terribly far from my home, and we'll set Flat Stanley on the railroad tracks (don't go there, it's too obvious) next to the final Golden Spike that was driven in the 1800's joining the East and West railroads.

We'll also get a picture of him with the old refurbished trains that run the tracks at the monument.

Next we'll drive a dozen or so miles down an old dirt road to one of my favorite places on the Great Salt Lake and take his picture. We will go to the spot where the water from the lake washes up on some large rocks, and the salt dries, leaving a coating one eighth inch thick that looks like cake icing, but is made completely of the dried salt and minerals from the lake. We'll take a small sample of that and package it carefully before sending Flat Stanley back to my grandson and his school class. No doubt on our journey we'll find some snakes or lizards that Flat Stanley can pose with for a picture. I hope he likes lizards and snakes!

Perhaps that evening we will bring Flat Stanley back home with us, and watch the movie *Signs* wearing our tin foil hats, so the aliens can't read our minds of course. We'll make a tin foil hat for Stanley and take his picture with all of us, wearing our hats. He can take his tin foil hat back home with him.

I may take him and the kids up to one of my favorite gold panning spots on the Green River. I'll take a picture of all of them gold panning and send back a small packet of dirt with a small gold pan for the kids to pan out. I'll 'salt' the dirt with a bit of gold of course.

This simple project will not only provide Braxton and his classmates with some interesting views of Utah, but will also give my kids a couple of days enjoyment in helping their distant nephew complete his class project. No doubt my kids will go back to school and tell their teachers of this project and perhaps one insightful teacher will continue the project for her class.

Continuing on with more fun projects for kids:

Plant a Row for Charity: I read on the Internet recently about a program begun in one community called Plant a Row for Charity. The idea was for those folks fortunate enough to have a garden, to plant one row in the garden, exclusively for a homeless shelter, or food bank, some organization that would provide this wonderful fresh produce for the needy.

Gardening is a wonderful activity for children. Children also have an innate sense, and closeness to other children of the world. I'm not going to give my ideas on where this sense comes from, but is more prevalent with children today, than when I was a child.

Spending a few hours a week in a garden with our children, and teaching them not only how to grow their own food, but to donate to those less fortunate will be lessons that will long outlive us.

When it's time to harvest the row, have the children help not only in the harvest but also in deciding which charity is going to benefit from your labors. Take them with you to donate the food, and visit with the folks at the food bank or homeless shelter or charity of your choice. Can we possibly imagine, if half of the people in this country that had gardens would use this method to help our countries needy, the impact this would have on our food banks? The happiness that good fresh produce would bring to those that are scraping to put together a meal. We would have much less food shortage and malnutrition in this country.

It might be wise to check with your local food bank or shelter and see what guidelines they may have on natural gardening, or chemicals, or what foods would be most beneficial to them.

I had the opportunity recently to take my ex and all of our younger children on a camp out to the mountains. As this was an annual event for us, we all looked forward to it very much. The highlight of the trip was to float down the river (stream) using inner tubes. This year, however, the water was quite low, making for a rocky ride for the kids and lots of bruises on the backsides of the adults. This was something we so looked forward to, and the children were disappointed it wasn't all they'd experienced other years. As the children toted the tubes up the old dirt road through the trees to try another bumpy ride down river, the ex and I were in camp cleaning up. We agreed the trip had been fun, and we'd have many memories. It still needed *something* to make it more memorable.

Being a resourceful single dad I still couldn't come up with an idea to make the river float more enjoyable short of digging a half mile long channel in the center of the stream. But I hit on another idea borrowing from an email I'd read on the Internet from some other creative parents. I grabbed a couple of bags of marshmallows from our supplies, grabbed the ex by the hand and headed off into the woods asking her to be my "lookout."

Well I went from tree to tree and bush to bush, while my ex kept an eagle eye out for the kids. I stuck those marshmallows on any little twig and thorn I could find. Surely she thought I had lost my marbles. When finished, I had four or five marshmallows left, and we high tailed it back to our picnic table to await the children's return.

Not long after, they came from the opposite direction, egos bruised as much as little bodies. "Well that's not much fun!" one of them said.

They milled around the picnic table, obviously bored. We were munching on the marshmallows, five weren't enough for all of them of course.

When they were gone, the question came that I was waiting for.

"Are there any more marshmallows?" Michele was the first.

"Yep." I replied, smiling.

She looked at me, sensing I was teasing "Dad!"

"Papa!" Garth chimed in.

"What?" I asked.

"Where are they?" she shouted.

I chuckled, enjoying my fun. "In the woods," I said seriously.

"No, Dad!" my seven-year-old wasn't going to be taken in.

"I'm serious, there's tons of them. We just picked these." Knowing they wouldn't buy this.

My son chuckled "You picked them?"

"Yup." I replied.

Sarah looked at me "He's lost it Cam."

They chided me for several more minutes, convinced I wasn't going to give up my horde of marshmallows. My ex was laughing.

"You didn't know that marshmallows grow on trees? Oh come on!" I said. "They only bloom once a year and this happens to be the day! We ran into them this morning."

"Sure!" all four said.

"Seriously, you take those grocery bags and walk up that path," pointing, "Oh about thirty yards or so. If I'm lying, I will let you all throw me in the river, and throw mud on me." I could hardly contain the chuckles.

Sarah grabbed the bags "C'mon Cam, let's go look so we can throw him in the river." So off the four went up the path, convinced I was lying, as I couldn't contain my roar of laughter any longer.

"If they are there though, I get to throw all of you in the river!" I called after them.

"Nu uh!" they called over their shoulders.

Minutes later, we heard yells and shrieks, "We found them, we found them!"

"Come quick!" Came another voice. The excited voices died off as they were busily picking their newly found treasures. It wasn't long after our laughter died they came racing each other up the trail eager to show us all they had found. (Caution, don't do this in an area containing bears for obvious reasons). They were so excited as the piles of marshmallows spilled out on the picnic table.

"Who'd have ever thought?" Garth said, looking at all of the marshmallow piles. "Whoa!"

"And they're so fresh!" My ex winked at me. "Much better than store bought ones!"

My eternal thanks to the parents that came up with this idea, though I know not who they might be. What a wonderfully creative thing to do with your children! God bless you! This certainly turned a so-so camping trip into something exciting for the children.

Keep your mind open when you are with your children. They will *give* you the opportunities to be creative.

I took the children to the river two days ago and they, as always, had to bring home a couple of rocks. I don't know what the fascination is with rocks, but most kids seem to have it. My daughter found one stone, the size of an old silver dollar (larger than these modern ones) that was in the perfect shape of a heart. She wanted to bring it home. I've tried to teach them some Native American culture over the years so the rule is they always ask the rock (stick, flower, whatever it may be) for permission to take them home before they can. It also adds to the game. She did, and as always, the stone agreed.

I also noticed her teaching her younger sister how to ask permission. That brought me back to the memory of when I first taught her, and she gave me a look like she thought Dad was ready for the padded room but did it anyway. So they do indeed pass things down that you teach them.

When we arrived home, she asked if she could paint the heart shaped stone. So we rummaged around the house and found some nice sparkly paints they had used on another project, and she painted it beautifully, another treasure to add to her collection of memories.

The next day, they wanted to go to the river again, this is very inexpensive by the way, and of course, the water draws them. On the hike, they all found some walking sticks, and they wanted to take them home. Again, they asked the permission of the stick, and of course they brought the sticks home with them. After all, the stick had probably used up it's life in the forest and would soon decay and return to the earth. If the stick has the opportunity to be useful in another way, and spend time with these adorable children, of course it's going to be grateful!

On the way home, they asked if they could fix up the sticks. Making walking sticks is one of my hobbies. We arrived home and got some sand paper, and my Dremel rotary tool. I had been given the opportunity to teach them how to use the tools and to work with the natural beauty of the wood. They also used the tool to carve their names into them. On the next visit, we will pick out some nice wood stain to preserve another treasure for long past the natural life of the stick in the forest.

When they are grown and have children of their own, they will no doubt take their little ones to a river, perhaps the same one. They will relate and relive the many wonderful memories we have had on our fun filled river walks, and they will undoubtedly notice the difference in how the river has changed. They may one day be involved in projects to preserve these natural areas, in hopes that other children may have the opportunity to grow memories, as we had along one of our natural waterways.

I learned all too late in life that my dad was one heck of a storyteller. He and my mother used to travel with an Air Stream Club all over the country and other countries. He would be invited on stage at their big rally to weave a yarn as big as Paul Bunyon and Babe the Big Blue Ox. His stories were always original, very animated and entertaining for the youngest of children to the eldest member in attendance.

Following in the family tradition, I developed a little tale I like to tell my children from time to time. The story is entertaining not only in what is said, but how it's delivered.

I adopt an old, slow southern drawl. It's extremely slow in fact. When I pause, which is often, it lasts five to ten seconds, longer if I'm in the mood, and it entertains them to no end. Maybe they think Dad lost his marbles, which also delights them. Following is the story, remember, long slow words and very long pauses.

"Ol' blue, he was one heck of a dog." (pause)
"He sure loved to hunt." (pause) "Yep, he did." (pause)
"Well one day, I decided I was gonna have some fun with ol' blue." (pause)
"So I come out of the house," (pause) "With my shotgun."
"Well ol' blue, he comes runnin' from behind the house," (pause)
"Seen me with my shotgun." (pause)
"He sure loved to hunt." (pause)
"Well ol' blue run out to the field" (pause)
"To flush up some birds" (pause)
"So I turned around, went back in the house," (pause)
"And I thought for awhile"
(Long Pause)
"So I come out of the house with my deer rifle." (pause)
"Ol' blue come a runnin' from the field" (Pause)
"Seen my rifle." (pause)
"Ol' blue took off for the mountains to scare up some deer." (Pause)
"So I went back to the house," (pause)
"And I thought some more."
(Long pause)
"Come out of the house with my fishin' pole." (pause)
"Ol' blue, he come a runnin'" (pause)
"From the mountains" (pause)
"Saw my Fishin' pole," (pause)
"He runs around the back of the house" (pause)
"I said to myself..." (Pause)
"Hmmm..." (Pause)
"After awhile, I went round the back of the house..." (Pause)
"Myself." (pause)
"Ol' blue was back there diggin' worms..." (Pause for laughter)
"So I figured blue'd had enough." (pause)
"Took him to the field to hunt some pheasants." (pause)
"An' ol' blue hunted," (pause)
"And he hunted." (pause)
"After awhile he stopped." (pause)

"A pheasant jumped up," (pause)

"So I shot him." (pause)

"Another one jumped up," (pause)

"Shot him too" (pause)

"Another one jumped up," (pause)

"So I shot him" (pause)

"Too." (pause)

"After awhile I thought *this is odd.*" (pause)

"So I went over to see what ol' blue was doin'." (pause)

"Well that ol' dog had chased a bunch of 'em down a hole, and was lettin' 'em out one by one." (pause)

"One day ol' blue died."(pause)

"He did." (pause)

"Shook me somethin' terrible." (pause)

"So I skinned him," (pause for laughter)

"Made a rug out of him." (pause for laughter)

"After awhile, the rug wore out." (pause)

"So I made me a set of boot laces…" (Pause)

"For my boots." (pause)

"And do you know to this day," (pause)

"When I go bird huntin" (pause)

"And come across a bird," (pause)

"Them ol' boot laces just point straight out!"

You'll get some laughs, especially the first time you tell this story. My son has had me tell it to people over and over.

I've found another great use for this story. I usually tell my girlfriends the story at some point in our relationship. If we begin to argue about something silly, and I'm not into arguing, I'll look at 'em and say…."Ol' blue, he was one heck of a dog…." (Pause) They'll invariably laugh and walk away, throwing their arms in the air.

Hey, it works! Well, with one exception…. if you're ever tempted to tell this story, and her name is Tina, and she has gorgeous long brown hair, big brown beautiful eyes…Don't even go there. She goes OFF at the mention of "ol' blue"! Can't figure it out. 'Course I never could (pause) figure Tina out either.

One great influence you can have on your child's life is to provide them with a diversity of activities. You may find things on the lists above that you've never experienced yourself. Too many of us get locked into doing routine things in our lives. They're the things we've been raised with, or have bumped into on our path of life. Many of us follow in the family business, or at least do something that may be related to our fathers and grandfathers chosen occupations. This doesn't seem to be as prevalent as when I was a child, but it still exists to a great extent.

Being alive involves not only going through our routine activities but in experiencing life and all it has to offer. Getting your child involved with a variety of experiences can be measured in many ways. Last evening one of my children's friends, Kendra, was visiting for the night. I had purchased some oysters, which I am passionate for, and my 11-year old son Camden has acquired a taste for. Kendra had never experienced a raw oyster. Through no prodding from us, she decided she would like to try one. This isn't something I'd recommend for those that have no interest. After a great deal of consternation, she sucked the metallic delicacy through her lips and into her mouth. She struggled a bit, not with the taste, but with the texture. After what seemed like an eternity, she swallowed it.

This simple demonstration is surely a foreshadowing of what is to come in her life. She was not afraid, at a mere 13 years old, to try something new, something out of her comfort zone. When you build enough of these experiences into one's life a child begins to spread their wings, try things they might not have tried otherwise, and will be well versed in many aspects of their lives. To a great extent, I think we owe something as great as our global economy to this type of forward thinking.

When my son was seven years old, I was preparing to take a short summer holiday hike into the mountains and invited him along, for his first real hike into the mountains. Well, his first with me at least.

I like to go into some areas that are not well traveled, to get away from the other folks out enjoying the wild. We had gone off the trail a bit on the opposite side of a stream from the well-worn hiker's path, following a small game trail. We were laughing and having the time of our lives. It was apparent he was enjoying this special time with his dad.

I was leading as I rounded a tight corner in the trail and came upon a small skunk, only a couple of feet away. He had heard me coming and had his tail over his head in the firing position. I took a couple of steps back, laughing, and carefully showed my son from a safe distance.

He went off on me! Which of course made me laugh louder. We found a route around and let stinky go about his business. We headed back to the stream and main trail as my little explorer continued to bark at me, letting his thoughts on this hike being a stupid idea be indelibly branded into my skull. I continued to enjoy his first experience in nature.

We crossed the stream and began making big tracks down the trail, as his badgering was beginning to get to me (still found it amusing though). I was walking through some bushes overgrown to the path's edge, still in the lead, when we heard the buzzing of a rattlesnake I had nearly stepped on! My son froze in his tracks. Silence, thankfully.

I wasn't terribly concerned as this wasn't my first experience with rattlesnakes. I picked up a stick and moved the leaves aside so I could best see where he was. I had shades of the Crocodile Hunter. My foot had to have been less than five inches from him when his alarm went off as I passed. Whew, close call!

I gently prodded the snake, he was only two and a half feet long as he uncoiled and started heading up the hill to a little burrow. All the while, he continued to send his warning to us. He politely slithered into the hole, and the rattling grew fainter.

I looked at my son, still frozen in his tracks, his mouth hanging open, catching flies I'd imagine.

"You were saying?" I asked, chuckling.

"Not funny, Dad." He was not amused.

I told him he was gone, and he was determined he wasn't taking a step in *any* direction until he was certain. I pulled back the branches and poked around with the stick, giving him a good view, as he bent down, straining to see every inch of the shaded ground, his shoes still apparently cemented to the ground.

He was satisfied. His tirade began! Oh my god was I going to get it!

"I'm telling Mom! What were you thinking bringing a kid up here?! There are snakes and skunks, and spiders and bees, and we could die up here! What makes you think this is fun?! This isn't fun! This is stupid! I'm telling Mom as soon as we get home! You are going to be in big trouble mister! You're crazy! You're going to kill me!"

By this time my gait had quickened, I wasn't sure if it was because I was fleeing from the verbal assault, or if I was afraid he was going to use up all of the oxygen before we got back to my truck. And I heard it *all* the way home.

When I had him back safe in his mother's arms, he regaled her with a tale of survival unmatched by the greatest tellers of Tall Tales.

She asked me, "How big was the snake?" as she shot me a sideways glance.

"Oh, it was a baby! It was about (I held my hands a foot apart) that big." I couldn't help but laugh.

She knew me better. She gave me The Look, but it was his word against mine.

"Nu uh Dad! He was huge!" as he held his arms as wide as they would go.

"You didn't even see him!" I reminded him. I looked at the ex. "He was a bit scared." Whew! I would have rather gone back and faced the rattler.

So went my son's initiation into the wilderness. Do you think that was his last foray into the wilds? Not a chance! Next time he was invited, he was in the truck in a flash. He was still a bit cautious of course, as he should be. After all, his Dad didn't have the sense God gave sheep.

Two summers ago we had the opportunity to take the kids, my girlfriend at the time, and her children up a canyon neighboring the one with the snake, to see a waterfall.

I may have overestimated the trip for some of the young children, but have to admit, I was amazed at how well they did! They were troopers; they never complained; they hiked like mountain goats, and it was a long hike! On the way down, three of the girls were leading the way, followed by my son, my girlfriend and myself with the little ones. One of the girls in the lead let out a shriek, turned quickly on her heel and was beating feet back toward us as fast as they could, yelling "Snake!"

What did my son do? He was heading for the snake as fast as his legs would carry him! It was a narrow trail and sure enough, they all met head on in a tangle of legs and arms as they all collided, all determined to get to the snake or back to us as soon as possible!

My son has obviously outgrown his fear of snakes and most of the things we've run into. He has a healthy respect for nature and the wildlife.

By providing your child with a variety of activities, you'll likely stumble on one, or several that your child has a great interest in or a talent for. The hope of course is to find something hidden deep inside that spurns an awakening. Something that provides them with a creative outlet we may have never suspected.

This type of diversity provides many things for your child, things that aren't apparent on the surface. By experiencing many things, they will have a wide range of activities to choose from when they get involved in hobbies. They may find the line of work they would love to do as an adult, or have talent for providing them with a great future.

Most of us have met someone in our lives, maybe at a party or social gathering, or in our place of employment, that appears to have a wide range of knowledge on most any subject. Some of course have an opinion on most anything. Sometimes they have no first hand knowledge of most subjects, but rather they long to be included in the conversation or to be accepted.

I'm referring rather to those people that have experienced a great many things, have a very diverse background, are well read, and well experienced in all aspects of life. These folks have a great passion for life; they are generally quite popular with the crowd and have a terrific self-image. They don't generally have problems fitting in with most any crowd and are very appreciative of any new experience.

Being aware of the line of work our friends or acquaintances are involved in will provide many opportunities for getting our children involved in various activities. You may have a friend that is a policeman, fireman, doctor, nurse, artist, civil employee, fisherman, dock worker, autoworker, etc. Many times these types of jobs are open to having young ones tour their facilities, and learn of their chosen vocations.

By getting your children involved in a variety of interests, you will likely enjoy the experience as much as they do. You will provide a future for them beyond any college education.

We've talked of doing fun things with kids. Be careful not to fall into being a Disneyland Dad. Opportunities abound to experience exciting things with your kids but make sure there is a happy medium with those that are no cost, or at least inexpensive, mixed with the occasional spending spree. Be sympathetic to the ex, she may be struggling to make ends meet, and every time the kids come back from Dad's, all they say is what you did and how much money was spent. She may not have the money or the time to do all of those fun things with the kids. Appreciate what she is going through.

When someone does something nice, selflessly for us, we will return the favor. When you take the children home, just ask the ex, "Why don't you skip cooking tonight? Why don't you take the kids out for dinner tonight, on me." Give her a few dollars; even if all you can afford is fast food. When she pulls her jaw off the floor, she'll be grateful for a night off from the cooking and after dinner dishes. Better yet, bring dinner with you when you take the children home either as a surprise, or let her know ahead of time so she hasn't spent the day cooking. This will be a nice way of showing your ex you appreciate that she's taking care of *your* children. If she doesn't seem to appreciate it, keep doing it, she will get the idea.

When we show appreciation, it makes it easier for others to express appreciation for the good things we do.

ASSIGNMENT

Make a commitment to do something new often with your children. Pick out the craziest thing you can think of, or use some of the ideas above for inspiration. On your next opportunity with your kids, let yourself be a kid again. For a few hours or a day, shirk all of your responsibilities of working, paying bills, shopping (prepare ahead), and be a KID again with your kids. Do something completely crazy (but reasonably safe). Let yourself go back to when you were 10 or 11, when life was simpler. All of the other problems can be handled when you get back. Give yourself a break and visit a much happier time!

Don't let this be the last time you pay that visit to your child hood.

Get some one-on-one time with each of your children. If you have more than one child, it's important for them to have time alone with you. Do this on your off visitation days, take them to lunch, or on a hike, or to a movie theater. Don't let it cut into your time with the other children, but make it an extra.

Following are a couple of simple projects, foot, or sitting stools for your children. To be politically correct, if you are not carpentry inclined, with a few simple tools, your and your children can build these stools. These are items that with a little simple care can be maintained throughout your child's life and perhaps passed on to their children.

My Uncle John sends the first. This is one I had as a small child, and the memory of my red stool has stayed with me until today.

My Uncle John writes:

Uncle Johnny's Stool:

These boxes are real easy to make. I get a 12" board of white pine, and it takes 4 feet for each box. I make them in sets of 4.
The 12" board is really 11 5/8" so this is what you want to cut 3 boards to. The seat board should be cut 11" to fit in the space.

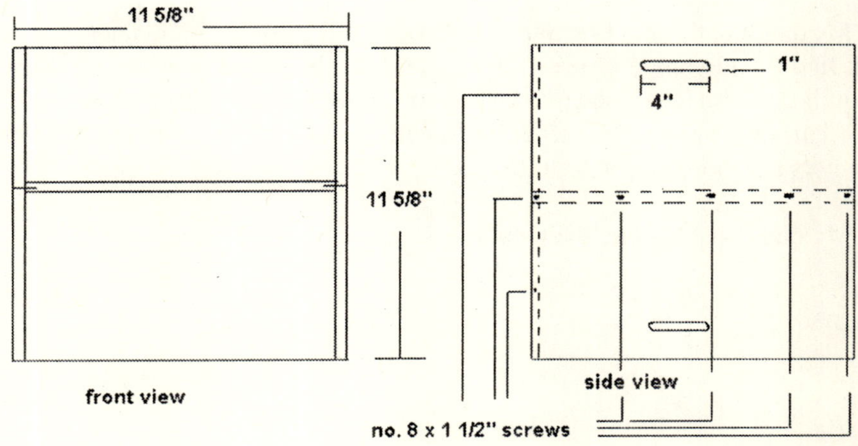

The paint job is up to you. I think it's neat to paint each surface a different color. (Author's note: my children call this a rainbow chair) It's a pain masking but looks great. Also one color per box is nice.

I'm using 2 of them as shelves in my bathroom since our grandkids are too big to use them. I don't know where the other 2 are. They must be around somewhere!

I'd like to send my special thanks to my Uncle John for sending these plans along to be included in the book. Build these and the smaller children will have a stool to sit and watch television, they'll have something sturdy to stand on in the kitchen while helping or watching, or reaching up into cupboards to get a drinking cup. You may find it useful for reaching up to top shelves, changing light bulbs on ceiling lights etc. These have so many uses; I can't begin to list them all.

My dad sent this next set of plans. Though this stool is a bit fancier, you'll still find a wide range of uses for it around the house, as will the children. They'll stand on it to reach into cupboards, to look in the mirror while doing their hair or brushing their teeth, or to help in the kitchen when the kitchen counters are too high for them to reach.

My dad calls this one the Grandpa Stool:

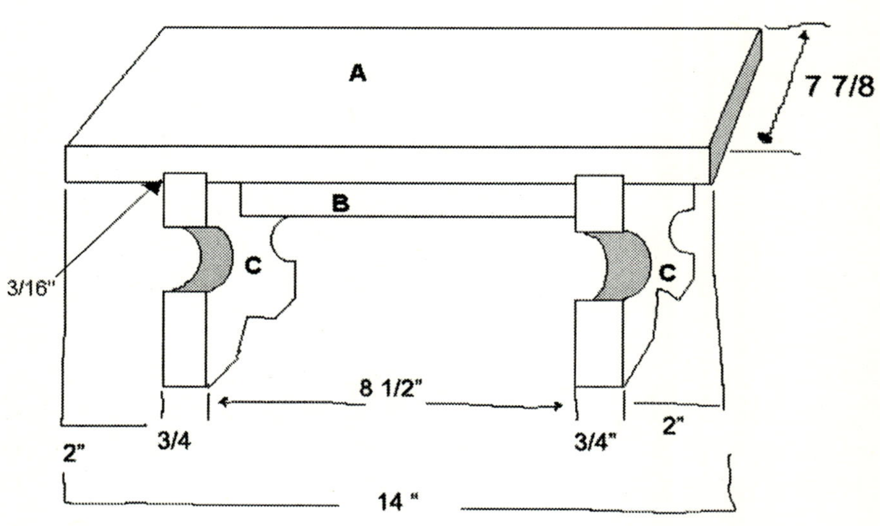

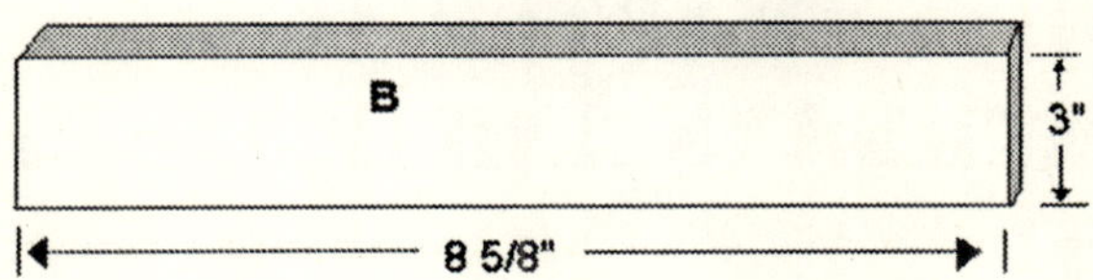

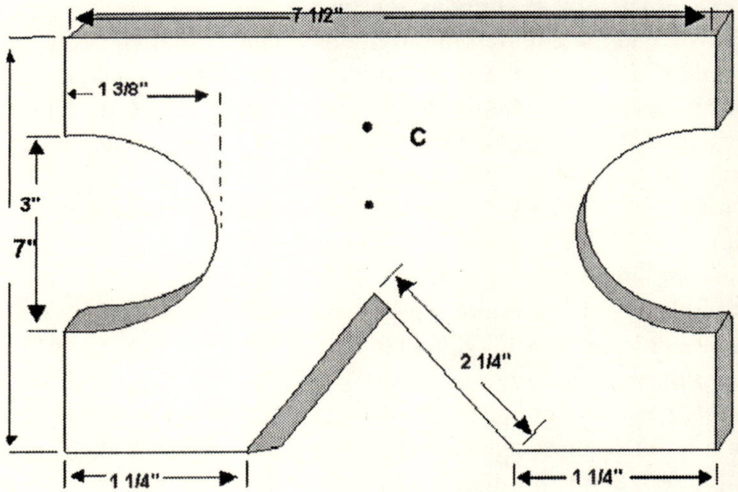

This stool can be made of any good wood, though my dad prefers hard wood such as Walnut or Cherry. With some nice wood stain to bring out the grain in the wood, it's quite elegant looking.

Recently Dad attended a big get together, and each person donated some item to be used as a give away or door prize. Dad made up one of these stools, along with the plans for building. The grandfather that won this prize was so elated he made it a point to thank my dad several times. You would think he had been given a million dollars! He was grateful to receive the stool.

He had an idea to make one for each of his grandchildren, to be passed down through generations.

CHAPTER 19
BIRTHDAYS AND HOLIDAYS

Most of us hopefully, grew up with loving families, and holidays were family oriented. Whether you're a single parent, or single without children, the holidays can be a very difficult time. If you're in a bit of loneliness, this can be exacerbated by the holiday season.

When we had the children in our home with W, we reveled in preparing for the holidays with the family, both immediate and the extended families.

I almost feel disgraced as the holiday season approaches. It's a promise of loneliness. I feel as though I've been forgotten while the world celebrates Christmas, Easter, Thanksgiving, or the others.

It's important to establish what works for you, to get through the holiday season.

As I mentioned previously, for a number of years after my first divorce that I found myself in another state than my children were living as the holiday season approached. Of course I would like nothing better than to be with them during Thanksgiving and Christmas, but since I wasn't a very responsible person when it came to finances this wasn't possible. I began to ache as a holiday approached, withdrawing into my own shell, making it impossible for anyone to sense my innermost feelings this time of year.

For six years I established my own tradition for Thanksgiving, Christmas, and New Years. On each of these holidays I would rise early, when my wee little neighbors were still snuggled tightly in their beds dreaming of the wonderful holiday that would soon be upon them. I would grab my shotgun, go outside and gather my dogs, load them all into the pickup and head for the river for a day of duck hunting or to the fields for a day of pheasant hunting. Being outside like this was something that recharged me and helped fight off the holiday blues.

Year after year I spent on the river or in the field. I'd sit at daybreak and think of everyone and the wonderful time they were having. I'd think of my children, probably climbing from their little beds, eyes twinkling in the Christmas lights blinking to survey all of the wonderful gifts Santa had brought them.

My dogs were my children. They filled me with joy and laughter. It was a wonderful time to be out hunting. It was rare that I'd see anyone else, and if so, probably another single person, out doing the same thing I was doing.

This may not be the best approach for many people, but being a bit of a loner, it was a wonderful serene time for myself and for my pets.

If you are the person that likes spending time with other people, you may have plenty of invitations around the holiday season. This may be a great way for you to spend time with other families and get to know a variety of traditions. Dinner with a friend and family can be a pleasant heart warming experience. You will have the opportunity to make more friends by accepting those invitations.

Be mindful of your own preferences at this time. After all, it's *your* holiday too! If, like me, you aren't comfortable in another's home this time of year, it may be time to spread your wings a bit and enjoy the time with a family, even if it's not your own. It may be that you would prefer to be alone doing something you like to do best. If so, politely thank any of the folks that extend the invitation and let them know for *this* holiday, you have other plans. It may be best to keep the offer open for the future and let them know you may be interested at another time. Otherwise, you may one day be wishing and hoping for an invitation *somewhere, anywhere* and your friends thinking you are perfectly content to spend your time alone *all* of the time.

The visitation awarded by the courts today usually consists of spending at least ½ of the major holidays with each parent. Your ex and you may want to decide individually on each of these and what is best for the kids. On Christmas, some children may want to spend the day at home, with one parent, enjoying the gifts of the day, not be shuttled back and forth, which can be hectic for the younger children. Think of their best interests and find a way to make it fit for both parents. If you have a close relationship with your ex, you may enjoy spending a Thanksgiving or Christmas together in one home with the children. W2 and I spend most Thanksgivings together, and it works well for both of us and for my son.

With many holidays and as the kids grow older there are questions that are going to spring up, and if you are not prepared, a proper response can be more trying than the holiday itself!

Christmas:

If you are Christian or have a basic Christian upbringing, some of the happiest moments in our lives belong to the Christmas holiday.

As a single parent, one of most daunting obstacles can be Christmas. I'm not sure in most cases if dads place the same priority on this holiday as mothers do, but we should. This is a HUGE holiday for the child.

When my three oldest daughters were in their younger years, they came to spend their first Christmas alone with Dad. I had been preparing for weeks. I spent a great deal of money on all of the "big" things that year. I took careful pains to make certain they each had at least some of the big things they wanted and had made sure they each had the same number of gifts. This is important.

Of course Christmas Eve is exciting for them, they stay up as late as they can, and I struggled to keep my eyes open until all were asleep. I stole out to my car opened the trunk and began shuttling all of the gifts into the house as quiet as a great Santa could be.

I carefully laid out the gifts all around the tree in the living room, on the chairs and sofa, and tip-toed quietly to bed content with the thought that tomorrow would be a great day.

I heard them stirring well before sunrise and gathered the sleepy eyed youngsters in my room, ready to assault the bounty that awaited them.

As we made our way into the living room and could begin to make out all of the gifts under the tree lights, I couldn't help but notice the look of disappointment on their wee faces. One of them commented, "There are no stockings, no candy, no little things. Let's go back to bed and wait until Santa comes."

My heart broke in a thousand pieces. Of course! I had all of the BIG gifts in place, but the little touches, the stuffed stockings, the little chocolate marshmallow Santa's, the little rolls of lifesavers had been neglected. I made a quick phone call to their mother, waking her from a sound sleep and explained my situation. She assured me that Santa got his wires crossed and had not understood the girls would be away from home that Christmas. He had left all of those things in their house!

Mom to the rescue! I packed up the kids, made the short drive to their house for their surprise. Mom had understood that I would miss "something" and was more than gracious in having the kids to her home for their real Christmas. Their happiness was all that concerned us, and it was never mentioned again between the two of us. She knew I wouldn't make this mistake again.

At some point, if your children are still young, sooner or later they are going to ask, "Is Santa real?" or something to that effect. Immediately your mind goes into defensive mode, waiting to fight off a barrage of questions and some verbal sparring to convince them they are mistaken. But they wait silently for an answer to a seeming simple question, "Is Santa real?"

You can handle this any way you would like of course. I've visited this conversation several times, not only with my young ones but others that are dear to me. I always answer with the question "What do you think?" A seeming cop out, but it's to get a good idea on where they stand, are they ready to hear the truth? Or is the adolescent truth going to hold for at least a few more months? The "Santa Truth" is a milestone in a child's life. This simple truth marks the first step on their way to adulthood. This marks the beginning of the end of the childhood fantasies.

Sometimes they'll respond with, "Yes, I think he's real."

BIG sigh of relief, Santa will be around at least a few more months.

Sometimes though, the response is "No, I don't think he's real." What a disheartening thing for them to say. They also sense this is the beginning of a new life for them. One that can be a bit scary, moving into teen years and on to adulthood, it all starts with the realization of Santa Claus.

When I hear of doubting Santa Claus, it's time to explain the real story of Santa and Christmas.

I begin to tell them that Santa IS indeed real, in the most wonderful sense of the word. He may not be a person as they've been led to believe. Or perhaps he is, I'm not real sure. But Santa is the Spirit of Christmas, the Spirit of Giving. Each time they give a gift to someone else, unselfishly, they will feel the warm glow of Santa. It doesn't have to be the Christmas season to experience doing something good for someone. This is Santa. Each time this feeling is present, it's the Spirit of Santa being kept alive. This is something they can always hold in their hearts.

Continue with a spiritual message, Christmas celebrates the birth of baby Jesus, and Heavenly Father's wonderful gift to the world. In the Spirit of Santa, we also celebrate His gift with the unselfish gifts we give others. The knowledge that Jesus is real is so very important for a Christian child. They will take reassurance knowing that Big Macho Dad, the man that has all the answers *knows* that Jesus lived, and loves us all.

It's important also to stress that it's important to let their younger brothers and sisters continue to believe in the *real* Santa until they ask the question. And if they ask their older brother or sister *The* Santa question, please refer them to Dad or Mom. We don't want to miss out on the wonderful memory of this child's graduation into the years beyond Santa!

Easter:

When finishing the Santa talk with that young one, and the most obvious question follows "But the Easter Bunny is real, right?" Smile and wink, and know their will always be a child inside. Note** the *Real* Easter bunny question, when it's time, can be answered in much the same way.

Easter is an equally important holiday for children especially for Christian children. You may want to tell your children the story of Easter, the resurrection of Jesus Christ and the reason he rose from the dead.

Easter celebration for us begins the spring season or at least we hope! Every year a passel of children descend on my home for the annual Easter egg hunt. Parents will gather early and stuff the plastic eggs with candy and gold $1 coins. The children get so excited every year in anticipation of the hunt for candy and gold. I always hold out a few of the gold coins for the little one that may not have been "lucky" in their hunt and came up short on their gold coins. I'll quietly slip them in their Easter basket as another parent distracts them. The grand prize every year is five $1 coins in one egg.

Having your own traditions at Easter, Thanksgiving, or Christmas offers a great stability in a child's life. You may want to stick with a traditional holiday with a big turkey or ham dinner, with all of the trimmings. The children know what to expect, what to look forward to, and may establish their own place in the kitchen preparing one of the dishes for a meal. As a teenaged youth, at Christmas we opted to change our dinner to lobster, which is one of my favorites. This was a fun, unique way to spend Christmas. Preparing party favors ahead of time, Santa Clauses, Easter bunnies, or turkeys for the holiday table can be a lot of fun *together* time. You will find some good books on making these in most Arts and Crafts stores.

You may opt for a walk together in nature or down the street after a large holiday meal, weather permitting or not! Whatever your plans have the children input their own unique ideas so you can celebrate these holidays in a fun way for all of you.

Birthdays:

One of my ex's sends a reminder as I'm writing this book:

Another holiday that's important for children of course is their birthday. Each child has been magically assigned one day each year that is to be a special day, only for him or her. This is one of my worst downfalls as a father. Few things are more disheartening to a child than to be forgotten on their special day by either parent (or grandparents). A simple card reaffirms they are loved and, of course we all like at least one present! Prepare your calendar with each child's birthday, and as I have to, mark a big B on the calendar several days before (I need a week on mine) as a reminder that a birthday is coming up and to get the card and present early enough to be presented to them, or mailed appropriately.

Your ex's birthday is also an important time in a child's life. In most cases, it wouldn't be inappropriate to take a younger child shopping before their mother's birthday to allow them to pick out that special present for Mommy. It teaches them the wonderful gift of unselfish giving, and they will look forward to her birthday perhaps more than she will. Especially when she is reaching her own milestones of the big 30 and 40 (or 50?). This one deed alone may put you into the "Big Book of Super Single Dad's!" a mainstay on all of our coffee tables!

Halloween:

Halloween of course provided us many memories as a child. When I was trick or treating in the small town I grew up in, we could safely blanket the entire town. Having to search through our bags for tainted candies, or fruit containing razor blades was literally unheard of. It saddens me terribly to think a person could commit such a tragic act toward an innocent child. Take steps to make certain your child is as safe as possible and still enjoys this miraculous holiday.

In our state, many of the churches have their members get together and bring the children to the church parking lot. The parents are careful to make certain they know each person in the lot and that they are safe and trustworthy. Parents are all dressed in costume, yet still recognizable as an upstanding parent in the church membership. The children go from car trunk to car trunk doing their trick or treating. Many of the trunks are seasonally decorated with ghost and goblins, witches and skeletons. Some offer spooky recordings that fill the parking lot with the wailing howls of the Halloween holiday. The children can have a wonderful time filling their bags with goodies and will experience much laughter and joy.

Local shopping malls are opening their doors more every year as the children can go from store to store picking their treats and enjoying the hospitality and safety of the shop owners. The mall offers a warm alternative to trick or treating on those cold Halloween eves. Generally a bench or two is available for us old fogies to sit and rest while the children scavenge the mall for treasures.

Children delight in Mom or Dad dressing up in costume to trick or treat alongside. Ask for their input on your costume each year, they will come up with some original ideas and may reveal some hidden parts of your personality that could be interesting!

New Year's:

New Year's Eve for all of us is a wonderful time to reflect on the past year and to look forward to the blessings we will receive in the coming year. If you are so blessed as to have your children on New Year's Eve or New Year's Day, it can be a fun time to sit and watch the celebrations on television, and share with each other the highlights or lowlights of the past year. During these times, you will notice how your child is growing. You may hear a happy or sad tale from the past year you were completely unaware of and may have an opportunity to teach (or learn) a lesson from the experience.

More and more towns are beginning to have a safe, alcohol free Street Fest or other celebration at New Year's. These are special events for the children to enjoy time with other families and friends in a safe holiday.

Establish your own traditions for each of the holidays. New Year's is a fun party for everyone. Let the children make a special holiday punch, or snacks for the occasion as you all sit around talking and enjoying them as the evening grows late. Take this time to review with them the wonderful (and perhaps sad) experiences the past year brought. Let them know this is a time to say goodbye to those times and to look forward to a New Year, with all of the opportunities it will bring.

Martin Luther King's Birthday:

No matter what color your skin, Martin Luther King gave our heritage some wonderful gifts. Take the time to learn the great gift Mr. King gave to our country. On his birthday teach your children about the great things this man did.

July 4th, Independence Day:

This is a celebration, deeply seeded in our country's history. Your children will learn of our nation's independence struggle through school, yet it's essential that your children know that *you* know the story, and how important it is for your way of life, and your children's.

Opportunities abound for family time during the Independence Day celebration. This is the time for parades; make certain your child has every opportunity to be *in* a parade! This is also the time for fireworks, gatherings at the park for fun activities, and family barbecues. Make certain the children have an appropriate amount of involvement in the celebration.

Memorial Day:

Memorial Day is a time to remember; not only those that have fought for our country in foreign wars; but also to remember all of our loved ones that have passed on. This provides a superb and solemn opportunity to visit a local cemetery and put flowers on the graves of those not forgotten. It's also an occasion to spend time during the evening talking of those in your family that have gone before, and a bit of family history. Your children will look forward to learning of their heritage on this holiday.

Labor Day:

Our country is steeped in tradition of hard-working men and women. Gone, for the most part, are the days of the sweatshops, the poor working conditions of the textile mills, mines, and factories. Begun in 1892 as a protest, union workers in New York City took the day off and gathered in Union Square to support the holiday. We think of it more as the last long weekend holiday of summer, or the close of the summer season, and a time for family and friends to join in a last barbecue or picnic. Let's share with our children, at this opportunity, this country was built on the common laborers sweat, blood and tears, to make this nation what it is today.

Hanukkah and other non-Christian holidays:

I am ashamed to say that because I am Christian that I have no knowledge of different religious celebrations. I would encourage you to find ways to include and increase your children's participation in such holidays.

This unique nation of the United States was founded as a veritable melting pot for all cultures and religions on earth. As a result, we have in many of our communities, a diversity of cultures and religions as well as family traditions unmatched on the planet. However, as we are all Americans, and we want to fit into that mold, we've taken a lot of our culture and congealed it into a blur of sameness, only to be brought out on special holidays. Celebrate our differences; learn from each other, we would not be this great nation without our differences!

For those of us that are Christian, I would encourage you to learn other religious holidays and take the time to help children understand, and celebrate the holidays their friends from other cultures enjoy. It is a splendid way to teach tolerance and an appreciation for others belief systems. You may enjoy it too!

Valentine's Day:

This can be a tough one for single dads if they don't have someone significant in their life. It's all a matter of perspective however. This can be a time to give thanks for the loved ones that are in your life, whether it's parents, children, or good friends. You'll get through it; maybe next year will bring that special someone.

The younger children traditionally will present their classmates with simple little Valentine's Day cards. Make certain they have theirs in order, ready for school several days before the holiday. The teachers will have the children present their valentines several days before the actual holiday, to give the students time to celebrate this holiday. Be aware that a special Valentine's friend may be important to the youngest child. This is a time when they may experience their first puppy love or as they get older, someone more significant. Help them to enjoy these first pangs in a healthy responsible way.

When picking out gifts for your ex from your children, it's important to have the children involved in the process, no matter what their age. It's not generally appropriate for Dad to pick out and purchase a Christmas Gift, Birthday gift etc, and pay for it, wrap it etc, for the children without their involvement. The child of a very young age can be along on the shopping trip and be involved in the gift giving process. This gives your child a sense of ownership in the gift, and is something Mom will cherish much more than a simple material item.

CHAPTER 20
KIDS AND THE KITCHEN

The kitchen can be the center of the house. Kids belong in the kitchen! A couple of weeks ago, my young son had a friend in for a sleep over during one of his weekend visits. It was the first time this particular friend had visited. As my son showed his friend around my tiny apartment, they came to the kitchen. "It's a small kitchen," my son told his friend, "But a lot goes on in here."

This brought warmth and a smile to my heart. It's sometimes difficult to see the things that are important to young ones. The kitchen should be a place for family and close friends to come together. I joke to my guests to "Get out of my kitchen," all in good fun of course, and that the only time I've ruined a meal is when someone was in my kitchen bugging me! Much warmth is generated in a loving kitchen, warmth that can't come from an oven. We've had some wonderful times in my kitchen, elbow-to-elbow or back-to-back with friends and family, with children underfoot, dodging and weaving each other as we rush to put a feast together.

With this madness, unless you've spent a lot of time in a kitchen, you may have a bit of trouble knowing how to set yours up in your new home. After all, you want to be able to find anything in an instant. Well, it doesn't matter! You can place items that are convenient for you. A couple of suggestions though, put glasses and cups on the bottom shelf of a cupboard. When your children are old enough and tall enough to pour their own drinks, you won't be asked constantly to come and get them a cup or a glass. Put silverware in a drawer they can reach at an appropriate age. It is best to keep sharp knives in another drawer or completely out of reach.

Keep an eye on your silverware! My youngest, when she was four would help by putting her silverware back in the silverware drawer when she was finished with her meal. The *thought* was there, the execution was lacking a bit!

Establish some basic rules at mealtimes. If you prefer the children to always bring their dishes back to the counter after dinner, certainly do that. They can begin doing this as soon as they are tall enough to reach up on the counter. You will find that they enjoy helping you.

You may also want them to scrape excess food in the trash, rinse the dishes, and put them in the dishwasher. Once you instill this simple task in them, it will not only cut down on your workload in cleaning up, but they may begin doing it at home for Mom voluntarily, and it will help her out.

Cleaning the kitchen can become a family affair, after all, everyone eats, there's no need for you to do all of the cleaning. It's a community effort in the home. You will also get a precious few moments more to spend with the children and help instill some basic values of hard work, teamwork, and some domestic skills as well.

If the children are too small to reach cups and glasses, you may want to build them a stool for kitchen uses. (Drawings attached in Chapter 18). My uncle built the first drawing 45 years ago, and he made one for each of five children. If you are not comfortable with carpentry, you may find some useable stools for sale in stores and thrift shops, but I have yet to find one that is so versatile. This doubles not only as a stool to stand on, with two different heights depending on which direction it's turned, but serves as a nice little chair for the young ones, and they will use it often. We wore the paint off of ours before it had outlived its usefulness.

Safety concerns are also something you will want to be mindful of in the kitchen. When cooking, make certain to always turn handles on pans toward the inside of the stove, so no curious youngster will pull a pan of hot anything on top of them.

I had the unfortunate experience of visiting a friend in the University Hospital burn unit many years ago when he was severely burned in a truck accident. One of his buddies that he came to know on the unit floor was a young boy, four years old that had been vacationing with his family at a cabin. Someone had a pan full of hot oil on the stove, getting ready for dinner. He reached up and pulled the hot oil down onto himself, burning over 90% of his body. The last word I heard the child had recovered well and had gone home, but the years of agony he suffered because of a simple oversight was tough to watch. Most likely the physical and mental scars will last his entire life. Don't let this happen to your child.

Kids love to cook. They love to be a part of fixing a meal, and they will announce their contribution to family and guests at dinnertime. Allow them to help where appropriate, if only putting water in a pan to place on the stove, or patting dough for biscuits. They love to be hands on and may surprise you at their rate of learning.

As they get older, they love to chop and mince vegetables, learn different spices, and they are more likely to at least taste or eat a meal they have helped prepare. I'm skeptical myself when eating something someone has fixed if I can't look and tell what's in it! Be mindful of safety and always supervise children in the kitchen.

My 11-year-old son has spent countless hours in the kitchen with me, and he has some of his own special recipes that only he makes. And these are not simple recipes! He loves to make things like smoked oyster spread, with canned oysters, cream cheese, a few spices, and minced onions. Last weekend he prepared pork chops and stuffing (it was wonderful!) while I was able to watch my first football game of the season, and the season is half over! He was very proud and did a wonderful job.

Benefits abound in teaching them to enjoy cooking. A benefit you may enjoy as they grow and become parents themselves, inviting Grandpa over for Sunday dinner.

ASSIGNMENT

Create a formal dinner with your children. Set the table with a tablecloth, burn candles, have a centerpiece. Fix your favorite meal, turn out the lights, light the candles, and turn off the television. Some soft music may be a nice touch. Use this dinner to talk and enjoy each other's company.

Make it fun for the kids. Let them drink their punch from a wine glass, or mix 7-Up with a bit of grape juice or cranberry juice for color, from the wine glass. Use this opportunity to teach them the salad forks, shrimp forks, the difference between soup and dinner spoons. Teach them the formal manners they will want to use in restaurants. Tell them some of your favorite stories from exotic or formal places you may have dined.

CHAPTER 21
KIDS ONLY!

Arguably, all of us need a bit more of our childhood in our lives. These recipes provide a great opportunity to show your fun side, as well as get the kids more involved in the kitchen. One of the great memories you can leave your children, no matter what their age, is the time spent together in the kitchen. For the little ones, start them with the smaller safe chores, dipping items in batter (they love it!) or putting water in the pan to boil. As they get older, move them on to the harder things, like dicing and slicing. Few things please a child more than to sit down to a meal and to be able to tell everyone they helped prepare dinner, no matter how small their part, their input of love into the meal makes it special.

Family and friends provided many of these recipes. I've provided credit, first names only where appropriate.

MAIN DISHES

Sesame Chicken Strips

1 cup mayonnaise
2 tsp. dry mustard
½ cup sesame seeds

2 tsp. dried minced onion
1 cup crushed butter flavored crackers
2 lb. boneless chicken breasts

Sauce:
1cup mayonnaise
2 Tbsp. honey

In a bowl, combine mayonnaise, onion and mustard. In another bowl, combine the crackers and sesame seeds. Cut chicken lengthwise into 1/4" strips. Dip strips into the mayonnaise mixture, then into the sesame seed mixture. Place in a single layer on large greased baking sheet. Bake at 425° for 15-18 minutes or until juice runs clear. Combine sauce ingredients serve with chicken strips. Yield: 10-12 appetizer servings.

Noodles and Eggs
My youngest children, picky as they are, love this variation on noodle soup!

2 pkgs. dry noodle soup mix (Top Ramen™, Cup-o-Noodles™ etc)
2 eggs
¼ tsp. butter or margarine

In small bowl scramble the eggs. Cook in small saucepan, over medium high heat in butter, until eggs are scrambled. Prepare noodles per package directions add eggs in bowl, top with noodles.

Hint: This can also be topped with a bit of shredded cheddar or jack cheese.

Easy Sloppy Joes
Judy

1 lb ground beef   1 can (8 oz) chicken gumbo soup
1 small bottle catsup   1 clove garlic (minced)
¼ cup onions (chopped) 1 pkg. hamburger buns

Brown onions and garlic over medium heat. Add ground beef, brown. Drain. Add most of the bottle of catsup (I leave about ½ - 3/4 inch in the bottom). Add chicken gumbo soup, stir until blended. Bring to a boil, turn down heat and let simmer for 20 minutes, stirring occasionally.

Old Fashioned Spaghetti

1 lb. ground beef   1 large onion (diced)
½ cup fresh mushrooms (sliced thinly)
4 garlic cloves (minced)   1 pkg. spaghetti sauce mix
1 lb. spaghetti noodles   1 6 oz. can tomato paste
2 Tbs. butter (divided)   2 tsp. garlic salt
1 tsp. pepper (fresh ground)   Olive oil
 Parmesan cheese (optional)

In large skillet over medium heat, in 1 Tbs. butter and drop of olive oil, sauté the onions and garlic until onions are translucent, add fresh mushrooms, and sauté two additional minutes. Add ground beef, brown and drain. Add tomato paste and 3 cans of water. Stir well until well blended, add spaghetti mix, and stir well, Add 1Tbs. butter, Garlic Salt and Pepper, Simmer 30 minutes. Cook spaghetti noodles per package directions.

Serve sauce over spaghetti noodles, topped with Parmesan cheese.

Hints: Serve with Vito's Garlic Bread or Quick and Easy Garlic toast. (See Breads.)

Kids' Individual Pizzas

1 pkg. pizza dough mix below (or 1 can biscuit dough)
1 can/bottle pizza sauce mix (or 1 bottle marinara sauce)
Favorite toppings (i.e.: pepperoni, sausage, onions, olives, pineapple, thinly sliced mushrooms, ground beef etc.)
8 ounces mozzarella cheese

Make pizza dough mix per directions, separate into dough balls sufficient in size to make a child sized pizza. If using biscuits, two large biscuits formed into a dough ball are usually enough for one child sized pizza. Let your child flour and roll out or pat out with hands pizza dough to make crust. Cover with sauce, then toppings, top with cheese. Bake at 425° 15-18 minutes on large, lightly greased cookie sheet or pizza pan until crust is golden brown on the bottom (or follow package mix directions).

Homemade Pizza Crust

2 pkg. active dry yeast
1 1/3 cup warm water
3 tsp. each salt and sugar

3½ to 4 cups all-purpose flour
2 Tbs. olive oil

Dissolve yeast in warm water in a large mixing bowl; let stand five minutes or until bubbly. Add 2 cups of the flour, oil, salt, and sugar, mix well.

Gradually beat in remaining flour until soft, but not sticky, dough is formed. Turn out onto a lightly floured surface and knead until dough is smooth and elastic, about ten minutes.

Transfer dough to an oiled bowl. Turn to coat dough with oil. Cover with plastic wrap, let stand in a warm place until doubled in volume, about 1 hour. Punch dough down, transfer to a lightly floured surface and let stand five minutes. Separate in half. Roll out dough to form 2-12 inch crusts. Transfer to a large baking sheet that has been lightly dusted with corn meal. Add toppings and bake as directed in recipe. Makes 2 - 12 inch pizza crusts.

Beer Batter Fish Balls

½ cup Beer (the alcohol cooks off quickly)   ½ cup Flour
1 egg (beaten)   Dash of Salt and Pepper
2 lbs. Catfish or halibut chunks (any good white fish, or dark meat chicken pieces may be substituted)
Oil for deep-frying   Lemon wedges

Mix beer and flour to make a nice batter on the thin side. Mix in the salt, pepper and egg. Wash fish pieces, dip one at a time into the batter, shake off the excess and place in deep fryer or 3/4" hot cooking oil in fry pan at 350°. Cook while turning until golden brown. Serve with lemon wedges and cocktail or fry sauce.

Barbecued Hot Dogs

Adults love this one too!

¾ cup chopped onion   3 Tbs. butter or margarine
1 ½cups chopped celery   1 ½ cups ketchup
¾ cup water   1/3 cup lemon juice
3 Tbs. brown sugar (softened)   3 Tbs. vinegar
1 Tbs. Worcestershire sauce   1 Tbs. yellow mustard
2 packages (1 lb. each) hot dogs   20 hot dog buns (split)

In a saucepan over medium heat, sauté onion in butter until tender. Add celery, ketchup, water, lemon juice, sugar, vinegar, Worcestershire sauce and mustard; bring to a boil. Reduce heat; cover and simmer for 30 minutes. Cut three or four ¼-inch deep slits into each side of hot dogs; place in a 2 ½ qt. baking dish. Pour the sauce over the hot dogs. Cover and bake at 350° for 40-45 minutes or until heated through. Serve on buns. (Yield 20 servings)

Quick Meat Loaf
Tina

Prep time: 1¼ hours

1 lb. ground beef (or venison)	½ lb. ground pork	1 egg
½ cup-dried bread crumbs	½ Tbs. onions, chopped	½ tsp. salt
1 cup milk		

Beat egg, add milk and bread crumbs. Mix thoroughly with the meat and seasonings. Bake for 1 hour in a greased pan at 350°. Serves 2-4.

Teriyaki Chicken w/ Ham Fried Rice

Many friends and guests have sought to find my secret to this chicken. Well, it's the brown sugar!

This dish is best done on the grill but works in the oven also. (Hint: don't try cooking the rice on the grill, it's very hard to keep the grains from falling through!)

1-3lb broiler/frying chicken cut up, skin removed
¾ cup Teriyaki marinade (Kikkoman brand)
1 Tbs. brown sugar

Heat teriyaki, add brown sugar, and stir well. Pour into non-metal bowl and cool. Set aside 2 Tbs. marinade and put remainder into non metal bowl or freezer bags, add chicken, marinate at least eight hours or overnight in refrigerator.

Cook over grill or preheated 350° for one hour or until juices run clear. Baste during cooking with the marinade only until the last 15 minutes of cooking. Once removed from oven, baste with reserved marinade before serving.

Rice:
5 cups Minute Rice
2 cups diced or shredded cooked ham
2 cups teriyaki sauce (Kikkoman)
1 Tbs. butter or margarine
2 cups water

2 cloves garlic minced
½ cup diced green onion
1 Tbs. brown sugar
1 cup baby frozen peas (thawed)

In a large cooking pot, on medium heat sauté garlic in butter until tender. Add teriyaki, brown sugar, and ham. Cook slowly for 20 minutes stirring occasionally until ham is tender. Add green onions, cover for another 10 minutes to allow onions to become opaque. Add 2 cups water and bring to boil. Add the rice, cover and remove from heat. Let stand for 5 minutes (or according to package directions.) Add baby peas, stir carefully and fluff with fork.

Hint:Strong Teriyaki flavor. Serve with something to contrast taste such as a tossed green salad, potato or fruit salad.

Dad's Special Burgers
Tina

1 lb. ground venison, browned (or beef)
¼ cup catsup
1 tsp. vinegar
1 tsp. sugar
1 dash of salt

1 Tbs. prepared mustard
1 Tbs. Worcestershire
½ cup milk

Mix all ingredients thoroughly. Spread thinly on hamburger bun halves, place under broiler for two to five minutes until done.

Hint: after cooking, top with grated monterey jack cheese and place under broiler long enough to melt the cheese. Serve.

Bleu Cheese or Ranch Burgers

This is an excellent break from the same old burgers!

2 lbs. ground beef	½ cup bread crumbs
3/4 cup ranch or bleu cheese salad dressing, divided	
1 cup grated onion, divided	Hamburger buns
1 medium tomato, thinly sliced	1 Tbs. butter or margarine

Mix ground beef, breadcrumbs, ½ cup ranch or bleu cheese dressing, and ½ cup onions with hands in large bowl. Cover (with towel) and refrigerate at least two hours. Form mixture into patties. Meanwhile in small pan, sauté onions in butter until slightly browned, keep warm.

Cook burgers in skillet on stove, or on the grill until done. Place the burger on a bun. Top with 1 Tbs. ranch or bleu cheese, sautéed onion, and tomato slice. Serve (messy but delicious!).

Sweet and Sour Venison
Tina

This recipe works well also with beef, chicken, or pork.

Prep time: 1 hour

1 lbs. cubed venison steak or roast (beef, chicken or pork)	
2 Tbs. oil	¼ cup water
1 15 oz can pineapple chunks	1/3 cup packed brown sugar
2 Tbs. cornstarch	¼ tsp. ground ginger
¼ tsp. cider vinegar	2 ½ Tbs. soy sauce
Salt	Hot cooked rice

In a large skillet, brown the meat in oil. Add the water, cover and simmer for 25 minutes. Meanwhile, drain the pineapple, reserving the juice. Combine the sugar, cornstarch, ginger and salt. Blend in reserved pineapple juice, vinegar and soy sauce. Add to the meat. Cook and stir until thickened. Stir in pineapple chunks heat through. Serve over rice. Serves four.

Sweet and Sour Wings

20 chicken wings (or up to 4lbs) separated
1 cup sweet and sour marinade
¼ cup water
3 Tbs. olive oil (or vegetable oil)
2 tsp Tabasco (or to taste)

Mix all ingredients in large bowl, add wings, stir, refrigerate and toss occasionally. Marinade at least six to eight hours in refrigerator. Place on baking sheet or in casserole dish, cook at 350° for one hour or until juices run clear.

Hint: Serve with bleu cheese or Ranch Dressing.

Wild Rice and Chicken
Recipe from Aunt Joyce, submitted by Judy

1-2 chickens, cut up
1 pkg. Uncle Ben's Long andWild rice
1 can Chinese mixed vegetables—not drained
1-can water chestnuts or bamboo shoots—not drained
1 can of mushrooms-not drained 1 can cream of celery or mushroom soup

Sprinkle rice in a 9 x 13 pan. Shake spice bag to mix and put ½ on top of rice. Mix cans (not drained) and put on top of rice. Top with chicken and sprinkle remaining spices on top. Bake 1 hour at 350°. If necessary, cover with foil during last half of cooking to prevent over browning. Dish is also good with pork chops.
Serves six.

Roast Chicken with Lemon and Herbs

The first time I made this chicken I only made one, for a small gathering. I learn my lessons well, and always make two. The chicken comes out tender, and so juicy, you may need to line your cutting board with tin foil before piercing the skin. The kids love brushing the oil and salt mixture inside of the chicken.

2 whole frying or roasting chickens (2-3/4 - 3-1/2 lbs each)
½ cup olive oil   2 Tbs. kosher salt
1 Tbs. black pepper (fresh ground)   1 lemon (in half)
6 sprigs rosemary   6 sprigs oregano
4 large garlic cloves (cut in half)
Chipotle Pepper sauce (optional, below)
Butcher Twine or Skewers

Preheat oven to 350°. Remove giblets from the body cavity, trim away excess fat, rinse and pat dry. Fold wing tips underneath the chicken.

Combine olive oil, pepper, and salt in small bowl. Coat the cavity of each chicken with some of the seasoned olive oil. (Reserve 3 tablespoons). Strip the leaves off of 2 sprigs rosemary and oregano, mince, reserve half, place remaining inside of the cavity each chicken and rub. Place 2 each of the remaining sprigs (leaves attached) in each cavity. Squeeze the juice from the lemon into the cavity, set lemon halves aside. (Repeat with the other chicken).

Separate skin from the breast and thighs by inserting fingers between the two. Squeeze in additional lemon juice and spread seasoned olive oil on the breast and thigh with a small basting brush. Rub remaining minced oregano and rosemary onto breast meat and insert 2 garlic halves on each breast. Insert lemon halves into each cavity and truss the chickens, legs together. Baste with Chipotle sauce if desired. (Or do one with, one without).

Place the chickens on a roasting rack in a roasting pan and roast until the juices run clear, or until meat thermometer inserted in the thigh reaches 180°. Remove and cool five minutes before carving.

Hint: I prefer to use bottled Chipotle sauce found in some stores. If you have trouble finding it, you might consider the recipe below (Chipotle Puree) to make your own.

Chipotle Puree

6 cups water
4 ounces dried Chipotle chili, stems removed
2 Tbs. achiote paste (available in Hispanic grocery)   1 cup tomato paste
1 cup firmly packed brown sugar   ¼ cup olive oil
¼ cup red wine vinegar   2 Tbs. salt

Combine all ingredients in a saucepan over high heat. Bring the mixture to a boil, decrease heat to medium-low, and simmer for 30-45 minutes. Remove from heat and cool completely. Puree the mixture in a blender or food processor until smooth. Store in an airtight container in the refrigerator until ready to use for up to three days.

Fajitas
Bruce

1 large steak or 3-4 chicken breasts
1 bottle of Alegro Marinade (usually found by A1 steak sauce)
½ head of lettuce   1 large onion (chopped)
1 package of grated cheddar cheese   1 carton of sour cream
1 jar of favorite salsa   1-2 packages of tortillas
1 can of refried beans (warmed)

Meat can be best marinated in zip lock bag for one to two hours while being refrigerated. May be done on fry pan but for best results cooked on gas or charcoal grill (marinade gives smoky taste). Tortilla shells are best if layered between wet paper towels and placed in warm oven or warmed in microwave and covered in dishtowels to stay warm on table.

Turkey Croissant Rolls

This is an excellent recipe for Thanksgiving turkey leftovers.

1 cup diced or shredded turkey
½ cup stuffing (leftover)

3 oz pkg cream cheese
1 cup turkey gravy
1 pkg Pillsbury Crescent rolls

Lay crescent dough out in triangles, top each with 1-2 Tbs Turkey, 1 Tbs stuffing and 1 tsp cream cheese, roll. Bake at 400° for 10-14 minutes or until rolls are nicely golden. Serve topped with warm gravy.   Yields 8 rolls.

Southwest Turkey Sandwiches

3/4 to 1 lb. thinly sliced cooked turkey (smoked, optional, deli turkey works best!)
1 can (4 1/4 oz) chopped ripe olives (drained)
½ tsp chili powder   ½ tsp ground cumin
¼ tsp salt   ½ cup mayonnaise
1/3 cup sour cream   1/3 cup chopped green onions
8 Large rolls cut in half (sandwich style)
2 medium tomatoes, thinly sliced   2 ripe avocados (thinly sliced)
¾ cup shredded medium cheddar cheese
¾ cup shredded monterey jack cheese

In a bowl combine olives, chili powder, cumin and salt, set aside 2 tablespoons. Add the mayonnaise, sour cream, and onions to the remaining olive mixture. Place bread on an un-greased baking sheet, spread 1 tablespoon of mayonnaise mixture on each slice. Top with turkey and tomatoes. Spread with another tablespoon of mayonnaise mixture, top with avocados and cheeses. Sprinkle with reserve olive mixtures to garnish.
Bake at 350° for 15 minutes or until heated through.

Oven Fried Potatoes

5 medium baking potatoes   1 tsp. salt or garlic salt
¼ cup vegetable oil   ¼ tsp. cayenne pepper
3 Tbs. melted butter or margarine

Wash potatoes. Do not peel. Cut lengthwise into 1/4inch slices. Cut slices in half lengthwise, if desired. Soak in cold water or ice water for ten minutes. Drain and dry thoroughly by patting with towels.

Arrange in a single layer in a 15 x 10 inch baking pan. Pour oil and melted butter over potatoes making certain they are well coated on both sides.

Bake at 450° in oven for 30-35 minutes or until crisp, turning once after 15 minutes of cooking.

Drain on paper towels and sprinkle with salt and cayenne pepper.

Texas Fries

3-4 medium Russet potatoes
Cooking oil for deep-frying
Dash cayenne pepper
Salt and pepper
Fresh lime (optional)

Cut potatoes into large fry fingers. Deep fry in oil or in ½"cooking oil in large fry pan until golden brown. Drain on paper towels. Sprinkle with salt and peppers. Squeeze lime juice over the fries if desired.

SAUCES

Fry Sauce

Recently the world came to Utah for the Winter Olympics, and all the talk from the visitors was of the fry sauce! (Of all things). I hadn't realized that this was so localized. It's simple!

½ cup tomato ketchup
½ cup mayonnaise or salad dressing

Put ketchup in a glass bowl first (it's important!) add the mayonnaise and stir with a fork. Stir until all lumps are gone. Serve with fries or oven fried potatoes.

(For some reason, if you add the ketchup TO the mayonnaise it comes out lumpy. But not to worry, you can beat it with a wire whisk or electric beater to smooth.)

Simple Tartar Sauce

¼ cup sweet pickle relish
¼ cup mayonnaise

Stir together well serve with fish sticks or seafood.

Cocktail Dipping Sauce

½ cup ketchup
A splash of Worcestershire

4 Tbs. horseradish (to taste)
A splash of Tabasco

Combine all ingredients and whisk, adjusting seasonings to taste. Chill.

APPETIZERS AND FUN SNACKS

Quick Popcorn Balls

2 quarts freshly popped popcorn
1 cup sugar
1 tsp vanilla

1 cup light corn syrup
½ tsp. salt

Turn popcorn into large bowl or pan; place in warm oven. In heavy 2-quart saucepan stir together corn syrup, sugar and salt. Cook over medium heat, stirring constantly, until mixture comes to a boil. Cook, without stirring four minutes. Remove from heat; stir in vanilla. Slowly pour over popped corn mixing well. When cool enough to handle yet still quite warm, quickly shape into balls. Makes about 12 (3 inch) balls.

Serve as appetizers.

Walnut Yogurt Dip

1 1/2 cups walnuts (6 oz bag)
1-cup plain yogurt (preferably live cultures though low fat is okay)
1 small clove garlic (finely chopped)
1 1/2 tsp sea salt
Freshly ground black pepper to taste
Lemon juice to taste (optional)

Soak walnuts overnight in water to cover. Drain walnuts and place on lightly oiled baking sheet. Toast in preheated oven at 350° for 15 minutes.

Place walnuts, yogurt, salt and garlic in food processor and whirl to puree. Remove to a bowl and add freshly ground black pepper and lemon juice (you may not need it if yogurt is very tart) to taste. Enjoy with whole-wheat pita chips, radish pieces, or celery. Makes 3 cups.

Green Onions and Cream Cheese
Angie

Kids absolutely love making these for your dinner guests.

8-green onions (remove very tops of green and roots)
1-3 oz pkg. cream cheese (softened)

Wet hands in water and shape cream cheese around lower (white) end of onions, creating 1/8" coating of cream cheese around the onion. Leave part of green stems to use as a handle. Serve as appetizers.

Easy Mushroom Crescent Snacks
Laurie

3 cups finely chopped fresh mushrooms	2 Tbs. margarine
2 Tbs. finely chopped onion	½ tsp. garlic salt
1 tsp. lemon juice	1 tsp. Worcestershire sauce

3 oz. pkg. cream cheese softened   ¼ cup. grated parmesan cheese
8 oz. can Pillsbury Refrigerator Quick Crescent dinner rolls

Brown mushrooms in margarine. Stir in next four ingredients. Cook until liquid evaporates. Separate crescent dough into two rectangles. Place in ungreased 13x9 inch pan. Press over bottom, 1/4 inch up the sides to form crust. Spread cream cheese over dough, add mushrooms, and sprinkle with Parmesan cheese. Bake at 350° for 20-25 minutes. Cool five minutes before cutting.

Crab Cheese Ball

2 cans crab meat (shells and cartilage removed)
2- 3 oz. pkg. cream cheese (softened)
¼ tsp nutmeg
¼ cup finely minced green onion

Mix all ingredients well in mixing bowl. Allow to cool, wet hands, shape into ball, allow to cool in refrigerator for ½ hour before serving.

Super Nachos

½ lb. ground beef   ¼ cup minced onions (or green onions)
1/8 tsp. pepper   1 Tbs. chili powder
1 tsp. garlic powder   ¼ cup chopped tomatoes
2 Tbs. minced Jalapeno (seeds removed for less heat)
1 jar Velveeta™ cheese
7 ounces tortilla chips

In medium saucepan, fill ½ full with water, insert bottle of Velveeta™, lid removed. Heat slowly, stirring occasionally with spoon until cheese is liquid. Meanwhile, Brown ground beef, drain, add chili powder and garlic powder, stir. Remove from heat. Spread tortilla chips on large platter. Sprinkle with ground beef, onions and jalapeno. Pour melted cheese over the top. Garnish by sprinkling tomatoes on top of cheese.

Hint: serve with Guacamole (below)

Guacamole

3 avocados (large, ripe)
2 cloves garlic (freshly minced, not in oil)
½ cup finely diced white onion
1 ripe tomato (medium, diced)
1 tablespoon lemon juice (fresh squeezed)
1 package guacamole mix

Peel the avocados, remove and discard the seed. Mash with a potato masher until smooth with small chunks. Add the garlic and onions, lemon juice and stir in gently. Add the avocado mix and fold gently but thoroughly. Add the diced tomato, fold gently. Chill in the refrigerator for ½ hour before serving to allow the flavors to blend.

Hint: for spicier mix, add ½ cup of salsa.

Pineapple Cheese Ball
Naomi

2- 8oz. pkg. cream cheese, softened
1- 8oz. can pineapple crushed and drained
½ cup chopped green onion
Worcestershire sauce (optional)

1 jar sharp cheddar cheese
1 cup crushed pecans

Mix all ingredients above except pecans (a dash of Worcestershire may be added optional). Form into a ball and chill for 1 hour. Once ball is chilled roll in the crushed pecans to coat. Chill until served. Makes one large cheese ball.

Camden's Venison Jerky
Tina

My son loves beef jerky, this was his first taste of venison, and he prepared this recipe himself.

2 lbs. venison
½ tsp garlic powder
¼ tsp pepper

½ cup soy sauce
1 tsp grated lemon peel

Cut venison into 1/4 inch strips, remove all fat. Mix all other ingredients. Dip venison into sauce and marinade at least 15 minutes. Lay strips onto baking sheet. Dry in oven or over wood stove for 10 to 12 hours at 150° to 175°.

Hint: My son likes his jerky very thin. Using a meat-tenderizing hammer to flatten the jerky very thin, it dries beautifully!

Hint: If you like your jerky spicier, add a dash of dried hot pepper flakes to the marinade. (Not much though, I added ¼ tsp and it was HOT!)

Holiday Squares
Sharon

2 sticks or one cup of butter
4 eggs
1 Tbs. lemon juice

1 ½ cups sugar
2 cups flour
1 can fruit filling

Cream softened butter with sugar. Add eggs one at a time, beating well after each. Add flour and lemon juice. Pour into a greased cookie sheet. Smooth the top out. Mark off into 20 squares. Using a tablespoon drop fruit filling into the center of each square. Bake at 350° for 45-50 minutes. While warm, sprinkle with powdered sugar.

Creamy Carmel Treasure Brownies
Laurie

1 cup finely chopped pecans
1 pkg. (18 oz) Nestle Toll House Refrigerated Brownie Bar Dough, broken into squares.

12 Creamy Caramel Nestle Treasurers (candy), unwrapped
½ cup Semi-sweet Chocolate chips
Cupcake papers

Place nuts in bowl, press brownies into nuts, coating well. Place into cupcake papers.
Bake 22 to 25 minutes or until the edges are set. Press one candy into each brownie. Cool completely.
Microwave chocolate chips in small, heavy-duty plastic bag on high power for 30-45 seconds: knead and microwave until smooth. Cut a tiny corner from bag; Squeeze to drizzle over brownies.
** *These are very large and VERY rich.

Lemon Cake Cookies
Suzanne

1 pkg. lemon cake mix
8 oz. Cool Whip
5 Tbs. lemon juice

2 eggs
Powdered sugar

Lightly beat eggs and mix all ingredients together. Drop by spoon onto powdered sugar (foil works well). Roll gently into balls and place on lightly oiled cookie sheet.
Bake at 350° for 8-10 minutes until lightly browned.

Date Squares
Judy from Carol

(Diabetic)

1 cup chopped dates
¾ cup chopped pitted prunes
½ cup dark raisins
1 ¼ cups water
½ cup margarine cut into pieces
1 tsp. vanilla
18 packets of Equal

½ tsp. cinnamon
¼ tsp. nutmeg
¼ tsp. Salt (omit)
¼ cup chopped walnuts
2 eggs
1 cup all purpose flour
1 tsp. baking soda

Combine dates, prunes, raisins, and water. Heat to boiling and reduce. Heat and simmer until fruit is tender and water is absorbed (10 min.). Remove from heat. Add margarine, stirring until melted. Cool. Mix eggs and vanilla into fruit mixture.

Mix and combine flour, equal, soda, cinnamon, nutmeg, and salt. Spread evenly in a greased 9 x 13 baking dish and sprinkle with walnuts. Bake 350° for 30-35 min. 24 servings.

117 calories per serving 17 g. carbohydrates 5 g. fat

Hattie's Peanut Butter Fudge
Judy

2 cups sugar	½ cup corn syrup
2 Tbs. butter	½ cup milk

Mix together and boil until a soft ball forms in cold water.

Take from heat and add:
2 Tbs. peanut butter   1 tsp. vanilla

Beat and pour into buttered pan.

Dana's Favorite Apple Pie
Laurie

Crust:
1 1/2 cup flour   1 tsp. sugar
1 tsp. salt

Mix above ingredients in pie pan. Mix with 1/2cup oil and 2 Tbs. Milk. Stir with fork, pat out like pizza crust—VERY EASY.

In bowl mix:
6 -7 cups peeled apples (I use McIntosh or mix a few varieties)
¾ to 1 cup sugar   1 tsp. cinnamon

Mound apple mixture in pie pan.

Topping:
½ cup brown sugar   ½ cup butter
1 cup flour

Stir above ingredients until crumbly—I use my hands. Pat mixture onto the top of pie.

Cook at 425 ° for 50-60 minutes. Let cool before cutting.

Hint : Cook pies on cookie sheet—they will probably overflow.

Skillet Chocolate Sauce
Judy

This was one of my favorites as a child. This chocolate shell is sold in stores, but it's not homemade!

¼ cup margarine   1cup walnuts (coarsely chopped)
1-6oz pkg. chocolate morsels (1 cup)

Melt ¼ cup margarine over moderate heat. Add 1 cup coarsely chopped nuts & sauté until nicely browned, stirring constantly, to prevent scorching. Remove from heat. Add one 6 oz. pkg. (1 c.) chocolate morsels immediately. Stir until chocolate melts and is smooth. Serve warm over ice cream or cake. It becomes a shell. Yield: 1 ¼ cup. Note: Sauce thickens on standing. Re-warm over hot water or over very low heat. Put it in a pint jar and set the jar in warm water. Does not need to be refrigerated.

Fruit and Honey Granola 350°
Judy

3 ½ cups Quaker Oats® quick or old fashioned uncooked
½ cup honey

1/3 cup coarsely chopped nuts
1/4 cup (½ stick) of margarine (melted)
1 tsp vanilla or other flavoring
½ tsp ground cinnamon
1 6oz package of diced, dried, mixed fruit (1 1/3 cup)
Trail Mix (or something similar)

In a cup, melt margarine in the microwave, covered with paper towel.
Chop the nuts. Heat oven to 350°. Combine all ingredients except fruit in a large bowl. Mix well. Spread evenly in a 15x10 jellyroll pan. Bake 30-35 minutes or until golden brown, stirring after 10 minutes. Cool completely and stir in fruit. Store in a tightly covered container or baggie, in a cool cabinet. This is delicious on morning cereal.

BREADS

Quick and Easy Garlic Toast

4 pieces sandwich bread
3 Tbs. butter (softened)

2 tsp garlic salt

Spread butter on the bread, sprinkle with garlic salt. Put under broiler until golden, serve.

Vito's Garlic Bread

Everyone that tries this bread wants to know who Vito is, Vito told me not to tell.

1 large loaf Italian bread
4 Tbs. butter (½ stick, softened)
¾ cup parmesan cheese (use fresh grated if possible)
Virgin Olive Oil (optional)

3 cloves garlic (minced fine)
¼ tsp garlic salt

Slice Italian bread loaf into 2 equal halves (important!) so you have a top and a bottom.

Mix butter, garlic salt, and minced garlic together well in a cup or bowl, spread liberally on the two halves of bread. Top with the Parmesan. Place halves on cookie sheet under broiler until browned (note: if one half is taller than the other it will 'brown' more quickly). Remove from oven, drizzle with olive oil, slice in serving size pieces, serve hot.

Breakfast Monkey Bread
Laurie

4 Refrigerator tubes biscuits.
White sugar
Ground cinnamon
1 stick margarine
1 cup brown sugar

Sprinkle some white sugar and cinnamon into a small bag or bowl.
Cut biscuits into quarters, place in sugar mixture to cover completely.
Place in greased bundt pan.
Melt margarine and brown sugar in saucepan. Pour over biscuit pieces. Bake at 375 degrees for 35-40 minutes. Turn over onto pan. Eat immediately.
*** Can cut this recipe in half using large loaf pan.

BEVERAGES

Orange Jules
Naomi

6 oz. frozen orange juice concentrate
1 cup water
1 tsp. vanilla-extract

1 cup milk
½ cup sugar
8-9 ice cubes

Combine all ingredients except ice cubes in blender. Blend for one to two minutes, adding ice cubes 1 at a time. Pour and serve immediately.

Z Punch
Laurie

2-3 pkg. Kool-aid (favorite flavor)
2-3 cups water
1-2 qt. ginger ale

2-3 cups sugar
1 large can pineapple juice (46 oz)

Mix all ingredients except ginger ale. Refrigerate or freeze. To serve, remove from the refrigerator or freezer. Set out to partially thaw. Add ginger ale.

Orange-Cranberry Fizz
Laurie

1 quart cranberry-raspberry juice
2 cups orange juice
Orange and lime slices

2 cups. ginger ale
2 cups lemon-lime seltzer

Mix first three together—chill or freeze. To serve, stir in seltzer, and slices. 10 servings.

Party Punch
Vickie

2 pkgs. lime gelatin
9 lemons juiced
Sugar to taste

1 tall can (46 oz) pineapple juice
1 Quart ginger ale

Combine all ingredients, chill. Makes 24 servings.

7-Up Punch
Vickie

1 16 oz. can orange juice
3½ cups 7-Up

1 12 oz. can frozen lemonade
6 cups water

Mix all ingredients, add ice, and chill. Serve.

Easy Punch
Laurie

1 large bottle Welch's White Grape Juice
1 large can pineapple juice (46 oz)
2 liters ginger ale

Chill or freeze first two ingredients, add ginger ale and serve.

More Party Punch
Judy

2 12oz cans frozen orange juice
2 12oz cans frozen pineapple juice
1 12 oz can frozen lemonade

Mix with 2 gallons of water and chill. Last, pour in 4 large bottles pale-dry ginger ale. Use food coloring or float ½ gallon of sherbet or sliced limes. Serves 50.

Red Satin Punch
Judy

1 quart apple juice
18-20 whole cloves

Sweetener equal to ½ cup sugar
2 sticks cinnamon

Peel of 2 oranges diced

1 quart diet cranberry juice

2 quarts diet 7-Up

A few drops of almond flavoring

Combine orange peels, cloves, and cinnamon in a spice bag made of cheesecloth. Place spice bag in apple juice in saucepan, bring to a boil, turn down heat and simmer 5 minutes. Set aside to cool. Remove spices and chill.

At serving time mix sweetener, spiced apple juice, cranberry juice and 7-Up. Makes 35 punch sized cups. (8 oz. equals 44 calories. Use as one fruit exchange.)

Fresh Squeezed Special Lemonade

I've made this cool summer beverage for friends and family on several occasions. One pitcher is never enough. They drink it up quickly!

5 lemons
5 limes
5 oranges
3 quarts water
1½ cups sugar (more optional)

Squeeze the juice from four of the lemons, limes, and oranges, pour ½ of mixture into a gallon pitcher. Reserve the remaining half in refrigerator.

Thinly slice the remaining fruit and set aside for garnish. Add water and sugar to juice, mix well. Store in refrigerator. Serve on ice with fruit slices as garnish. (12-16 servings)

Pineapple Punch
Vickie

2- 46 ounce cans un-sweetened pineapple juice
2-2/3 cups orange juice (may be made from frozen)
1-1/3 cups lemon juice (fresh, frozen or canned)
2/3 cups lime-juice
2 cups sugar

2 large bottles ginger ale (chilled)
2 large bottles plain carbonated water (chilled)

Mix all together in large punch bowl. Make 9 quarts.

Orange Nog
Judy

6 eggs separated
Pinch of salt
2 bananas (peeled)
8 oz. Cool Whip
Nutmeg

2 Tbs. grated orange rind
1 cup skim milk
4 cups orange juice
6 Tbs. sugar

Beat egg yolks, orange rind and pinch of salt until lemony colored. (5 minutes). Beat in 1-cup skim milk and the bananas. Stir in orange juice. Fold in Cool Whip, beat egg whites until stiff while gradually adding sugar, beat until smooth. Fold egg yolk mixture into egg whites. Will keep three days in the refrigerator. Stir before serving. Sprinkle with nutmeg.

MISCELLANEOUS

Play Dough

3 cups flour
6 Tbs. Cream of tartar
3 cups water

¾ cup salt
3 Tbs. vegetable oil

Cook on medium heat. Pull from sides of the pan. Let cool and play!

CHAPTER 22
MILESTONES AND CHILD SAFETY

When we're in a relationship, we see a division of labor between the mother and father. This method has worked for many thousands of years and is a very effective way to run a household. As head of the household we're pretty in tune with the children, how they are growing and what's going on in their lives.

The alarm clock goes off, we slowly open our eyes, and as we awaken to the real world around us, as we are forced to do when first becoming single dads, we find we are essentially as clueless as a newborn babe.

Hopefully you had the opportunity to be involved in the birth of your children. Ok let's give the ex credit for going through *that* nightmare! And hopefully you were able to at least pick up a modicum of knowledge in how to hold an infant, maybe slap the old diaper on that cute little butt, without having to call the local carpet steaming company.

Much of the knowledge of how to rear those kids, and what milestones in their lives are age appropriate, what little quirks are specific to each child, are locked away somewhere in the deep dark, dank recesses of that place we refer to as mother's mind. It goes to the same area that maternal instincts are born, and are guarded more secretly from us men than the Secrets of the Ya Ya Sisterhood.

So we find ourselves in this alien world of singles, surrounded by equally alien creatures and we have no clue what their needs are, how they are developing, and how to give them what they want to survive! And be careful; don't directly *ask* one of them, they are very good at taking advantage of a *clueless dad*.

At least one unlucky soul out there is separated and stuck with a newborn (good at least you're laughing bud, that's the spirit). I wish you luck my friend, it's been many years since I've had to do that not that I haven't continued to change a diaper here and there. You may want to ask the ex for some pointers on infant care. Though I've tried to include all of the things you may encounter you may have things come up that are not covered in this book, in such an instance, look toward a family member or close friend for support.

Be aware of your child's development and search out information on where they should be in their development. Be very aware, that *all children develop at their own unique pace.*

My son quit nursing at a very early age. I don't remember how old, but it was much earlier than we expected. He had no interest in it any longer.

My youngest Michele on the other hand, was still in diapers beyond her fourth birthday! I was very concerned! Michele though, didn't have time for such things. She is extremely active and is only interested in playing. Taking the time to go to the bathroom, seemed counter productive in her playtime, which is *all* the time. When she was old enough for preschool, and was getting some teasing from other children her age, it didn't take her long to make her decision, she was done! In one day, like that, she was potty trained.

I have six children as I've mentioned. All have developed completely differently. They've started on baby food and solid food at different ages, been potty trained, crawled, walked, and began using silverware all in their own good time. I've seen no apparent correlation in their growth because of this. All of them are as bright and outgoing, socially adapted and joyful as any of the children their own ages and school grades. (Mine are much brighter and more beautiful though of course!) Don't be concerned if your child appears slower or don't necessarily expect a child prodigy if they learn faster. No matter what speed they seem to develop, delight in their accomplishments, comfort them through disappointments, and support them always.

To assure that your child (or infant) reaches a healthy age, you will want to baby proof or child proof your home, as is age appropriate.

Children are naturally curious. You *are* to encourage this, but make certain they live in an environment to be curious safely.

Some of the more obvious things you'll want to be aware of:

Get electrical covers for the electrical outlets in your home. You can find these little plastic plugs to go into any unused outlet, thereby assuring baby or small children cannot stick their finger, or other objects in the socket.

Be aware of any electrical cords in reach of small children, they may pull on them and pull something on top of themselves. They may also wrap them around their neck, encourage the puppy to chew on it, or chew on it themselves. Get a plastic tie, or industrial stapler to secure the cord.

Be aware of any plants in your home, which may be in reach of the children, and is possibly unhealthy for a child to eat. Many common household plants can make your child sick if ingested. Make certain to put them out of reach by hanging them on hanging plant holders, or up on the entertainment center or on top of cabinets.

Check all chairs, stools and tables, make certain they are stable and will not tip over on a child when they attempt to climb on them, or pull on them.

Keep lit candles out of reach of children. They are fascinated by fire. Don't be alarmed that your child may be a pyromaniac; this is normal behavior.

When cooking, make it a habit to turn the handles of all pans inward, so that they cannot be accidentally pulled or knocked off by you and your child. I have personal witness of a young child that reached up and pulled a hot pan of cooking oil onto his little body. I met him in the burn unit of a hospital some years ago, severely burned over more than 90% of his body. He recovered, but will be scarred for life, physically and emotionally.

Be mindful of your child's age as it relates to any stairs in your home. Child gates to restrict their movements are a wonderful blessing.

When your child is particularly small, they will chew paper, especially wrapping paper, or writing paper, envelopes, etc that may be within reach. Their tiny windpipes cannot accommodate chunks of any kind, and they will choke.

Make certain your carpet and floors are always clean, they will taste anything that comes in their path as they crawl around the house.

Have child safety seats in the car; use them per the manufacturer's instructions. Don't put them in a seat that has an air bag, unless the manufacturer specifically designed it for children (none are available at this time) or it can be switched off while they are riding.

Look for any sharp objects, including corners of tables and desks, they will find a way to bang their head, bump a knee, or eat them.

Check furniture for any chipping or peeling paint, varnish, or furniture finish. Children will also eat this.

Make certain their beds are safe; the slats on cribs or railings are sufficiently narrow that they cannot put their heads through. A child can put the largest part of their body in some amazingly tiny places.

Turn down the temperature on your water heater to 125°. When your water heater was installed, the temperature may have been set from 150° up to 180°. At 150° a burn may result in less than three seconds.

Fire resistant pajamas are an essential in today's home.

Make certain clothes irons and hair curling irons are unplugged and put out of reach of the little ones.

Make certain you have sufficient smoke detectors, and maintain them regularly.

Have a plan in place so the children have a viable escape route from the home and their bedrooms should a fire start in the home. Also have a meeting place outside if you should ever be separated in such an instance.

Medicines particularly pills, though this includes liquid, looks like candy to children. I don't know why either the pharmaceutical or the candy companies can't put two and two together and one of them make some change. Keep all medicines out of the reach of children. If you're into illegal narcotics, the same goes. It's a great idea to keep such things in a lock box, out of reach. A small toolbox, with a padlock on it will prevent you packing the kid off to the hospital.

Be mindful of your bathroom items, toothpaste, bath powders, razors, and shaving cream. It's a good idea to keep these absolutely out of the children's reach, or keep them locked up as in the above.

Household cleaners are also very dangerous for children. Baby proof any cupboard doors with baby proof latches that may hold cleansers, bleach, floor cleaners etc. They will find a way. But at the same time, encourage their explorative spirit by leaving latches off of cupboards with pots and pans that they can bang on! Make certain "manly" chemicals are also out of reach such as solvents, paints, and lighter fluid we might keep in the garage.

One of the most dangerous items that may be in your household to little ones, oddly enough is baby oil. This is something that is not widely known. Generally the warning on the bottle (if it's present) goes unheeded, and the caps are not baby proof, at least not at this point in time. A baby becomes very familiar with the oil that feels so good, that Mommy or Daddy uses on them. When ingested, it's very dangerous, not only going into their stomach and intestines (a powerful laxative I'm sure), but they will also take some of it into their lungs. This coats the air sacs in the lungs, making it impossible for oxygen to be taken in. Essentially your baby may smother or drown.

You'll want to keep a close eye on young ones while they take a bath. They love to play in the water, and may want to be in the tub much longer than you have time for, but indulge them. What is the right age when they don't need to be closely monitored during bath time? This varies, but the age is usually long after they've learned to walk. Filling the tub with a few inches of water and allowing them to play safely can only be accomplished after they have achieved great muscle control.

Teach children the technique of stop, drop, and roll should a fire ever catch their clothes. A child's natural instinct is going to be to run for help if their clothing catches fire. Running will only fan the flames and make the situation critical. When panic sets in, it's tough to remember the stop, drop, and roll. During playtime, mealtime, whenever it's least expected, yell out "Stop, Drop, and Roll!" Do it yourself. Watch your children follow. This will teach it eventually as an instinct or reaction. They'll get lots of giggles from doing it as well as watching you roll around on the floor.

The above are the basics. When you've done all of the above, put your child on the floor and watch them closely. They will soon alert you to anything you've forgotten. Keep a notepad but *rescue the child before writing it down*!

You will find many additional tips in the Bright Futures booklet listed in the assignment below.

Your child will reach the age they would like some privacy, and begin to be more modest when they are not fully clothed. The young children run around naked, with reckless abandon, and won't see any need for restrictive clothing. Your ideas on this are probably pretty set in your mind, no need to change that. Teaching them when it's appropriate to wear clothes will be determined by your own ideals. It will serve you well to teach this without instilling shame in your child. The human form is very beautiful in its natural state, yet our society dictates modesty in our dress and actions. You will know when your child is old enough and are feeling more modest. Be open to any uncomfortable feelings they may experience in this regard.

Make certain they have places to dress, and can lock the doors, and have a lock on the bathroom so you, or their siblings won't barge in to catch them in a compromising situation. This is especially important for female children as they become more aware of the differences in their bodies, from their male counterparts.

Unfortunately, no matter what measures we take, our children are going to encounter accidents, injuries, and have health issues. You will want to make certain your children have adequate health insurance. You may obtain this through your place of employment, purchase it on your own, or be sure they are covered through some government Medicaid etc. If you have yet to get them insurance, make certain to do it soon, before you need it. Get the best medical and dental care you can afford. Life insurance and other forms of coverage are at your own discretion.

Unfortunately also, no matter what we do to protect our children from child predators, children are going to continue to be abducted until we as a society have raised our entire consciousness to a level that it is no longer an issue. Sadly, I don't see us coming to such a place in our society anytime in the near future.

When a child is abducted or goes missing for other reasons, the best proactive system being presented today, in my opinion is the Amber Alert. Information on this system is very prevalent in the news media today. If you are not aware of such a system, please investigate further.

Several states have enacted the Amber Alert system, as ours has one also called the Rachael Alert. I'm not certain if they are different but both work essentially the same way. If your state has none, I encourage you to investigate it and support it. Sign any petitions that support it, or any program that will protect our children. If need be, start a petition and contact your local congressman and appropriate government officials. We *all* must protect *all* children.

If you are a member of America Online, you will find the Amber Alerts listed at keyword Alerts. You may subscribe to this service (this is a free part of the America Online service) and receive an automatic email on any Amber Alert issued that may be pertinent to your area. Other Internet Service Providers will either have access to the same or may be getting it soon.

Digital signs on the freeways in your area may post the Amber Alerts, as will news and television reports anytime a child is abducted or missing. It is critical to make as many persons aware of a missing child, as quickly as possible.

Should you become aware of a child that may have been abducted, missing or is being exploited contact your local authorities or The National Center for Missing or exploited Children at 1-800-THE LOST.

As more and more households begin to go online, the danger of your child meeting a predator online is rapidly amplified. Some surveys suggest one of five children; between the ages of 10 and 17 have received some form of sexual solicitation while online. I have no doubt the number is probably higher. This cyber world allows the predator to remain anonymous and safe in his or her own home. They cruise the children's chat areas disguised as a child, searching for their next victim.

If your child is into the online world, I would suggest keeping the computer in a main area of the house. Many things can happen if your child has Internet access in the privacy of their bedroom.

These predators are extremely well versed not only in the Internet but also in ways to obtain information from your child, who they are and where they live.

Of course children know that they don't give out their names or addresses on the Internet. And the predators know this too. They will gather information over time, creating a profile of your child, retaining information gathered. With enough time he will fit the pieces together like a puzzle.

For instance your child may feel safe revealing the state they live in. This in itself appears harmless. Their screen name, email address or online identity may contain something personal, part of their name, gender or age. Two pieces of the puzzle are in place.

As your child becomes more familiar with their online friend, they begin to exchange other information, "I play on a softball/football team" etc. They may reveal the name of the school they attend. More pieces of the puzzle fall into place. The name and address of most schools can be found online. So what? Your child is one of a few hundred children in town X, Y, Z.

As they grow closer, the predator may ask, "What is the name of your team?" Or "What number are you on the softball/football team?" When the child reveals this information, they have been narrowed down to one. Most anyone could locate this child with the above information.

Many websites offer help with online safety. Your particular Internet service may have one. Since I'm a subscriber to America Online, I'm aware they have several safety features for children. One is the screen name AOLSafetyBot. This is a screen name you can send an Instant Message to, asking safety questions or reporting suspected predators. AOL also has keyword AOLGuardian. This area will allow you to set controls for your child, and you can subscribe to receive an email containing your child's online activities, including who they are emailing, who they are speaking with in instant messages, areas they visit or attempt to visit and which chat rooms they are visiting.

Programs such as NetNanny, Cyber Patrol, and Cyber Sentinel (with it's Predator Guard) can be useful tools in your monitoring and controlling any unwanted activity.

A few more websites worth visiting:

www.missingkids.com brings you up to date on missing children

www.netsmartz.org is full of helpful safety tips. Both you and your child should visit the site and learn what it has to offer. The site has areas for any age group that would be using an Internet or online service, as well as a great area for parents to help them educate their children on child safety while online.

Your child may be more adept at computer usage than you. Your life experiences will be essential in teaching safety. It is difficult for us to believe such animals, as the child predator exists. It may be difficult for them to realize they are to be the target of such a being.

Your job as protector is to use all resources available to provide your child with a safe environment, allowing them to be a kid for as long as it takes.

ASSIGNMENT

As a single dad, you will want to make certain you have all of the necessary information available when caring for the children. Make certain you have received any medical cards from the mother if appropriate, insurance information, and doctor and dentists names addresses, phone numbers. Also be aware of the nearest hospital, as well as the hospital the children's particular physician may be associated with. Make certain you have the children's social security numbers in a handy accessible place.

Stop by your child's pediatrician or doctor's office. Ask if they have, or where you might obtain specific literature that may help you.

One booklet I highly recommend is "Bright Futures, Guidelines for Health Supervision of Infants, Children and Adolescents, Second edition, Pocket Guide:2001 Update." This may be found at your pediatrician or doctor, or you may contact the organization responsible for the booklets publishing:

National Center for Education in Maternal and Child Health
Georgetown University
2000 15th Street North, Suite 701
Arlington, VA 22201-2617

The booklet contains information and is organized from birth through teen years. It has helpful information on milestones to look for in your child. It also provides many safety tips that may prove essential.

Your local library may also have a copy, as well as other informative books on raising children. This would be a beneficial outing for your children to visit the library while you research materials that may be helpful to you as well.

CHAPTER 23
THE MAGIC FORMULA

In the grand scheme of things, when compared to universal time, the few short years you have to make the difference in a child's life is only an instant. In the time it takes for you to snap your fingers the opportunity has been grasped or lost. The results of the action performed in that instant will remain for an eternity.

Something has been eating at me since I first began this project a few months ago. When I had decided that I would write something I know in the preceding pages, I went on an Internet search to find what was available for single dads in printed form.

I was saddened, yet excited to see very little in print on how to be a single dad. I was excited because of the need for this book, yet I was saddened because of the millions of single dads in our country with no reference books to help them in their journey.

In my quest to research what was available, I found one book that was dated a few years ago, and I started going through the reviews, or customer comments on the book. One gentleman's comments hit me, "Nope, don't buy this book, nothing new in here." I was curious as to what he was looking for when he bought the book? Kids have been around since the dawn of man, literally. Over the past 50 years, a library full of research has been printed on kids' thoughts, feelings, what they are doing and eating. What new could anyone offer? I'm assuming by his comment that he had meticulously studied all of these works though I could be mistaken.

It was apparent from his few words however, he must be missing *something,* or he wouldn't be wasting his time reading books on the subject.

For many of us that have been single dads for years, we certainly have some idea of how to do it, and what we are intending to accomplish. My concern is for the newly single dad that is looking for some guidance on this path they've been thrown on. It's very difficult for me to remember what it was like when I was divorced from my first wife. The distance of my home from theirs made it easy for me to ignore the fact that I had kids somewhere, and I didn't think of what I should be doing. I didn't have to live with the fact they were growing up, asking questions, some of them questions a dad *should* be answering. When I did move closer to them after a number of years, I was allowed to ease into the situation, which made it at least a bit less painful.

What about the single dad? He may *want* to step up to the plate but is either without any sense of direction, or is receiving mixed signals from anyone that may have had an encounter with this little alien creature. Which foot goes first? What do they eat and drink? What is considered wet as it refers to a diaper?

I have intentionally avoided all of the years of psychological research done on children. I've avoided quoting all of the greats like Jung, Dr. Spock from my days, Dr. Seuss, Boone and Crocket, Pope and Young, and all of the others.

This research is available from most bookstores and libraries. I've found books with all of the technical jargon, that frankly I have trouble translating into plain English. When faced with a screaming child after burning her hand on the stove, I don't see the point of opening a number of reference books to know which ointment to put on it, hot or cold water, and how to best deal with her psyche after the tears have stopped. Get me in touch with what she's feeling and I can figure it out for the most part. If not, the hospital emergency room is only a short drive.

Frankly, I find their books a bit dry, and best suit me after a hard day with the kids and I need some sleep.

I think what is most needed and what I have tried to offer is a fresh perspective. A perspective that will help us see the humor in some of the things they do, and I'll admit, they do the same stupid things I did as a kid. When a kid has taken a swat at a bee on a flower, and missed, and is making a mad dash for the house, or any nearby water source, let's admit it, it's funny!

Or when my six year old, after being interrupted in her story, begins again with "Um…. as I was saying…." it brings a giggle. I wonder when she learned to preclude her continuing thought with such an adult phrase. These are the little miracles that happen daily with my children, whether I am present to appreciate them or not

Some things they've learned from me, and of course I try to help them separate the good words, from the words Daddy uses. But hey, they get a taste of the real world when they are with me. It also helps me keep my reality in perspective and to realize what is important. I see how Daddy's carelessly or carefully chosen words can make a difference in their perspective.

No matter whether you are involved in their lives or not, your kids will likely still grow up. They will go to dance class or to football games. They will graduate Junior High and High School. They will have their first crush and get their hearts broken. They will meet the love of their life, and they will marry and will likely have children of their own. They will raise them as best they know how, as you and your ex did. If you're not involved, they will still be forced to go down the path.

If you are being Dad, and you do the best you can, they will see life differently. They will have you to share their experience with. They will learn how to express their love for Dad, and how to speak their mind when it's called for. They will be raised with different ideals than if you were absent. They will be much more likely to have a successful marriage themselves, if they have learned of the great gift that true love is, from their Dad.

There is no magic formula to raising children. Everyone does it differently. What I consider dos or don'ts may be viewed completely differently by someone else. The important thing for you is to find what method works for you. Which is healthiest in reaching the goal you want with your children, and to be *consistent*. Of course you will adapt, but you can adapt *consistently* without throwing your child into an utter state of confusion.

I doubt you will have found any groundbreaking techniques in the previous pages. That's ok, that wasn't my intention. My intention was only to provide a different view, to view those little breakages or the destruction of property as precious angelic learning experiences from your children. If you were running a furniture store, it may be one thing, but you're not raising furniture, you're raising children. Keep it in perspective.

The simplest things in most of our lives are the ones that are the most memorable. My fondest memories aren't of Disneyland or a great trip to the Bahamas, but rather family get-togethers or the taste of that pizza in a little tiny Michigan town where my family would stop after a long hot day at the beach. My memories are of swatting at that bee, and him stabbing the palm of my hand, as I ran home to the comfort of my mother's arms. Or the first time I teed up a ball with my dad on hole number one of a nine hole course. It was just the two of us.

I remember going to a small lake with my dad on my 16th birthday. We didn't do anything spectacular. We walked and talked. I let him in on one of my great secrets, that I was big enough, and fast enough to outrun him. Turned out it was no secret at all, the words had no sooner left my lips than he bowled me over in the grass after running me down. Later, my mother showed me the trophy he had won as a State High school track star in his younger days. Wish I had known this earlier.

I remember as a young boy, our family was completing a vacation trip to Florida. In preparation of returning home, I hurried to my room and packed my suitcase. I took special pains to conceal some adult magazines I had procured in the clothes that they would not be seen. These were treasured magazines that I intended to delve into later, to help me understand more of this birds and bees stuff.

My dad had come by the room to check on me, and spied my open suitcase, and was aware of my inability to pack neatly. Of course he saw this as a great learning experience for me. I knew it was lunchtime and begged him to help me after we had our lunch. He was never one to waste an opportunity. A late lunch was no deterrent. Beginning to remove each article of clothing and instructing me on the importance of careful folding of each item, he had lifted all but one shirt, which would reveal the magazines I had so carefully stowed away.

By this time I was sweating bullets! My head began to spin trying to come up with some explanation, so wild he would have to believe it, when those magazines were revealed. I sorely hated to disappoint my dad, and this would be something I would be severely punished for. I knew at the very least I would have a very long ride across Florida and the neighboring states to reach our home, if I were allowed to live that long.

He completed the folding of a pair of pants, and his hand moved to lift the shirt. From down the hall echoed my mother's angelic voice, "Dad! You two come and eat your lunch, now!"

Time stopped or at least my heart did, could it be? A small grin spread over my father's lips as I looked pleadingly into his eyes. "Well," he said as he withdrew his hand "Let's go have lunch, I think you can finish this after."

I dropped to the floor. I began to twitch. I had witnessed my first miracle from God! Dad picked me up, threw me across his shoulder laughing as we headed down the hall to the kitchen. I carefully reached up and wiped the sweat from my brow so that he wouldn't notice.

To this day, I've never asked him, nor do I have any clue as to whether he knew what secret treasure was concealed under my clothes. I do know, those magazines never made it home with us. I wasn't going to put my life on the line a second time to let him come and check again after lunch! Did he not know? Or *did* he know and not quite know what he was going to do when he lifted that shirt? That doesn't sound like my dad. He may have known, but knew the lesson had been taught and left it at that. That sounds like my dad.

I wonder if I will ever let myself go back into my childhood, for the few moments it will take to ask him and know the truth. I hadn't thought of that story for years, but now, it's important. It's important to know who my dad was that day.

That's the *magic* in raising kids. The magic is in the energy created when you are together. When you allow the curtain of the father to be raised, to reveal the kid again. One who can see the humor in the precious gift of fatherhood.

It's not always in *what you do*, rather in the fact that *you are there to do it with*. It takes both of you to bring that energy to its magical magnificence. Without you or without them, it's not going to happen. It's important that you be Dad when you are with them. Not the father or some stranger trying to teach all of the lessons of life. Just be Dad. The most effective method of teaching is not to teach, *be* what you want them to refer to as Dad. Be the person you want them to be when they grow up. Let them make their own choices after living with your example.

Any child that has not had the opportunity to have a Dad will understand completely that magic missing in their life. They may not believe in magic any more. How can they believe in something they've never seen?

We've read the words from the ex wives and we understand what they are *saying* they would like us to do differently. We read "Understanding the Ex," and we understand them completely. Well maybe that's an impossible task, but for a brief moment I hope, you've been able to step into their shoes, or into their minds and hearts and see the difference in perspective than that of our own.

We have a list of things to do with the kids that may last years to accomplish them all. But more importantly, it's a mind set to keep your psyche open for new opportunities and possibilities. Notice the things they might point out while driving in the car, those are the things they might like to do. Go ahead and pull the car over and go into that pizza place, try to create the experience I had as a child. Or as we pull into the neighborhood amusement park or arcade, realize that life is precious don't drive by.

We are who we are, your ex, the kids, and yourself. There is no changing them. To a point you will influence your children in who they become. Your ex will be influenced to a degree by your behavior. However, you have the power and choices to be that which you want to be. The type of dad your children want and need, and the type of ex that will most benefit you, your ex, and your offspring. I'm not suggesting a change so much in you, but rather to allow yourself to be who you intended to be. Be the person that makes your life exciting. This alone has a great influence on so many others around you.

Fortunately or unfortunately, no final chapter is written for the single dad. We'll always be present. One day in the not so distant future you may have the opportunity to walk into one of those establishments you used to frequent, after your kids are grown and have kids of their own. You may see some other single dad, or your grown son with his rug rats in tow, dropping coin after coin into the games. You may notice he has a furrowed brow, a worried look in his eye, or a bead of sweat rolling down his forehead. Smile, pat him on the back and let your words of experience comfort him "You're doing great, Dad. Everything's going to be fine."

You might notice as you walk away that the cycle continues. You have contributed your years in service, and it's time to leave the task to others. Hopefully seeing him with his children will bring back many fond memories.

Perhaps a small tear will roll down your cheek.

You'll know that you were loved, and you were the best *Dad* in the world.

ASSIGNMENT

1. Take care of yourself.
2. Be Dad.

Printed in the United States
22690LVS00008B/24